THE HANDHELD
LIBRARY

WITHDRAWN

THE HANDHELD LIBRARY

Mobile Technology and the Librarian

Thomas A. Peters and Lori Bell, Editors

 LIBRARIES UNLIMITED

AN IMPRINT OF ABC-CLIO, LLC
Santa Barbara, California • Denver, Colorado • Oxford, England

Library of Congress Cataloging-in-Publication Data

The handheld library : mobile technology and the librarian / Thomas A. Peters and Lori Bell, editors.
  pages cm
Includes bibliographical references and index.
ISBN 978–1–61069–300–4 (hard copy) — ISBN 978–1–61069–301–1 (ebook) 1. Mobile communication systems—Library applications. 2. QR codes—Library applications. 3. Electronic reference services (Libraries) 4. Public services (Libraries)—Technological innovations. I. Peters, Thomas A., 1957– editor of compilation. II. Bell, Lori, 1960– editor of compilation.
Z680.5H36 2013
027.4′2—dc23   2012051415

ISBN: 978–1–61069–300–4
EISBN: 978–1–61069–301–1

17 16 15 14 13   1 2 3 4 5

This book is also available on the World Wide Web as an eBook.
Visit www.abc-clio.com for details.

Libraries Unlimited
An Imprint of ABC-CLIO, LLC

ABC-CLIO, LLC
130 Cremona Drive, P.O. Box 1911
Santa Barbara, California 93116-1911

This book is printed on acid-free paper ∞

Manufactured in the United States of America

Contents

Introduction: The Mobile Revolution and Libraries, Librarians, and Library Users

Lori Bell and Thomas A. Peters

Key Points

- The mobile revolution has been one of the largest, fastest revolutions in the history of humanity.
- The history of mobile communications and devices is briefly summarized.
- The impact and key issues of the mobile revolution for libraries and librarians are explored.
- Possible action avenues for libraries and librarians, especially in light of heightened competition and marginalization, are enumerated.

INTRODUCTION

The challenges and opportunities presented to libraries, librarians, and library users by the mobile revolution are massive, exciting, and sometimes daunting. The mobile platform has become the twenty-first-century service platform for most sectors of the economy, society, and culture—especially the information-services sector. The mobile revolution is a huge, global revolution, more pervasive than the previous Internet and web explosions. Librarians have a proven aptitude for taking large technological innovations and applying them both effectively and efficiently to advance the missions of libraries. Just as we needed to begin offering services on the web in the 1990s, now we must offer mobile services because library users need, expect, and demand them. Thomas (2012) notes, "Indeed, a new wave of mobile-savvy users have arrived in our libraries: not only texters but also eager patrons adept with e-readers, smartphones, and tablets."

The rapid pace of technological development in the area of mobile computing and communication is amazing—perhaps unprecedented in the history of humanity. The plethora of devices, device types, operating systems, apps, standards, and protocols is dizzying. Given the magnitude of this revolution—perhaps one of the largest revolutions in the history of the human endeavor—how should librarianship best invest its limited time and other resources? Should we be developing services? Content? Standards? Apps? Mobile websites? Metadata? Devices? Probably most if not all of these. The earlier emergence of first the Internet and then the web may provide some guidance about how libraries can effectively respond to the mobile revolution. The mobile revolution challenges librarians to determine which content types and what services—existing and new—will be needed to serve mobile library users well. Also, for certain types of services, such as reference, the addition of service options (phone, email, chat, IM, SMS, etc.) has resulted in serious sustainability concerns as reference continues to spread into new communication channels.

As any technology gets adopted and diffused throughout a population, eventually it recedes from our collective consciousness. We just use the technology without thinking about it too much. Now that the first wave of the technological mobile revolution has passed, successive social and cultural revolutions are building. Those follow-up phases of the mobile revolution may not yet have fully manifested themselves on the global stage. How people communicate and connect socially seems to be undergoing some profound changes in diverse areas ranging from dating to political revolutions.

The mobile revolution also is changing the information lives of many individuals. Where and how we access, apply, and create information is expanding as we collectively grow accustomed to having a net-connected personal portable device always available. At the very least, libraries and librarians need to try to make the services we provide, the content we manage, and the systems we offer as mobile-friendly as possible.

BREADTH, DEPTH, AND RAPIDITY OF THE MOBILE REVOLUTION

It is nearly impossible to overestimate the breadth, depth, and rapidity of the mobile revolution, especially during these early adoption and diffusion stages. The mobile revolution involves the use of any mobile device (smartphone, tablet, laptop, ultrabook, dedicated e-reading device, gaming device, etc.) and any mobile network to engage in one or more of four fundamental activities: communicating, finding and using information, being entertained, and creating content. The mobile revolution is arguably one of the fastest, most pervasive diffusions of any technology in human history, rivaling things such as TV sets, toilets, cooking utensils, and clothing in terms of the breadth of diffusion and outpacing just about everything in the rapidity of such a globally pervasive diffusion. The mobile revolution began as a technological revolution, but it probably will beget significant social, cultural, legal, and economic revolutions as well. The use of mobile phones currently far surpasses any other mobile technology. It is a truly global phenomenon. Although the adoption rates and speeds vary from country to country, almost every nation on earth is moving rapidly toward a state of almost universal adoption. The International Telecommunication Union (ITU 2011) estimates that at the end of 2011 there were over 6 billion active mobile phone subscriptions. If those subscriptions were spread evenly across the estimated 7 billion people on earth, the diffusion of the mobile phone alone would be approximately 86 percent. For comparison purposes, approximately one-third of the 1.8 billion homes worldwide now have Internet access (ITU 2011), up from 20 percent saturation only five years ago. A mobile revolution clearly is occurring. Perhaps even the word "revolution" is insufficient to describe what is happening. Barbara Fister (2012), in writing about changes in access to reading material, calls it an apocalypse.

When the personal desktop computer entered the consumer market in a big way over 30 years ago, it was considered a remarkable technological advance. In late 2010, the global market for smartphones surpassed the market for personal computers when measured in terms of the number of units shipped (http://www.pcmag.com/article2/0,2817,2379665,00.asp). This trend probably will never reverse, and eventually desktop computers may go the way of rotary dial phones, or at least the desktop computer will become a marginalized, niche market, such as LP records have become for the music industry.

The United States is neither the leading edge nor the trailing edge of the global mobile revolution phenomenon. In summarizing the Pew Internet Project's analyses of the mobile revolution in the United States, Brenner (2012) notes that approximately 87 percent of all adults in the United States report owning a cell phone. The adoption percentage for adult Americans has been hovering in the mid to upper 80 percent range for almost three years. This diffusion rate far outpaces the number of adult Americans who own a laptop, a dedicated e-reading device, or a tablet computer. Approximately 63 percent of adult Americans have gone online using one or more of the mobile devices they own. Not surprisingly, adults in the United States who have higher income, more formal education, or are younger tend to have adopted mobile phones at a higher rate. Perhaps surprisingly, at least in the sense of how the popular media tend to portray cell phone use in the United States as dominated by young whites (Yelton 2012) (with male dominance thrown in for good measure), the adoption of smartphones by U.S. blacks and Hispanics outpaces that of whites (Brenner 2012). Text messaging and taking photos currently are the most-used functions of mobile phones.

HISTORY OF THE MOBILE REVOLUTION

Today when we speak about wireless networking, we tend to be thinking of mobile devices and 3G, 4G, or WiFi networks, but the original wireless was radio, which offered advantages over the existing wired forms of communication and data transfer, such as the telegraph. Frenkiel (2002) notes, "it is impossible to overstate the impact that broadcast information and entertainment have had on the world." The revolutions in radio (and later, television) broadcasting paved the way for the current mobile revolution. Although the concept of sending invisible signals out in waves at nearly the speed of light had been discussed and tested by scientists since the mid-nineteenth century, it wasn't until September 1899, when Guglielmo Marconi sent a radio broadcast announcing the return to New York City of Admiral Dewey from Manila, that wireless radio broadcasting became practical and poised to become pervasive (Frenkiel 2002).

While the early decades of the development of radio centered around military and ship-to-shore communications, it was the Detroit Police Department in 1928 that conducted the first practical application of vehicle-based (and thus land-mobile) radio communication (Frenkiel 2002): Car 54, where are you? Three times between 1947 and 1958 the Bell System petitioned the Federal Communications Commission (FCC) for a band spectrum to develop a broadband urban mobile telephone system, and three times the FCC denied the request, in part because of the "vast educational and entertainment opportunities thought to be offered by the newly proposed UHF TV band" (Frenkiel 2002). Evidently the Summer of Love (1967) inspired even the FCC, because by 1968 they had soured on the promise of UHF TV and were ready to give something else a try. This was followed by 15 years of earnest discussions and saber-rattling among the various stakeholders, who almost unanimously saw the proposed new system as an undesired threat to the status quo. "The first cellular system in the U.S. was put into operation by the Bell System in Chicago, in 1983" (Frenkiel 2002). In a cruel irony of history or of government regulation, in 1984 the Bell System, which had the vision and expertise to advocate for a truly mobile (i.e., for both sender and receiver) communication system for decades, was broken up.

The early mobile cellular devices were about the size of an automobile. In fact, they were automobiles. It took some time for mobile technologies to shrink in size and become truly personal and portable. March 6, 1983, was a red-letter date in the history of the mobile revolution. That's when Motorola put its two-pound DynaTAC mobile phone on the market, with a manufacturer's suggested retail price of $3,995 (http://en.wikipedia.org/wiki/Dynatac)—equivalent to over $9,000 in 2012 terms. DynaTAC stood for dynamic, adaptive, total area coverage, which is not hopelessly obsolete as a catchphrase for the mobile revolution as a whole.

Then came the personal digital assistant (PDA). The Apple Newton, first released in 1993 (http://en.wikipedia.org/wiki/Apple_Newton), was arguably the first PDA. It didn't fare well in the marketplace. The first PDA to really capture the imagination and use of the general public was the Palm Pilot, which became available in March 1996 (http://en.wikipedia.org/wiki/Pilot_1000). It was designed to keep track of appointments, contacts, notes, and so forth. Soon third-party software developers were creating apps for the Palm Pilot. Microsoft soon developed Windows CE, which some wags dubbed WinCE, designed for portable devices. Palm and Windows began competing to dominate the mobile OS market. Shortly thereafter, some employees from Palm left to develop their own company, Handspring, and their own device, the Visor, which became available in September 1999 (http://www.computinghistory.org.uk/det/5781/Handspring-Visor-deluxe/). The 1990s clearly were the PDA decade.

Enter the dedicated e-reader device, which had been imagined and discussed for decades but didn't launch a revolutionary first strike until the late 1990s. The Rocket eBook from NuvoMedia, available in 1998, was one of the first commercially released dedicated e-reading devices. The Softbook was another. Other devices, which combined PDA functionality with e-reading functionality, soon emerged, such as the Franklin eBookman. None of the first-generation dedicated e-reading devices sold well. With the failure of these to thrive, many thought e-books would never become accepted by the general consumer, that they were a bunch of hype like the longstanding idea—far from realized—of the paperless office.

Although the IBM Simon, arguably the first smartphone, went on sale by BellSouth in 1993, it wasn't until the early years of the present century that smartphones began to become broadly adopted. When this happened, mobile phones began to include PDA-type functionality. This was the death sentence for the "standalone" PDA, and it also heralded the era when people began thinking about doing more than just talking into their mobile phones. Now, most members of younger generations don't consider voice communication to be the primary purpose of their mobile phones. Texting long ago eclipsed talking as the primary means of near-simultaneous communication via these mobile devices.

Internet access came to mobile phones in the 1990s, but initially the data speeds were agonizingly slow. In 1989 the Bloomington Public Library in Illinois operated the first bookmobile in the nation with cellular connectivity for circulation functions on the go, at the blazing speed of 1200 baud. "A baud rate of 2400 was tried but was very undependable" (Logsdon 1990). The onboard computer was housed in a padded wooden box to protect it from bumps and jolts (Logsdon 1990). This promised to improve library services not only in the metro area but also in surrounding rural areas, but the slow data-transfer speed necessitated the reversion to offline circulation transactions.

Internet speeds on cellular devices really did not achieve broadly acceptable rates until the first decade of this century. Also, the memory capacities of most portable electronic devices were insufficient to handle many media types, such as audio books, until several years into the current century. Audible.com, which launched its business in 1999, was the first big audiobook vendor to implement a business model that delivered audiobooks to portable devices, such as the beloved Otis. They also developed the direct-to-consumer business model, eschewing sales to libraries and other organizations for the most part. This direct-to-end-user business model, always a threat to libraries, has escalated as Amazon, Apple, and other major e-content vendors have pursued direct-to-consumer business models with a vengeance.

Library vendors of portable e-content soon emerged, however. OverDrive, for example, launched its downloadable digital audiobook service in November 2004, followed closely by NetLibrary, Recorded Books, and others. This enabled libraries to lend e-content, often on portable devices, either library owned or patron owned, in a big, popular way.

The Playaway self-contained portable audiobook device also emerged in 2005. It offered libraries, other institutions (such as branches of the military), and individuals the ability to listen to audiobooks on a self-contained, extremely portable device without all of the hassles of moving content onto and off of portable MP3 players. Their service seemed to be popular with people who were not averse to portable e-content experiences but didn't want to mess with the technical aspects. Playaway also offered libraries a circulatable and shelvable object, which fit well with existing library systems, shelving, and procedures. Until Playaway, most mobile audio devices were too expensive for libraries to consider loaning them out.

Audiobooks that could be distributed to listeners go back to the 1930s, when the National Library Service for the Blind and Physically Handicapped participated in the development of the 33-1/3 RPM record format (the "LP") to accommodate long audiobook narratives. The audiocassette really revolutionized the portability of audiobooks and music. It enabled the listening of recorded music (not broadcast over radio) and spoken-word content in cars, on boomboxes, and so forth. Of all the types of content available on today's portable devices, audio content (e.g., music and audiobooks) played a crucial early role.

The compact disc (CD) also played a role in the mobile revolution. Portable CD players had their moment in the sun. Many of them were designed like clam shells. Of course, they required moving parts to spin the disc, and they had to be large enough to contain and play back a CD, so their battery life and portability were limited.

Portable MP3 players—and, more generally, portable media players—also played a large, early role in the development of the mobile revolution. Although MP3 players often played back more than just MP3 files, the name has stuck. For libraries and library users, the MP3 player opened up significant opportunities for listening to digital audiobooks on the go. Digital audiobooks were a hit with library users long before e-books came to the fore.

The tablet computer, particularly the Apple iPad, also has contributed to the mobile revolution. The concept of a tablet-like computer has been around for decades, but the adoption and diffusion of tablet computers really accelerated in 2010 when Apple released the iPad. The impact of tablet computers on the overall mobile revolution has been varied. In terms of portability, tablets generally seem to be perceived as more portable than the typical laptop computer and even more portable than the newer ultrabooks, but less so than a smartphone. However, because of the larger screen on the typical tablet, many people in education and business often adopt and use tablet computers. On the interaction front, tablet computers have popularized swiping, pinching, and other ways of interacting with a mobile device that are not heavily reliant on a mouse and keyboard. In terms of key functionality, while tablets enable all of the four key functions we've identified (communicating, finding and using information, being entertained, and creating content), tablets seem to excel as media consumption devices.

IMPACT OF THE MOBILE REVOLUTION ON LIBRARIES AS ORGANIZATIONS

Libraries are the innocent bystanders—or civilian casualties—of this mobile revolution. Inouye (2012) explores how the mobile revolution and the e-content explosion are revolutionizing the organization of libraries. He notes, "It is natural enough to focus on digital content, whiz-bang technology, and how libraries should provide innovative services for our communities. Yet there is more going on than meets the digital eye." The underlying struggles center on control and organizational change: "The digital revolution is essentially an organizational revolution for libraries" (Inouye 2012). The Online Computer Library Center (OCLC) report on U.S. public library perspectives, released in March 2012, noted that only five percent of respondents listed "mobile access" as one of the three top priorities for their library (OCLC 2012). However, e-books and other e-content were rated high by 37 percent of respondents, far outdistancing the second most mentioned priority—buildings and facilities issues—at nine percent. Libraries as organizations are still coming to grips with the challenges and potential of the mobile revolution.

The mobile revolution also has put a strain on libraries as organizations in the general area of resource allocation. Because most libraries are cultural institutions that take the long view, any revolutionary period with rapid changes can be unsettling. The mobile revolution certainly has created challenges in managing and balancing the library's investment of e-resources and printed resources, but it also has placed some interesting strains on other library resources, including human resources and space. The number of person-hours devoted to various existing and emerging initiatives can place a library ahead of or behind the curve in terms of embracing and exploiting the affordances of the mobile revolution. The way that people will use the library as a built space as we move farther into the mobile revolution is an interesting design and management problem.

IMPACT OF THE MOBILE REVOLUTION ON LIBRARIANS AS PROFESSIONALS

The mobile revolution presents librarians with a third major service platform, after in-person and sedentary web-based platforms. Our content, systems, and services have to be retooled, and sometimes reconceptualized, for mobile devices. In this era of limited budgets and scarce resources in general, trying to spread library services across these three platforms is proving to be difficult and probably unsustainable. Each library must not only assess the current information practices and preferences of the community it serves but also make informed predictions about rapidly evolving and expanding community needs and expectations.

Because there are so many mobile device types, operating systems, apps, content providers, and service providers, and because most of this crazy quilt of options was designed for individual users, the challenges of providing even rudimentary instructional and tech support for mobile library users are not trivial. Librarians have been struggling not only to keep up with fast-paced developments in the mobile revolution, and how these affect the provision of library services, systems, and content, but also to maintain current knowledge about the wide variety of portable devices, operating systems, file types, file transfer and sharing mechanisms, and other facets. No particular device, operating system, or file type seems poised to dominate its market. Patrons are flocking to libraries not only for content to put on their portable devices but also for tech support. Thomas (2012) notes, "Staff technology training and skill development must be part of the planning, not only to avoid staff burnout and alienation from tech initiatives but to ensure adequate backup, tech support, and succession planning."

Librarians also are using mobile technologies to improve and extend their professional activities related to librarianship, research, and service. Examples in the fertile field of librarianship include roving reference with a tablet computer, the use of portable devices to deliver instruction, multimedia tours, enhanced experiences of special collections, and so forth. Also, the mobile revolution opens up interesting possibilities for mediated and unmediated library services beyond the walls of the physical library. In the area of research, librarians are using mobile apps and on-the-go access to and creation of information to bring their research closer to the field of actual information use. For example, one methodology used by the recent Ethnographic Research in Illinois Academic Libraries (ERIAL) project (http://www.erialproject.org/project-details/methodology/) involved giving portable digital cameras to college students and academic librarians so that they could capture their information lives as they happened.

Librarians also are using mobile technologies to assist in their current awareness and professional development activities. For example, Twitter can be a very good tool for professional development and current awareness, if you follow the right individuals and organizations. Twitter, Boopsie, and other mobile apps have made in-person conferences and workshops more participatory, communal, and useful for both attendees and those following the conference hot topics and developments from afar.

KEY ISSUES

The mobile revolution will change not only where people interact with information and information services but also how. This has resulted in some key issues and challenges for libraries and librarians.

- *Control*: How the information experience, which increasingly will blur the distinction between creating and consuming content, evolves as the mobile revolution advances is a huge ponderable. One facet is how the struggle for locus of control over that experience will develop. For instance, the "Big Six" trade book publishers in the United States probably will experience declining influence and control over the next decade. Companies such as Amazon, Barnes & Noble, Kobo, Apple, and Google, which are using the end-user device as their foot in the door to build an enduring, vertical presence in the information lives of millions, if not billions, of individuals, probably will gain control. The types and levels of control that will be exercised by authors (content creators) and readers may be the key battles for control. For libraries, the mobile revolution has resulted in the loss of control (or sharing of control) regarding controlled and uncontrolled vocabularies; the end-point information appliance used by the user to access, interact with, and create information; and the locus and ambient environment in which the user accesses library content, systems, and services.

- *Evolution of the Information Experience*: The mobile information experiences includes several facets, including content, interface, services, value-adding opportunities, social media and community interaction, the end-user device, and the situational characteristics of the place where the information experience occurs. All of these facets combine to create an overall information experience. Librarians need to engage in experience visioning and design. We cannot forget or slight the major components, such as the user interface, the content, and the metadata, but the winning information services in the mobile era will spend considerable time and attention on the overall experience.
- *The Experience Is King*: Years ago the declarative statement "content is king" was making the professional rounds of spoken and written utterances. The underlying sense was that ultimately, for libraries, the delivery of content to users was more important than services, systems, organizational structures, mission statements, and so forth. As the mobile revolution continues apace, however, a new monarch appears to be emerging. Sure, content remains important, but for many mobile users the complete experience is king. Also, the context of the current experience of the mobile user affects the type of information and information service they want and need from libraries. For example, when a mobile user sends a text message to an SMS-based reference service asking for an address, usually they want directions to that location, not a mailing address, because they are en route. As a service provider, you need to think in terms of freeway exits, not ZIP codes.

OPPORTUNITIES OPENING UP FROM THE MOBILE REVOLUTION

The mobile revolution opens up several fundamental opportunities for libraries and library services. A few are listed below.

- Closeness to the place and moment of information needs. Information needs can arise at any time, in any place. In the "good old days," users often had to wait until they got to a library before they could seriously pursue most of their information needs. Mobile library services make it easier for libraries to respond to information needs where and when they arise.
- Different types of information experiences in and outside libraries. Mobile technologies have added interesting new wrinkles to library tours, scavenger hunts, and other in-library activities. Libraries also have served as venues for "big games" or "urban games" where the library itself becomes the game board. Players use their mobile devices and their wits to solve the mystery or win the game.
- The ability of mobile users to add value to and "give back" to an information system or community of library users. Often simply by using a mobile information system, the users are helping to refine, define, and improve the system.

POSSIBLE ACTION AVENUES

The mobile revolution should not be a spectator sport. We need to take action, probably sooner rather than later. Even if librarians, libraries, and library-related organizations accept the basic argument of this book that the mobile revolution is huge and hugely important for the future of libraries, library content, and library services, the question remains concerning what action avenues should be pursued, given the scarcity of basic resources—money, time, talent, and others. "Take a hard look at how you are doing business, assess what resources you have, and consider whether you are well positioned for the challenges ahead" (Inouye 2012). Outlined below are some of the basic action avenues, particularly regarding the disturbing trends with e-content, which are not necessarily mutually exclusive.

- *Protests and Boycotts*: Protests and boycotts traditionally have proven to be effective in the short term, but their long-term implications for an information ecosystem remain suspect. The ability of social media such as Facebook and Twitter to accelerate and expand the short-term impact of protests and boycotts seems to be forcing the issue of the long-term efficacy of these strategies. The ability of mobile populations and crowds to self-organize, share information, and perhaps converge on specific locations to engage in protests and boycotts seems to be expanding and improving as a result of the mobile revolution.
- *Talking with Publishers*: In 2012 the American Library Association ratcheted up this strategy for addressing disturbing trends in the evolution of the e-content ecosystem. The president of ALA, the executive director of ALA, and others had high-profile meetings with representatives of the major trade publishers, trying to persuade them to sell or lease more of their frontlist e-books to libraries.
- *Talking with e-tailers*: Because the U.S. Department of Justice decided to move forward with its action to sue Apple and five of the Big Six publishers for price collusion centered around the agency pricing model (i.e., where the publishers set the prices and the e-tailer merely acts as the sales agent), this probably will be the death knell for the agency model and a further erosion of the power of the large trade publishers. Librarians should be having serious, ongoing discussions with the major e-tailers (Amazon, Apple, Google, Barnes & Noble, Kobo, and others).
- *Appeals to Altruism*: Making appeals to altruistic behavior and the almost intangible benefits of libraries for the culture of reading and democratic societies is another action avenue that librarians, libraries, and library-related organizations can pursue. Appeals to altruism may have some positive impact on legislative bodies and charitable foundations but little if any positive impact on publishers, tech companies, and others.
- *Focus on Content*: Libraries began as collections of content, and metadata and information services grew up around and in support of library collections. As the impact of the mobile revolution reverberates through the library ecosystem, the meaning and value of content has become under scrutiny. When it comes to e-books, it is amazing how quickly nonlibrary entities (Amazon, Google, Barnes & Noble, Apple, etc.) have been able to amass and offer e-book collections of more than a million titles. All but the largest libraries and library consortia have had a difficult time ramping up their e-book offerings so quickly.
- *Focus on Services*: Libraries may want to focus more on "wraparound" information services than on the provision of basic content per se. For instance, rather than serve as the tax-supported last mile in the provision of bestselling books, perhaps public libraries should continue to develop services that help readers to connect with good books, authors, and other readers. Thomas (2012) provides a good overview of the state of mobile library services in late 2011, including Mosio's move toward patron relationship management, where mobile communication engenders an ongoing relationship between the mobile user and the library.
- *Focus on End-User Devices*: Most mobile devices are intensely personal. They are designed to be accepted and used as personal devices, and most users do indeed develop intensely personal

relationships with their portable devices. Nevertheless, not all library users can afford to own and operate a personal device—or they simply choose not to. Libraries and other organizations have to acquire and provide access to these devices that are designed and marketed as highly personalizable, sole-owner devices. This takes commitment on the part of the library because the devices evolve rapidly and are not designed for constant use from a wide variety of users. The need for libraries to provide end-user devices for a portion of the population served will continue indefinitely, but it probably will remain a peripheral—not core—service in the mobile era. The stripped-down, institutionalized dedicated e-reading devices available in conjunction with the 3M Cloud Library service are an interesting experiment in this area.

- *Process Improvements*: One of the more interesting outcomes of the explosion of interest in mobile access to e-books and streaming media is the rapid improvements in online sales and fulfillment systems and services. Amazon set the de facto standard in this area with its ability to offer sales of e-books and other e-content that involved, on the user's part (after initial setup of the service, including purchasing a Kindle/Fire device or downloading the free Kindle software to their device of choice), only one click and waiting less than a minute for delivery of the content. Because Amazon, Apple, Barnes & Noble, and other e-tailers are focusing on the direct-to-end-user market rather than on the institutional market, their fulfillment and distribution systems have made amazing progress in a few short years. In contrast, the fulfillment and distribution processes in libraries (which we call document delivery, circulation, and interlibrary loan) have come to look increasingly archaic and cumbersome. Just as the initial simplicity of Google's search interface had a ripple effect throughout the entire web, these amazingly good fulfillment systems serve as a challenge to fulfillment systems throughout all sections of the economy and society, including libraries.

- *Focus on the Gestalt Experience*: Our profession has developed a healthy regard for information objects—books, primarily, during the past several hundred years. We collect them, describe them, provide access to them, and sustain them. However, because the mobile revolution is enabling deep, immersive interactions with information objects from just about anywhere, while people are doing just about anything, perhaps as the mobile era unfolds we librarians need to focus as much or more on the gestalt information experience as we do on content, metadata, and services. These three pillars of our profession will continue to be vitally important, but we need to think about and plan for the complete user experience. While the mobile revolution seems to be encouraging us to think and act in this way, one of the ironies is that our control over key aspects of that gestalt information experience is declining. For instance, we don't have much control over the devices people use, where they use them, what applications they use, or how they customize the interface.

- *Litigation*: Suing individuals and groups that appear to be engaged in behaviors that seem to inhibit libraries from pursuing their missions certainly is an action avenue worth considering. The Authors Guild appears to be following this basic action avenue, among others, with brio. Litigation can be expensive and time-consuming, with uncertain and often inscrutable outcomes. Because libraries generally have high social and cultural capital—most people love libraries and have fond memories of library visits—we probably should pursue this action avenue only with extreme forethought and caution.

- *Legislation*: Libraries also may want to pursue local, state, and federal legislation that would protect libraries and the library model of delivering information content and services as we move farther into the mobile era. Appeals to altruism, the public good, and the future of a democratic society may resonate more with legislators than with for-profit organizations such as most publishers and tech companies.

CONTENT COMPETITORS IN THE MOBILE INFORMATION CONTENT ARENA

The mobile revolution has fostered an e-content revolution of sorts as well. Content had been going digital—either at the moment of creation or retroactively via digitization—well before the mobile revolution gained force and momentum, but the mobile revolution has added some interesting new wrinkles to the e-content revolution. The mobile revolution also has created a new cohort of content competitors in the mobile information content and services arena. The Big Six trade publishers in the United States currently have much sway, but they may be at the zenith of their collective influence and profitability, much as the Big Three television networks had in the 1970s prior to the onslaught of cable and satellite television. Fundamental changes in the basic environmental conditions surrounding e-content creation, distribution, and use seem to be putting a downward pressure on prices and expanding the distribution channels. The primary aggregators and retailers of e-content, such as Amazon, Google, and Apple, may gain more influence as a result of these environmental changes. It remains to be seen if their values will align well with the values and missions of libraries.

SERVICE COMPETITORS IN THE MOBILE INFORMATION SERVICES ARENA

The types of library content and services offered to mobile users on their gadgets of choice are varied and growing. Wang, Ke, and Lu (2012) list several: "A variety of mobile web applications in libraries have been developed, including mobile library websites and MOPACs (Mobile OPACs), mobile collections, mobile library instruction, mobile databases, mobile library tours, mobile learning, library SMS notifications, mobile library circulation, QR codes, access to services (such as reserving study rooms and checking out laptops and e-book readers), and SMS reference." If we concentrate only on services, broadly defined, one noteworthy development over the past several years has been the development and launch of library-like mobile services by nonlibrary entities. Cha-Cha is answering reference questions, Amazon is lending books to users of mobile devices, and a plethora of startup companies are fostering mobile, real-time (i.e., as-you-read) e-book discussion groups. Mobile library service development is a worldwide phenomenon. For instance, the National Digital Library of China offers a customizable mobile-phone app, a free mobile newspaper service offering the full content of 40 newspapers, and a collection of hundreds of thousands of e-books, which can be downloaded to users' mobile e-reading device of choice, or to one circulatable from the National Library of China (http://www.nlc.gov.cn/newen/newVisitUs/nlcss/bysemr/#11). Charles Darwin University in Australia is using QR codes to provide both online and in-person treasure hunts that provide a fun orientation hunt for new students (Cummings 2011).

PRIVACY, CONFIDENTIALITY, AND INTELLECTUAL PROPERTY

The mobile revolution involves a lot of service collaboration between libraries and other entities. Unlike during the era when print dominated, librarians do not have much control over private and confidential information about how people seek information and what they actually access. "Today, the tools and platforms that enable user access to digital content put reader privacy in peril. Borrowers' personal information and materials-use records are in the hands of intermediary companies and content providers" (Inouye 2012).

The mobile revolution also may be quickening a general social and cultural reassessment of the value of privacy. Many mobile users seem at least somewhat comfortable about sharing formerly privately held information with mobile information and services providers, as long as these providers use this personal information to add value to their services and wares and do not sell or give this information in personally identifiable ways to third parties. Although there have been many relatively minor security breaches and poor corporate judgment surrounding confidential data, collectively we have not yet experienced a major, cathartic privacy disaster. If and when that happens, we may see many users revert back to old-style attitudes and behaviors toward privacy.

The mobile revolution may be affecting intellectual property in other ways, too. For example, for a system of intellectual property rights to work, there needs to be a way to generally establish beyond a reasonable doubt who is the author or creator of a work, such as a digital utterance of some type. For books and articles, this usually is a straightforward process. The author or authors claim most or all of the intellectual property rights unless they convey those rights to some other legal entity (such as the publisher). The creation of a motion picture entails a more convoluted establishment of intellectual property rights. That thorniness may look like a smooth surface when we contemplate the challenges of establishing, asserting, and defending intellectual property rights in a full-blown mobile era, where everyone is online and connected almost all the time and works are created through robust social media environments, open-invitation crowdsourcing, and other collaborative group efforts. In short, the real challenge of the mobile revolution to intellectual property may not lie so much in enforcing appropriate use but rather in establishing authorship.

MEASURING THE SUCCESS OF MOBILE LIBRARY INITIATIVES

As more libraries begin to deploy mobile library services, several are undertaking systematic attempts to assess the impact and success of these mobile services. For example, Wang, Ke, and Lu (2012) used the logs and reporting capabilities of the integrated library system (ILS), as well as questionnaires administered to the user population, to assess the success of a due-date-reminder SMS service delivered to mobile devices, as well as a renewal request service at the Oriental Institute of Technology in Taiwan. Patrons could renew their library materials directly on the mobile devices. This research found that users of the SMS-based overdue and renewal alerting service actually improved their behavior, in the sense that they checked out more books and had fewer overdue fines. Furthermore, this SMS messaging service was used more by continuing education students than by regular undergraduate students (Wang, Ke, and Lu 2012). This type of "proof in the pudding" research is needed for all the various types of mobile library systems and services being implemented by libraries.

INTO THE FUTURE

Now that just about everyone in the world has (or has ready access to) a mobile device, the future of the technological aspect of the mobile revolution may be more incremental than disruptively different. The idea of mobile computing may be supplanted by even more integrated human-computer interaction in human life, such as ubiquitous computing or pervasive computing. The devices will get progressively smaller and more integrated into our persons. Eyeglass-based mobile devices are already here, followed probably by contact-lens-based devices, culminating in subcutaneous mobile devices. Perhaps the smart tattoo will displace the smartphone, just as the smartphone displaced the PDA. On the other hand, large-screen interactive displays seem to be gaining interest and momentum. Although they probably will never be mobile devices, the trend seems to point to both significantly larger and significantly smaller devices.

The mobile revolution will transition into the mobile era, but there seems to be no going back. Libraries and librarians need to constantly assess the changing environmental conditions and their value proposition. The mobile revolution is not a "problem" to be solved once and forever. Thomas (2012) observes, "It's a race without a finish line." Today's wise decisions and moves will need to be assessed and revised tomorrow and tomorrow and tomorrow.

CONCLUSION

It is difficult to envision, let alone predict with confidence, how the mobile revolution will affect libraries, librarians, and library users over the coming years. The mobile revolution demands active discussion, earnest thought, thoughtful play, careful but accelerated planning, and determined action by librarians. "We need more librarians who will seize the initiative—people who can assess the new reality of digital content and figure out how libraries fit into this world. Unfortunately, there isn't a lot of time to make this shift" (Inouye 2012). We do not need to abandon our core missions and long-held values, but we do need to be innovative and proactive in our thinking and planning about the role of libraries in the mobile era.

We have designed this book of contributed chapters so that each chapter provides an in-depth, action-oriented look at a specific aspect of this huge mobile revolution and how it is affecting libraries, librarians, and library users.

REFERENCES AND FURTHER READING

Brenner, Joanna. 2012. "Pew Internet: Mobile." [Blog post] February 23. http://pewinternet.org/Commentary/2012/February/Pew-Internet-Mobile.aspx.

Cummings, Sally. 2011. "QR Codes in the Library—An Investigative and Fun Orientation Program." [Blog post] June 14. http://www.sallysetsforth.com/index/qr-codes-in-the-library-an-investigative-and-fun-orientation-program-14-june-.

Fister, Barbara. 2012. "Recommended Reading, Apocalypse Edition." *Inside Higher Ed* (February 16). http://www.insidehighered.com/blogs/library-babel-fish/recommended-reading-apocalypse-edition.

Frenkiel, Richard. 2002. "A Brief History of Mobile Communication." *IEEE Vehicular Technology Society News* (May): 4–7. http://www.winlab.rutgers.edu/~narayan/Course/Wireless_Revolution/vts%20article.pdf.

Harris, Christopher. 2012. "Going Mobile." *School Library Journal* 58(1): 14.

Inouye, Alan S. 2012. "The Revolution Isn't Just Digital." *American Libraries* (January 11). http://americanlibrariesmagazine.org/features/01112012/revolution-isn-t-just-digital.

International Telecommunication Union (ITU). 2011. "The World in 2011: ICT Facts and Figures." http://www.itu.int/ITU-D/ict/facts/2011/material/ICTFactsFigures2011.pdf.

Logsdon, Lori. 1990. "Bookmobile Online Circulation via Cellular Telephone." *Computers in Libraries* 10(4): 17–18.

OCLC. 2012. *U.S. Public Libraries: A Snapshot of Priorities & Perspectives.* Dublin, OH: OCLC. http://www.oclc.org/reports/us-public-libraries/default.htm.

Thomas, Lisa Carlucci. 2012. "The State of Mobile in Libraries 2012." *The Digital Shift* (February 7). http://www.thedigitalshift.com/2012/02/mobile/the-state-of-mobile-in-libraries-2012/.

Wang, Chun-Yi, Hao-Ren Ke, and Wen-Chen Lu. 2012. "Design and Performance Evaluation of Mobile Web Services in Libraries." *The Electronic Library* 30(1): 33–50.

Yelton, Andromeda. 2012. "Bridging the Digital Gap: Mobile Services Can Help Libraries Reach Out to All Populations." *American Libraries* 43(1/2): 30.

Part I

Mobile Tech Trends in Libraries

1

Serving Your Mobile Users: The Essentials

Robin Ashford and Alex Rolfe

Key Points

- Texting is still enormously popular.
- Libraries can use quick response (QR) codes to bridge the gap between the physical and the virtual.
- Users who have to pinch and scroll around will not be impressed.
- Libraries need to decide which apps to showcase.
- E-book content is becoming optimized for reading on mobile devices.
- There are many simple, low-cost ways to market your mobile services.
- Hit counts and other basic statistics should be easy to come by.
- We can look forward to new ways to provide service.

INTRODUCTION

The mobile revolution is in full swing. Libraries can no longer afford to be passive. We need to recognize the importance of this societal change and strategize accordingly. The adoption of mobile devices is surging: in 2011, Americans purchased more smartphones than PCs, and there are more wireless subscriptions than people (Mobile Future 2011). Libraries need to be alive to the implications of this rapid growth. Many already are, but may be wondering how to address it. The rapidity of change and the array of mobile technologies out there create a bewildering environment. Here are the elements we recommend for a library to serve its mobile users successfully.

TEXT MESSAGE REFERENCE

Short message service (SMS) reference was one of the first services libraries offered for mobile users. SMS allowed short text messages to be sent over phone networks. The standard was in place as mobile phone networks grew, and it now remains as just about the only mobile service available for users with feature phones. Now texting is moving away from traditional SMS to other messaging services using the Internet rather than phone networks (Troianovski 2011). Even so, texting is still enormously popular. Some 83 percent of American adults own cell phones, and three-quarters of them (73%) send and receive text messages; the typical young adult cell owner sends or receives 50 messages a day (Smith 2011). Texting for reference help is a service well worth offering.

There is not necessarily any monetary cost, though those wanting the best features may find it worthwhile to pay. Meebo and Pidgin are popular free instant messaging (IM) services that allow the library to send and receive text messages as well, while also connecting to a wide array of IM networks. Mosio's Text a Librarian and Altarama are two SMS services, of several available, that provide features like transcripts and statistical reports. Libraries need to make sure the service is staffed and responsive. This service has its unique considerations: messages have to be kept short—under 160 characters (although some services will break up longer ones for you)—and there is a possibility that you are incurring costs for the user. It is a fairly low-barrier service for the library to offer, however, and consumes a lot of resources only if it gets heavily used, which may justify the cost.

QR CODES

Many libraries are implementing quick response (QR) codes in their physical and online spaces. Though they may not be mainstream in your part of the world, smart implementation of QR codes makes sense in libraries, where we aim to best serve all of our constituents, including our ever-growing population of mobile users.

Practically speaking, QR codes excel at bridging the digital and physical worlds, and libraries—now more than ever—are places where the two are intertwined. A low-threshold technology, QR codes are easy and inexpensive to create and implement. Whether they become mainstream or are replaced by something even simpler in the future, they are a technology we can easily implement to add value for our library users now. When used wisely, QR codes provide a lot of bang for the buck.

On the technical side, a QR code is a matrix barcode developed by the Denso Wave division of Denso Corporation in 1994. The barcodes were originally designed for the automotive industry for easy, rapid scanning of information (Denso Corporation

Figure 1.1
CCPL.

2011). Because they are two-dimensional, QR codes can contain more data than a standard barcode, such as contact information or a link to a website, audio file, image, or video. Libraries, with their mix of print and digital formats, are a natural place for using QR codes to bridge the gap between the physical and the virtual. QR codes can place movie trailers on DVD cases and put book reviews on print books. From adding information to purchased content or library exhibits to providing audio tours, these little codes can truly add value for mobile users. Some of our content is already enriched with QR codes by publishers: the journal *Neurosurgery* recently began using QR codes to link readers to related videos or further data ("QR Codes in *Neurosurgery*" 2011; MacRae 2011).

QR codes are also increasingly embedded on web pages; the goal is often to simplify a task the user would have done more laboriously without the QR code. A good example is QR codes in library catalogs. The benefit here is that instead of needing to have paper and pen and time to write, users can scan the code to get the title, author, call number, and location of the item on their mobile device. They may have done this from their computer at home, but the next time they visit their library they can easily pull up that information from their barcode-reader history and walk directly to the item on the library shelf—and no worries about remembering what they did with that little piece of paper! Some library catalogs with QR codes also take users to the full mobile catalog record. Users getting help at the reference desk can just scan the code to bring the record up on their phone, where they can place a hold, share it with a classmate, or simply save the information for later reference.

Much has been written and presented on the topic of QR codes and libraries, and examples of QR code usage in libraries abound. A good starting place for ideas is "Library Success: A Best Practices Wiki," which includes a page dedicated solely to libraries using QR codes ("QR Codes" 2011). A search for "QR codes libraries" on www.slideshare.net also yields many valuable presentations on QR codes and libraries.

The usefulness of QR codes is debated, and, indeed, not all QR codes provide a value-added experience for the user. This is unfortunate and is something libraries should consider when preparing to implement QR codes. A negative experience scanning a library QR code lowers the likelihood users will try scanning other useful codes. Commercial marketers regularly make the mistake of creating QR codes that take users to nonmobile sites that, on top of being difficult to read, offer the user nothing in return other than advertising to purchase a product or service. When users take the time to open a barcode reader on their device and scan a library-created QR code, they should be rewarded with something of value, not punished with advertising, a nonmobile site, or other low-value content. After all, we want to serve our mobile users better, not "sell" them something they don't care about. Labeling, or some text that explains what the QR code does, is also important so that users can avoid scanning codes to content that is of no interest to them.

These are the sorts of QR-code implementations that cause a user to come back for more: bringing the user to a mobile library app or site that they can add to their home screen, a gift or cash reward in a scavenger hunt, or a short, useful video tutorial. Best of all are those that meet a real-time need, such as reserving a room on the spot, checking the availability of computers in real time, or learning more about a library display or art show while viewing it.

Figure 1.2

Use of QR codes in poster, Albertsons Library, Boise State University.

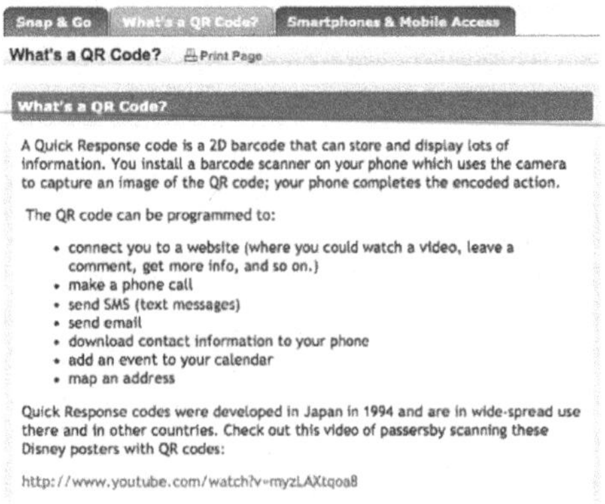

Figure 1.3

Explanation of QR codes for the Snap & Go project, Contra Costa County Library.

However, the greater challenge lies in the fact that most people still don't know what a QR code is or what to do with one. In June 2011, only 6.2 percent (14 million) of mobile users in the United States scanned a QR code (comScore 2011). Also, not all users own a device that can scan the code, so it is important to provide a URL along with a QR code whenever possible. In this environment, it makes sense to provide information on QR codes; whether it's a sign, a handout, a page on the library website, or face-to-face instruction, it's important that we provide some means of educating library users about QR codes. Boise State University, Albertsons Library, Contra Costa County Library, and many others have done an excellent job in this area by creating extensive online guides about QR codes, as well as print posters and cards to educate and at the same time advertise their mobile sites.

Malicious codes and privacy have been raised as concerns. Barcodes can link to browser exploits or could include other malicious content to manipulate your mobile device. It is safest to know and trust what you are scanning. As long as you made the code, you know it's safe. And of course, QR codes, like links on websites, may need to be updated from time to time. As for users, most barcode-reader apps can be configured to show the URL they are going to open up before they actually load, which is one preventive option. Branding the library-created QR code with a logo can instill confidence. If somebody were to put up a rogue QR code of his or her own, it would look odd to your users because it would have no logo as part of the code. In the end, as with other online content, there are risks we may not be able to foresee or preclude.

MOBILE SITE AND MOBILE CATALOG

A mobile website is an important component of mobile library services. Many libraries have their eye on this already; the *Library Journal* Mobile Libraries Survey 2010 revealed that a mobile site and mobile catalog interface were at the top of the list of services currently offered or planned for (Thomas 2010). It is relatively simple to provide a few mobile-formatted pages showing hours, phone numbers, and other information users may want to check while out and about. Given the small screen size, mobile users do not expect or desire sites as robust as standard websites. Users who have to pinch and scroll around a full website on their handheld devices will not be impressed. The mobile site also serves as an access to point to other services for mobile users. Some are discussed below; others, such as applications showing real-time availability of library computers, may not be essential but are nonetheless wonderful. Many users expect to find such services through a mobile site and are not likely to get to them solely through a standard website, QR code, or other means.

One of the first services to go online was the library catalog; before the World Wide Web was invented, libraries provided

Figure 1.4

Customized QR code used by the Harold B. Lee Library, Brigham Young University.

dumb-terminal access to their catalogs. Similarly, the library catalog is one of the first things that ought to appear in the mobile realm. Exposing the collection is one of our basic responsibilities. Certain catalog features, such as account access, make particular sense for mobile users. The ability to renew books and place holds should be part of any mobile catalog. Because this is more difficult than simply putting up a mobile-formatted page, many libraries will need to pay a vendor. A side benefit of doing so is that most vendors' products can double as a basic mobile website as well.

To help users take advantage of your mobile catalog and/or site, you will want to have a redirect script on your main website and catalog pages. Often it can be placed in a header, but if your catalog is also your proxy server (we use Web Access Management from Innovative Interfaces), you may need to go through some implementation gyrations to keep it from redirecting users to your catalog when they authenticate on the way to your library vendor apps.

Mobile catalog vendors are adding features and functionality rapidly. In the 14 months that LibraryAnywhere, the product we use, has been in general release, its makers have added greater freedom to customize, better statistics, new search options, and support for more devices. Boopsie, another vendor offering a mobile catalog interface, recently added the ability to scan any book's universal product code (UPC), check for availability, and place it on hold. Both Boopsie and LibraryAnywhere work with a variety of integrated library systems (ILSs); another option may be a mobile interface offered by your ILS vendor, such as Innovative Interfaces' AirPAC.

LIBRARY VENDOR APPS

Database vendors now offer mobile sites, apps, and sometimes even mobile-friendly features within databases, such as the Alexander Street Press QR codes permitting music downloads to mobile devices. Specific databases often merit their own app; the Nursing Reference Center app from EBSCO downloads a library of information on diseases and drugs that could be useful in a wide variety of health-care settings. Many individual journals, such as *Nature* and the *American Journal of Transplantation*, provide their own apps as well. The impressive amount of development by vendors and publishers constitutes another signal that the mobile landscape is increasingly important for libraries and their users.

The number of library-related apps is already overwhelming. Some libraries have made informational web pages or LibGuides listing mobile apps; MIT and the University of Arkansas are particularly good examples. These guides are useful both to their users and to those of us who have yet to make such pages for our own libraries. What quickly becomes apparent, though, is the need for criteria and policy. Given the plethora of apps available, libraries need to decide which ones to showcase.

Promoting these apps implies some level of library support for them, and this may also need to be a consideration for libraries putting information about them online. It has always been a challenge to keep abreast of the changing functionality of our web-based databases; learning about all the apps and the details of how they work is no less daunting. Most vendors include a help page that library staff

Figure 1.5
Library-related app logos.

can point to. For the more popular apps, such as EBSCO, we may need to assist our users with the initial authentication process. In some cases authenticating is more intuitive than in others; Gale and EBSCO, for example, solve this problem in different ways. The good news is that once a person has been authenticated, they usually do not have to worry about going through the process again. The move to mobile platforms by our vendors presents definite challenges for library workers, but getting these apps into their hands is nonetheless a very important way we can provide value to them.

E-BOOKS

With a mobile site in place, and with vendors offering content via their own apps, expectations soon follow for the library to provide its content in a mobile-friendly format too. Many users read books on their mobile devices already and would love to have access to their library collection in this way. Librarians too are eager to meet this growing demand.

Ebrary's recent download survey found that the most-desired feature is the ability to "check out directly to mobile devices," with more than half of the 395 respondents ranking it highest (McKiel 2011). Ebrary followed up in the fall of 2011 by rolling out a surprisingly generous two-week download option. For those wanting only a chapter, they can download a PDF with no digital rights management (DRM), which means there are no restrictions on how or how long they use it. But to get the entire book, one must have Bluefire or another app that has Adobe Digital Editions; this is what enforces the two-week limit. Allowing downloads to devices equipped with Adobe Digital Editions is becoming the norm, at least for aggregators like EBSCO, EBL, and ebrary. E-books purchased directly from certain publishers, such as Springer or Cambridge, allow the downloading of chapter PDFs with no DRM; users can open these with any PDF-reading app and keep them forever.

One way or another, e-book content from all sources is becoming optimized for reading on mobile devices. As more and more users acquire mobile devices, libraries with solid e-book collections will see use statistics accumulate in part from people standing in lines, riding on buses, sitting in parks, and so on. Libraries with few or no e-books will not be available to their users in this way. With mobile devices becoming ubiquitous, and now that our vendors accommodate them, why wouldn't we want our content available through those devices?

Figure 1.6
Use of QR code to promote the George Fox University Library's mobile website.

MARKETING

Libraries with a mobile presence will want to advertise these valued products and services. There are many simple, low-cost ways in which to get the word out. The library mobile website or app can be easily promoted on the main library website with a banner, button, or text link to a web page containing a URL to the mobile site, as well as a QR code. Information can be included about what the mobile site offers. Libraries can also promote their mobile presence via posters and signage inside the library. On college campuses, postcards promoting the mobile library site—with a QR code to scan—can be placed in student lounges, dorms, and computer labs, as well as in the library. Public libraries can place post-cards or posters in community centers and other public areas such as bus stations. Contra Costa County Library, for example, put up eye-catching billboards with a word cloud and large QR code at various Bay Area Rapid Transit (BART) stations.

Services such as SMS reference can be promoted via a QR code and accompanying explanation, as the Calvin T. Ryan Library at the University of Nebraska has done.

Figure 1.7

Use of QR code to promote the SMS reference service at the University of Nebraska—Kearney.

ASSESSMENT

In a time of shrinking or stagnant budgets, assessment is very important. For mobile library websites, even those developed in-house, hit counts and other basic statistics should be easy to come by. Expect low numbers at this relatively early stage, but do not necessarily be deterred by them. The *Library Journal* Mobile Libraries Survey 2010 found that mobile offerings accounted for only 5 percent of use (Thomas 2010). Our own mobile site serves between 1 and 2 percent of the number of pages our website serves in any given month. The number of users is between 3 and 4 percent of those using our standard site. (There are fewer pages per user for the mobile site because our standard site is so much more robust.) Yet the number of mobile users has increased 325 percent for us from a year ago, and the number of hits has climbed 67 percent year over year. We expect this trend to continue as more of our students acquire handheld devices and as our mobile services mature.

Statistics can also reveal how mobile users are using your services. Our EBSCO statistics, for example, show that the EBSCO Mobile interface produces far fewer full-text downloads per session than their main interface does. This implies that users are e-mailing results rather than opening them on their device. They have also been avoiding downloading PDFs; they have downloaded HTML full text more than PDF, instead of half as often, as is the case for the main interface. Their obvious dissatisfaction with reading PDFs on a mobile device may affect how we instruct mobile users as well as what apps we recommend. Our mobile site statistics also tell us which devices people are using, information that can also be used to tailor services.

QR-code use can also be tracked, depending on which service you use. It is possible, too, to simply make a batch of QR codes and find out later that you have no means of tracking them, so be sure to factor this in when deciding what kind of QR-code generator or URL-shortener to use. There is more than one way to go about it, but statistics would be worth having. It is important to identify implementations that are not working, as well as to provide evidence of successes.

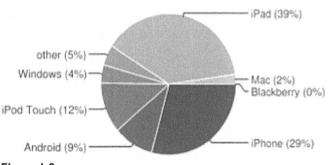

Figure 1.8

Mobile site usage by device type at George Fox University.

A FUTURE OF SMARTER SMARTPHONES

New mobile technologies are being developed and evolving at a dizzying pace. The exponential growth of smartphones is well documented (International Data Corporation 2011), and the mobile revolution is in full swing. Planning how best to move forward with ways to serve our mobile library users can be a challenge even when we are certain of the benefits a known technology can provide.

For planning purposes, and for those libraries with budgets that allow for experimentation, keeping abreast of some of the technologies in development is helpful. Should you implement QR codes in your library if newer, better technologies are just around the corner? Predicting what will be the next great thing that will benefit your mobile library users is tricky business. What we know for certain is that the development and evolution of technology will continue. Smartphones and other mobile devices will get smarter. Below are brief descriptions of technologies worth following.

Augmented reality (AR) enhances one's view of the physical world by overlaying digital information. This magical technology, developed over the past few decades, is rapidly evolving in the mobile space. Better known for fun and games at this stage, a real effort is being put forth to develop it in the more practical and educational space. In the future we may be able to hold up our mobile devices to augment library displays with 3D interactive images, or perhaps have a 3D movie trailer come alive on top of a DVD or book, or enjoy something as practical as a demonstration on how to fix the printer in front of us.

Nate Hill of San Jose Public Library created "Scan Jose," an AR project supported in part by funding from the Institute of Museum and Library Services. While walking around San Jose, people can go to the Scan Jose mobile website for directions to the next point of interest; when they arrive, they will be shown historical pictures pertaining to that location. For the full AR experience, people can use the Layar browser; if they hold their mobile device up in front of them, Layar will use the device's camera to show them what's really in front of them, while overlaying the historical photo appropriate to that point of interest.

Another technology that will soon be part of our mobile users' repertoire is near-field communication (NFC). NFC-enabled mobile devices allow users to interact with posters or anything with a "tag" (an unpowered NFC chip) by simply touching their device to it or waving it nearby. This is the technology behind Google Wallet ("tap to pay" is now available at check-out at stores in test cities), Google Places, and several other applications in development. Many believe that NFC will replace QR codes. Before long, perhaps our mobile library users will see posters with NFC tags, and instead of opening a QR scanner, they will simply wave their device near the sticker to be taken to additional content.

Push technologies may also prove useful to libraries. Urban Airship, a small start-up in Portland, Oregon, specializes in "push notifications," a technology that enables apps to give mobile device owners pop-up notifications about breaking news, social network activity, or discounts. Their recent acquisition of a San Francisco startup, SimpleGeo, will allow location-specific technology to be added to the notifications. This addition could make push notifications far more interesting and useful. Rather than just buzzing when new messages arrive, your device could present a coupon to you because you walked by a store. Walking into your library might trigger a notification of recommended books that are currently available or a reminder while you are there that you have books on the hold shelf. If given the ability to customize their personal notification settings, mobile users might find this very convenient.

Apple's Siri and Google's continuous development of translation and voice-recognition software promise other interesting developments in mobile behavior in the slightly more distant future. As more of our users become mobile users, and as mobile devices become more sophisticated, we can look forward to new ways to provide service.

REFERENCES

comScore, Inc. 2011. "Press Release: 14 Million Americans Scanned QR Codes on Their Mobile Phones in June 2011" August 12. http://www.comscore.com/Press_Events/Press_Releases/2011/8/14_Million_Americans_Scanned_QR_or_Bar_Codes_on_their_Mobile_Phones_in_June_2011.

Denso Corporation. 2011. "About QR Code." http://www.qrcode.com/en/index.html.

International Data Corporation. 2011. "Worldwide Smartphone Market Expected to Grow 55% in 2011 and Approach Shipments of One Billion in 2015, According to IDC." June 9. http://www.idc.com/getdoc.jsp?containerId=prUS22871611.

MacRae, Duncan. 2011. "Introducing QR Codes: Linking Print and Digital Content via Smartphone." *Neurosurgery* 68(4): 854–55. Accessed December 27. DOI: 10.1227/NEU.0b013e318214ccad.

McKiel, Allen M. 2011. "ebrary's Download Survey." Accessed December 27. http://www.ebrary.com/corp/collateral/en/Survey/2011_ebrary_download_survey.pdf.

Mobile Future. 2011. "2011 Mobile Year in Review." December. http://mobilefuture.org/page/-/images/2011-MYIR.pdf.

"QR Codes." 2011. *Library Success: A Best Practices Wiki.* Accessed December 27. http://www.libsuccess.org/index.php?title=QR_Codes.

"QR Codes in *Neurosurgery*: Linking Print and Digital Content via Smartphone." 2011. *Neurosurgery Report*, March 11. http://neurosurgerycns.wordpress.com/2011/03/11/introducing-qr-codes-linking-print-and-digital-content-via-smartphone.

Smith, Aaron. 2011. "Americans and Text Messaging." *The Pew Internet & American Life Project.* September 19. http://www.pewinternet.org/Reports/2011/Cell-Phone-Texting-2011.aspx.

Thomas, Lisa Carlucci. 2010. "Gone Mobile? (Mobile Libraries Survey 2010)." *Library Journal*, October 15. http://www.libraryjournal.com/lj/ljinprintcurrentissue/886987-403/gone_mobile_mobile_libraries_survey.html.csp.

Troianovski, Anton. 2011. "Carriers Sweat as Texting Cools Off." *Wall Street Journal*, June 9. Accessed December 27. http://online.wsj.com/article/SB10001424052702304778304576373860513481364.html#ixzz1hfOEY7nE.

2

Mobile Present, Mobile Future

Lisa Carlucci Thomas

Key Points

- Develop a mobile strategy for your library that matches the needs and interests of the community served.
- Identify the key priorities that can be met in the short term on a tight budget and set a foundation for future development.
- A well-developed mobile strategy encompasses a broad range of library services.
- Mobile-patron relationship management builds upon the SMS reference concept to combine marketing, outreach, and sustained interaction.
- Mobile users self-select information streams, seamlessly prioritizing attention based on immediate impulse.
- Cultural and communication forms are irreversibly changing as a result of mobile technology.
- Use the minimum viable product (MVP) method to design and deploy mobile services.
- Think mobile first, web second.

Libraries today operate in uncertain times. Whether you count your library experience in months, years, or decades, you know firsthand that mobile technologies are changing the way we interact with information and that evolving mobile and social information trends are placing new demands on libraries. The migration to digital content and delivery, collaborative creative production and social media, crowd-sourced development of resources, ubiquitous and customizable data streams, and nearly instantaneous point-of-need connectivity to a seemingly infinite amount of information raises increasingly high expectations about how, when, and where one might access content. These factors prompt fresh skepticism about the library's place, function, and utility in the mobile environment and present libraries with a mandate to adapt programs, services, workflows, and collections to suit mobile needs.

In this chapter, we explore existing challenges to developing mobile library services, preview what is next as libraries expand mobile offerings, consider emerging roles and priorities as librarians become active providers of mobile information, and discuss ways for libraries to plan for the future and relevantly engage in the mobile revolution. Libraries offer unique services and support found nowhere else. Library collections include outstanding resources, in multiple formats, designed to meet the various needs of beginning library users to advanced researchers. In addition to printed books, periodicals, and resources, libraries offer e-books, licensed databases, born-digital and digitized items, archives, special collections, ephemera, multimedia resources, and much more. However, for many individuals, the mere mention of libraries stirs a nostalgic soup of teeming stacks, quiet reading rooms, and neatly organized card catalogs. As librarians well know, the modern reality is quite different from that vision. Libraries offer technologically current information resources to meet new demands daily, yet they continue to be defined by outdated assumptions. These assumptions, both internal and external to the profession, restrict our ability to dynamically respond to change. We suffer a fracturing of professional identity and label ourselves "techies" or "non-techies" in support of the new or old ways of being, thus charting the course of our professional, and technological, skill development.

Libraries as dynamic, technologically relevant institutions languish in this debate. Aside from mode of delivery, librarians' professional creed supports access to information content in all forms. We share the responsibility to work together to keep ourselves and our profession current as the information society advances. We are also responsible for talking with our boards, donors, legislators, and communities to modernize expectations about what we already do and to provide the voice and the data as advocates for what's needed to do it better, such as resources, staff, technology, training, and support. Fortunately, librarians are no strangers to shaking things up for the greater good. We work hard to organize and facilitate access to resources, promote freedom of information, ensure patron privacy, demonstrate ethical practices, and rally for fair use. Libraries are community-focused by design and provide an essential foundation for a literate citizenry. In short, librarians face risks and take risks, and embracing the value of new technologies and mobile trends is part of a bigger picture.

CHALLENGES TO MOBILE

Over the past five years, since the introduction of the Apple iPhone and Amazon Kindle, mobile devices of all types, including smartphones, e-readers, and tablets, have become mainstream technologies, and the landscape has broadened significantly. Current iPhones and Kindles are now fifth-generation devices, and Apple's iPad and Amazon's Kindle Fire are leading the pack among portable tablets. Likewise, Android and Windows devices are steady competitors in the smartphone and tablet markets. Without question, we're in the midst of major change. Librarians around the world are working together to learn about, experiment with, and implement mobile technologies by adopting and developing best practices with library peers, institutional partners, vendors, associations, and organizations. In a 2010 study of public and academic libraries in the United States, *Library Journal* asked how many libraries "currently offered" or "planned to offer" services for mobile devices (Thomas 2010). At that time,

44 percent of academic libraries and 34 percent of public libraries reported providing some type of mobile services to their customers. Approximately two out of five libraries had mobile services planned or in discussion. Leading services included text-messaging reference, SMS notices and alerts, mobile-optimized websites and online catalogs, as well as native apps (either developed by the library or purchased). Survey respondents who were not planning mobile services reported several reasons for the decision: limited budgets, lack of priority, insufficient technical skill among staff members, and varying perceptions about the importance of mobile library services. These factors, combined with the cost and constant evolution of device hardware, inhibit libraries' ability to experiment and innovate. And while any one of these barriers could block mobile development in a library, together they impede libraries' collective ability to develop a public awareness of our role in this market as providers of mobile access to information and to engage mobile users at a critical time of patron demand. If we are not making our services available to mobile users and marketing effectively those that we do offer, we risk having patrons go elsewhere.

So how do libraries keep pace with mobile trends in the midst of these concerns? The obstacles to mobile library services are challenging but not insurmountable. Since 2010, we have seen the expansion of mobile offerings and new services on the scene as mobile proficiency among librarians and library users increased. Today's mobile patrons can just as easily search Google via smartphones as they can search a library website or send an text-message reference question. Libraries providing mobile services elect options with added value that will capture the interest and attention of mobile users and offer ongoing engagement. In addition, libraries are steadily improving mobile access to library information, e-books, research databases, and digital collections and are employing mobile technology to maximize access to point-of-need information: from circulating e-reading devices, to developing creative uses for QR codes, to enhancing special collections with augmented reality and geolocation, to the expanded integration of interactive mobile and social platforms and library services.

Libraries seeking to establish an action plan for assessing and implementing appropriate mobile strategies can work with vendor partners, library peers, and information technology consultants to plan both short-term and long-term solutions. As third-party mobile platforms become more readily available, there are new opportunities for experimentation on a shoestring budget, and library vendors are making more mobile features and options available to customers, often at low to no cost. Libraries are also key mobile development partners for vendors creating and improving mobile technologies. For example, Mosio, SirsiDynix, Boopsie, and Fanngle all work closely with library experts to obtain direct feedback from the field.

Library Journal's "Patron Profiles" reports that "[the Gartner Group] expects U.S. sales of smart phones to have grown from 67 million in 2010 to 95 million in 2011" (Patron Profiles 2012, 3). That's a giant leap in a fraction of time. The Pew Research Center reports that "one in every ten American adults now has an iPad or similar device" (Patron Profiles 2012, 4). Mobile-savvy users are arriving, eager and adept with e-readers, smartphones, and tablets, along with a new and evolving set of expectations. Such changes highlight the opportunities presented by the push of mobile technology and underscore the need for libraries to develop a mobile strategy, that is, a tiered approach to meeting the mobile demand, aligned with the institutional goals, and developed along with an action plan based on the specific characteristics of the library and the community.

MOBILE LIBRARIES: NOW

Even if you are still learning about what mobile services are right for your library community, it is necessary to be aware of the opportunities presented by mobile interactivity and to develop a mobile strategy for your library. Your library's mobile strategy, furthermore, will need to evolve as the mobile revolution continues to unfold. As I noted during a 2012 interview on this topic,

Meanwhile, patron expectations continue to evolve, and mobile users seeking mobile access to library services and collections expect to find what they need readily available. What they're actually finding ranges from splendidly concise library mobile websites and mobile searchable catalogs to advanced and complex apps; from straightforward SMS reference services to mobile-social communities via Facebook and Twitter; from value-added mobile services (QR codes, augmented reality, place-based digital collections, research guides, and more) to no mobile services at all. . . . Early adopters are now adept at navigating the mobile information experience, and fledgling users expect those delivering the information to anticipate their needs. (Mosio 2012)

A well-developed mobile strategy encompasses the broadest range of library services, including those mentioned—mobile websites and online catalogs, reference services, and access to collections—and much more, including but not limited to community information, events and programs, room reservations, course materials, and a full suite of patron-account management features, such as renewals, holds, fine payments, virtual bookshelves, and self-checkout. Consider how existing service offerings translate to the mobile environment, and remember that not everything needs to be mobile-accessible immediately. Identify the key priorities that can be met in the short term on a tight budget and set a foundation for future development. Next, work on defining the methods and milestones for establishing quality service transactions with customers across these new delivery methods and platforms. The M-Libraries wiki entry (Library Success Wiki 2012) offers a wealth of information about libraries experimenting with and implementing mobile services, which will be helpful when setting benchmarks for your institution.

Once the services, methods, and benchmarks are determined, creating a patron-relationship management plan ensures that mobile library communications align with existing services, represents the mission of the institution, and maximizes the efficiencies and opportunities of the technology. Mobile patron-relationship management tools offer solutions to help libraries meet their key priorities as well as obtain and assess feedback and strengthen customer relationships. Mobile platforms that offer two-way communication, direct interaction with patrons and library staff, and archived messaging maintain continuity and context and encourage repeat conversation via mobile devices.

A study of the "Text a Librarian" statistics at Southern Connecticut State University, where I implemented and managed SMS reference services from 2010 to 2011, determined a 60/40 split between reference and nonreference mobile interactions. Reference questions included circulation and collections inquiries, requests for assistance with course reserves and citations, research support, and numerous technical and e-resource questions, most related to off-site access. Nonreference inquiries ranged from questions about building hours and holiday schedules to asking about library technology and equipment, from direct requests to contact subject librarians to feedback and complaints about services and spaces. These reference and nonreference questions alike are potential springboards to further conversation, offering new prospects for improving point-of-need patron satisfaction and amassing qualitative data for future assessment.

By promoting direct, responsive communication via text messaging, libraries can both assess and address the mobile information needs of their unique customer base. Moreover, as more libraries provide mobile offerings, expect these types of nonreference communications from mobile users to increase. Libraries need a better way to manage these interactions effectively and assist patrons for whom text-message communication is the preferred point of contact. Mobile-patron relationship management expands upon the SMS reference concept to combine marketing, outreach, and interaction to meet a broader need for information services beyond the basic reference inquiry. In addition, it is applicable and relevant to the widest range of mobile library users, as users can use any type of mobile phone.

As emerging information technologies have driven demand for new library communication channels, we have seen increased interest in the use of mobile tools to promote interaction, expand outreach, market programs, and connect the physical and virtual library experiences. Libraries today are at widely different levels of mobile engagement, and when you factor in the outstanding shift taking place in the way we collectively communicate and interact with information, what is needed now and what is realistic for libraries to implement right way become very different conversations. It is up to the librarians and administrators to evaluate the barriers and options, the risks and benefits, of providing mobile services. With the mobile landscape in constant flux and library budgets equally changeable, having a mobile plan mapped out in advance ensures that informed decisions and quick action are within reach.

MOBILE LIBRARIES: NEXT STEPS

Cultural and communication norms are irreversibly changing as a result of mobile technology. Furthermore, not only does mobile communication offer convenience for remote users, it connects individuals to multiple places concurrently, diverting attention from information in close proximity. Sherry Turkle describes a common scene: "Walking through a college library or the campus of a high-tech start-up, one sees the same thing: we are together, but each of us is in our own bubble, furiously connected to keyboards and tiny touch screens" (Turkle 2012). Mobile users self-select information streams, seamlessly prioritizing attention based on immediate impulse. For libraries to relevantly compete under these circumstances, we have to take a proactive role in establishing and maintaining patron relationships, and seek creative ways to promote fortuitous and responsive communications with mobile library users. We can do this by examining our present information services, determining specific steps to take toward mobile implementation, and consciously refining our mobile-oriented programs and services. Consider it a steady work in progress. Next steps require taking a creative, entrepreneurial approach toward mobile innovation.

1. Write a "State of Mobile" report for your institution, assessing and evaluating the challenges to mobile innovation. This document will serve as the foundation for planning efforts and the baseline for assessment of mobile services. The mobile report should include:
   a. Budget and resources for mobile technologies
   b. Priority and value to the library community

    c. Technical skill and ability, including staff training requirements

    d. Perceptions and awareness of mobile library trends, technologies, and services

2. Plan "Mobile First, Web Second": "[mobile devices] occupy a lot of people's leisure time. Therefore if your app is geared toward leisure activities (games, communications with friends, etc.) then mobile is awesome" (Suster 2012). The more we know about mobile behavior, the more we can customize content and services to appeal to the mobile audience and keep users interested. As more data are hosted in the cloud, as more social networks allow for institutional accounts, and as more mobile options include gamification and incentives for participation, the more creative libraries can be about integrating these options into their suite of mobile library services. Key points to remember include the following:

    a. Design new services for mobile first.

    b. Adapt existing web content to the mobile web.

    c. Integrate, don't abandon, web development efforts.

    d. Third-party mobile social platforms expand library presence and engagement.

3. Go lean. *The Lean Startup* method suggests creating a "minimum viable product (MVP)" to begin the "process of learning as quickly as possible" (Ries 2011, 93)" Once an MVP has been created, author Eric Ries recommends "a full turn of the Build-Measure-Learn loop with a minimum amount of effort" in order to determine whether to "pivot or persevere" (Ries 2011, 75–78).

    a. The MVP, by definition, is a rough draft, just thorough enough to test and measure.

    b. Test to establish a baseline for your library or consortium.

    c. Obtain both qualitative and quantitative feedback.

    d. Pivot (revise hypothesis) or persevere (improve and assess).

4. Predict the future. "Emerging technologies are a matter not only of qualitative challenge, but also of sheer quantitative overload," says Bryan Alexander, Director of Research at the National Institute for Technology and Liberal Education (NITLE) (Alexander 2009). Such overload can paralyze the decision-making process. Future modeling provides a means of navigating uncertain times based on reasoning and expertise. Alexander (2009) details these future modeling techniques:

    a. Environmental scanning—surveying immediate trends from a variety of sources

    b. The Delphi method—consult the experts via a collaborative process

    c. Prediction markets—use economic models to "trade ideas"

    d. Scenarios—create a projected story and examine the variables using role playing

    e. Crowdsourcing—solicit open feedback from a wide range of voluntary participants

Mobile technologies are a driving force for innovation in libraries. They are influencing research behavior and patron expectations, and these norms will continue to evolve. By evaluating the present possibilities for mobile services, reviewing web content from a mobile perspective, demonstrating flexible and agile development models, and anticipating the future, we position libraries favorably as effective providers of mobile information. Expanding public interest in mobile services, including access to e-books and digital content, is fueling controversy related to digital publication, distribution, and licensing, for libraries, publishers, vendors, and individuals. Fortunately, "early [library] innovators are amassing and sharing the knowledge gained through their experiences, assessing the multiple variables that define each library's unique operating environment and community" (Thomas 2012). Mobile library services well supported by a functional mobile strategy, clearly defined goals, and innovative processes provide a solid foundation for ongoing development and participation.

Libraries today are indeed operating in uncertain times. These are times of constant change and technological advancement. The swift influence of mobile culture has long-term, widespread, cross-industry implications. Next-generation devices and new applications with increased functionality and complexity will continue to vex and inspire as consumers of all ages purchase and upgrade to new models. Even for the mobile-proficient, it is a culture of new, newer, and newest. As we actively seek ways to go mobile within the context of organizational priorities and community needs, we can design services that are workable, scalable, and adjustable. Learning about the changes that are taking place in the mobile sphere, overcoming barriers to implementation, creatively enhancing existing services, and employing new mobile methods to interact with and support patron needs are all part of the process. The lasting potential of mobile library services will only be realized through endeavor, experimentation, and experience.

REFERENCES

Alexander, Bryan. 2009. "Apprehending the Future: Emerging Technologies, from Science Fiction to Campus." *EDUCAUSE Review*. May/June. http://www.educause.edu/EDUCAUSE +Review/EDUCAUSEReviewMagazineVolume44/ApprehendingtheFutureEmergingT/ 171774.

Library Success Wiki. 2012. "M-Libraries." Accessed April 28, 2012. http://www.libsuccess.org/ index.php?title=M-Libraries.

Mosio. 2012. "Library Thought Leaders Q&A: Lisa Carlucci Thomas." *Text a Librarian – Library Help Desk Software* [Blog], January 12. http://www.textalibrarian.com/ mobileref/library-thought-leaders-qa-lisa-carlucci-thomas/.

Patron Profiles. 2012. *Patron Profiles: Mobile Devices, Mobile Content and Library Apps*. New York: Library Journal.

Ries, Eric. 2011. *The Lean Startup: How Today's Entrepreneurs Use Continuous Innovation to Create Radically Successful Business*. New York: Crown Business.

Suster, Mark. 2012. "Web Second, Mobile First." *Both Sides of the Table* [Blog]. January 28. http://www.bothsidesofthetable.com/2012/01/28/web-second-mobile-first.

Thomas, Lisa Carlucci. 2010. "Gone Mobile? (Mobile Libraries Survey 2010)." *Library Journal*. October 15. http://www.libraryjournal.com/lj/ljinprintcurrentissue/886987-403/gone _mobile_mobile_libraries_survey.html.csp.

Thomas, Lisa Carlucci. 2012. "The State of Mobile in Libraries 2012 (Mobile Libraries 2012)." *Library Journal*. February 7. http://www.thedigitalshift.com/2012/02/mobile/the-state-of -mobile-in-libraries-2012.

Turkle, Sherry. 2012. "The Flight from Conversation." *New York Times*. April 22. http://www .nytimes.com/2012/04/22/opinion/sunday/the-flight-from-conversation.html.

3

The New York Public Library and the World of Tomorrow—*Biblion: The Boundless Library*

Deanna Lee

Key Points

- *Biblion*, a scholarly journal devoted to the New York Public Library (NYPL) collections, has been reimagined as a mobile experience that brings to new audiences a magazine-like reading experience of serendipitous discovery.
- The multimedia experience builds upon how people move through physical collections, stacks, and exhibition spaces.
- The first collection presented in the new *Biblion* highlights the records of the New York World's Fair 1939/1940 Corporation.
- The storytelling model is based upon a new spatial construct of information: the story/stacks exist on multiple planes, versus single-layer consecutive magazine pages or digital information presented one-dimensionally, with every item one equal click, one equal link away.
- Options for different reading experiences and different journeys through content are a key component of NYPL initiatives, especially important for digital, multimedia, and mobile projects.
- The goal is not to tell and present stories in one way only but to give readers many visual pathways to understanding the nearly infinite number of possible narratives.

Thanks to today's fast-evolving and ever more creative mobile technologies, we can fulfill libraries' mission of extending public access to information to record numbers of people in myriad ways. We can redefine what it means to read and to explore. And, with e-readers and touch capabilities, we can allow people to hold the documents and treasures that tell the stories of humankind—right in their own hands.

This game-changer turns on its head the widespread misconception that libraries' role and usefulness are being diminished by the advent of e-books—which are of course being checked out free from public library websites by ever-increasing numbers of people. For, in addition to circulating collections, libraries are chock full of special collections—with the very rarity of holdings necessitating limited access. Too many people have not been able to actually see and hold, much less be inspired by, some of the greatest treasures documenting our history and lives.

The New York Public Library's collections of more than 65 million items have long been compared to the holdings of the world's great national libraries. The vast majority—over 50 million—are rare, noncirculating items, many held in 88 miles of stacks in the library's landmark Stephen A. Schwarzman Building alone. Treasures safeguarded at the 42nd Street library include the Honus Wagner baseball card (perhaps the world's rarest), the first Gutenberg Bible to cross the Atlantic, a 1672 map showing California as an island, the personal papers of performing-arts giants ranging from Lillian Gish to John Cage, Malcolm X's briefcase, Jack Kerouac's harmonica, and not only the handwritten manuscript of Virginia Woolf's *To the Lighthouse* but her walking cane, which she left at the River Ouse when she took her own life. Items like these are generally physically accessible only to those with a demonstrated research need, for obvious reasons of preservation.

To both promote and broaden the impact of the library's vast collections, NYPL Communications had been considering a digital rebirth of *Biblion* (1992–2001), its scholarly journal devoted to the collections, which had reached only a somewhat limited list of subscribers, primarily research libraries. The first iPad came on the scene in 2010. With its (then) unique touch capabilities, we realized the time had come to reimagine and realize a new kind of presentation of our collections and of *Biblion*—one that would bring to new audiences a magazine-like reading experience of serendipitous discovery.

Working in concert with the very talented designers and developers at Potion Design, we plunged forward with the goal of making an innovative app providing unparalleled access to the unique and magnificent collections of the library, one that would meet both the mission and some of the most important challenges faced by NYPL, and indeed all libraries, today:

- to provide a multimedia, online experience different from but building upon how one moves through physical collections, stacks, and exhibitions spaces
- to make the past relevant, connecting it not only to the present but to a future full of potential for libraries and anyone in the information business
- to broaden our definition of audience not only demographically but to one eager for more active engagement

What we ended up with was *Biblion: The Boundless Library*—named Apple's 2011 Education iPad App of the Year, approaching 150,000 downloads in just seven months, far exceeding our hopes for an app about a World's Fair that took place more than 70 years ago.

GIVING THE CONTENT SHAPE

Biblion is based on the idea of the library's unlimited stacks (throughout the app's design one "sees" metaphorical linear stacks, sometimes in shadow as in

Figure 3.1
Metaphorical linear stacks of the Biblion app. Image copyright The New York Public Library.

Fig. 3.1)—and that once you give readers visual pathways through those stacks, *infinite narratives emerge.*

The potential for unlimited storylines was one of the reasons we chose the "World of Tomorrow" extensive records of the New York World's Fair 1939/1940 Corporation, contained in the library in over 2,500 boxes. Among scholars, it is one of our most requested collections—full of official and unofficial documents, letters, drawings, photographs, ephemera, and rare sound and film archives. In the app, we present over 700 of those rare items for people to hold, turn over, flip through, and zoom into, organized in an "infoscape" allowing the visualization of that content as part of a world or storytelling whole.

The entry point is referred to as an "exhibition wall" of organic groupings or themes that emerge when the original sources are given shape—processed and organized by NYPL archivists and curators and made easily browsable through an amazingly extensive 700-page finding aid to the collection. Users moving through the theme areas can see how the fair, like the library, has something for everyone—from a world dealing with economic despair and war ("A Moment in Time"), to starlets and exotic animals ("You Ain't Seen Nothin' Yet"), to food and pop culture ("Fashion, Food and Famous Faces"), and technological innovation ("Enter the World of Tomorrow").

Entering the World of Tomorrow, one sees stories organized as "stacks" comprised of a real visualization of the exact items that make up story lines:

- galleries of photos and documents—the blue, yellow, and white stripes—with introductory text on the left, as in "Mad Science" (Fig. 3.2a)
- essays by leading scholars such as Ron Simon of the Paley Center writing on the introduction of television at the fair, naturally more text-based (Fig. 3.2b)

Figure 3.2a
The Mad Science gallery of images and texts. Image copyright The New York Public Library.

Figure 3.2b
Example of a primarily text-based essay introducing television. Image copyright The New York Public Library.

• stories, like "48 'Typical' Families at the Fair" chosen from each state for their personification of all-American values, which provide narrative text about the contest and contestants in addition to the wealth of photographs, audio interviews (the red stripes), and more in the collection (Fig. 3.2c)

Through these different formats and visual presentations, the *content is given shape.* The storytelling model is based upon a new spatial construct of information: the story/ stacks exist on multiple planes, versus single-layer consecutive magazine pages or digital information presented one-dimensionally, with every item one equal click, one equal link away. By showing items individually and as part of a whole, *Biblion* allows the reader to see the length, the breadth, and the types of content that comprise a story. One can feel its weight and be inspired to dive right into the narrative.

For example, diving into "48 'Typical' Families at the Fair," stunning photographs are interspersed with a governor's introduction of his state's selected family and even detailed applications (Fig. 3.3), which can be read and zoomed into to glean, for example, the "ambitions of children." The Burdin siblings of Miami, 14 and 12, wanted "to be a certified public accountant" and "to teach music . . . until I'm old enough to get married and have three children." Their father made $2,000 a year, was a Purple Heart recipient, and listed the Bible as his preferred book.

Figure 3.2c
Example of a multimedia story about 48 typical families. Image copyright The New York Public Library.

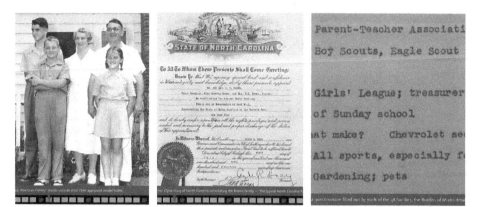

Figure 3.3

Images and documents regarding "typical families." Image copyright The New York Public Library.

OPTIONS FOR MULTIPLE PATHWAYS OF DISCOVERY

At the same time, in aiming for a magazine-like reading experience, touch-and-swipe capabilities provide the reader with the option of flipping through a story, even skipping forward to the end. So a scroll bar at the bottom of the frame—again, representing the exact items that make up a given story—allows one with a simple slide of the finger to, in the case of "48 'Typical' Families," move forward right to the champions, the ultimate all-American family: the Leathers, hailing from Texas.

A novel and important part of *Biblion*, especially as a library app, is the option to "see less and read more." Thus, while the landscape or "gallery" view allows one to experience the content in a computer-screen-like, media-heavy view, with the focus on the gallery items themselves filling the frame, a simple rotation to "book" view turns the device into a text-heavier e-reader. From a gallery photo of that proud Leathers family (Fig. 3.4a), a reader turning to "book" view can digest details not only about them but about how winning families were chosen (by newspapermen), what prizes they received (including baseballs autographed by Babe Ruth for the boys), and more (Fig. 3.4b).

Options for different reading experiences and different journeys through content are a key component of NYPL initiatives, especially important for digital, multimedia, and mobile projects. Our patrons come from many walks of life, and they come to libraries for an array of needs; at the same time, they are widely varied in their technical facility. Digital and touch-technology exploration come naturally to many, and to an increasing numbers of users, but not all; others for a variety of reasons prefer a more classically directed presentation.

Towards this end, and in acknowledgement that many of our patrons come to the NYPL for our communities of scholarship and expertise, *Biblion* includes a number of

Figure 3.4a

Gallery view of the most typical American family. Image copyright The New York Public Library.

STORY
48 "Typical" Families at the Fair

The winning Leathers family poses in front of the Ford car that brought th the Fair.

TYPICALLY TYPICAL IN EVERY WAY
But there could only be one ultimate winning family. On October 15, 1940, the Leathers family from Clarendon, Te was voted "Most Typical Americans" and invited to return the Fair in November. The family consisted of John Leath 19; his sister Margaret Joan Leathers, 16; and Mr. and Mr E. Leathers, whose first names and ages were not provide the PR department in their press release.

Figure 3.4b
Book view of the most typical American family. Image copyright The New York Public Library.

FASHION, FOOD & FAMOUS FACES

Tales from the Fair

e Czech Consul, wrote this letter asking for help.

War and the Czech Pavilion

The building of the Czechoslovakia Pavilion at the World's Fair proceeded amidst political uncertainty and intense negotiations; the fate of the country hung in the balance as Fair planning progressed. Intimations of the unfolding conflict in Europe can be found in the files, correspondence, and photographs related to the status of the pavilion and of Czechoslovakia itself. Throughout 1938, Czechoslovakia was under threat from Nazi Germany to cede its western border areas, known as the Sudetenland. In September, the Munich...

READ MORE ➡

Read about war and the Czech Pavilion.

unknown, the all-American feast never came Gaige did assemble regional recipes in his *Fair Cookbook: The American Kitchen*, which hed in 1939.

spired was the proposal by Althea Lepper of anted to operate a small restaurant that sold ern corn bread with bacon, ham, and maple e my idea, too, to have a real southern : and good Negro serving help," she wrote. rejected, and I assume, although I do not that the poignant plea of Marie Hanc, wife ak consul, also failed. Her letter, written nd's back, is one of the saddest documents l a sharp reminder that the Fair that

Figure 3.5
Example of an inter-story connection with Biblion. Image copyright The New York Public Library.

essays that serve as guided tours through the collection and through the app. Reading contributions from a wide group of researchers and authors—from professors and graduate students to *Daily Show* writer Elliott Kalan to *The New York Times*'s William Grimes—users can share in and follow along with, for example, the "Gastronomic Tales from the Fair" that Grimes unearthed during his culinary travels through the collection.

One particularly notable discovery, a surprise even to the library, was a 1939 handwritten letter from Marie Hanc, wife of the Czechoslovak consul to New York mayor Fiorello H. La Guardia, asking for the opportunity to run a sandwich stand at the Fair to support her family, stranded far from their country. Grimes calls this "one of the saddest documents in the archive, and a sharp reminder that the Fair that promised the World of Tomorrow sounded the last note of optimism in a very dark time."

A major goal of the Library being to provide historical and cultural context—underscoring and bringing to life, for example, the "very dark time" leading to Marie Hanc's poignant plea—*Biblion* aims to maximize the breadth and depth of the World's Fair collection by providing dynamic links or interstory connections, recreating the serendipitous discovery of research. These links provide context in a new and integral way, showing how the stories and subject matter of our lives are interconnected, from food, to history and politics, to commerce and culture, and more.

To learn about Hitler's annexation of Czechoslovakia and how that played out at the Fair, a reader of the Hanc letter can follow a yellow interstory connection (Fig. 3.5) to the story of the building of the Czech Pavilion. That story in turn can lead to one documenting 18 months of negotiations for a German Pavilion, which showcases telegrams to Berlin,

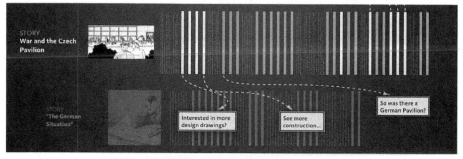

Figure 3.6
Countless possibilities for serendipitous discovery within the Biblion infoscape. Image copyright
The New York Public Library.

rare design sketches proposing that the German Pavilion abut that of Yugoslavia, and
newspaper articles and photographs covering a heated feud between Joseph Goebbels and
La Guardia, whom the German propaganda chief called "New York's gangster-in-chief."

The goal is not to tell and present stories in one way only but to give readers many
visual pathways to understanding the nearly infinite number of possible narratives.
Readers choose their own progression and journey through the app's stories, essays,
and galleries—not unlike browsing through library stacks, but here in the app the reader
explores and jumps from stack to stack, story to story.

While one reader might move from food to Czechoslovakia to Germany
(Fig. 3.6), another might be led from a mosaic in the Czech Pavilion to view a gallery
of public art throughout the Fair, and from there to see and learn how one prominent
sculpture took shape in a gallery of Augusta Savage's *The Harp*, the very popular work
inspired by the African American anthem "Lift Every Voice and Sing." One can read
about it through original Fair captions and hold precious views of a work that did not
survive the Fair. (A small bronze version of the original is held by NYPL's Schomburg
Center for Research in Black Culture.)

In gently guiding readers through links to thus move and explore between stories and
stacks, the app provides countless serendipitous moments of discovery in a world of information unlike any other—an "infoscape" or charted world of library holdings laid out with
multilinear stories. *Biblion* thus moves beyond a traditional progression through items or
stories as in a book or magazine. Each story exists on its own within the compendium of
stories. Not only does this equalize the information, it creates a more user-driven experience of content. Someone using *Biblion* can choose different entry points to a world of
information instead of being presented with a static collection of articles. Once in a story,
the user can follow contextual links to jump to different narratives without losing a sense
of structure. The experience is not only a new paradigm; it replicates being in an environment with multiple stimuli (such as the Fair or a library).

Biblion clearly demonstrates that libraries have the creativity and potential to be at the
forefront of new forms of communication and, critically, innovative digital design with a
purpose. Throughout the process of making the app, design aimed to reflect the
physical-library experience of exploration, browsing, and delving into research or a book;
to increase access to information through new formats in new ways; and to involve and
inspire diverse communities of learners. As with any content-driven enterprise for the

NYPL, the institution's mission is the constant creative guide: to inspire lifelong learning, advance knowledge, and strengthen our communities. The full name of the app speaks to these goals of opening up the unparalleled resources and riches of the library; we invite all users to experience NYPL through *Biblion: The Boundless Library.*[1]

NOTE

1. *Biblion* and its 1939/1940 World's Fair collection items are also accessible free on a website drawing from the same content management system (CMS) at exhibitions.nypl.org/ biblion/worldsfair. In addition, virtually every image in the app is available to view and purchase in the NYPL Digital Gallery at digitalgallery.nypl.org (digital ID numbers for items are included in the app).

Part 2

Mobile Library Users

4

Mobile Learning: The Teacher in Your Pocket

Meredith Farkas

Key Points

- Mobile learning presents pedagogical possibilities for seamless, interactive, contextual, and individualized learning.
- Library applications of mobile technologies for learning cover several areas of need.
  - Orientations and tours become self-guided, engaged learning.
  - Point-of-need instruction is enhanced when delivered to mobile devices.
  - In-class use and classroom response systems are improved by smartphones and tablets.
  - Instructional outreach involves making content accessible where the users are.
- Considerations for the use of mobile devices in library instruction include knowing the mobile habits of your community, their instructional needs, and how to optimize instructional content for mobile use.

Mobile computing has exploded around the world over the past several years. Morgan Stanley suggests that mobile Internet use will exceed the use from fixed devices, and Ericsson projects that 80 percent of people will access the web from a mobile device by 2015 (Ingram 2010; Ericsson Corporate Public & Media Relations 2010). Mobile devices are being used for content creation, communication, information seeking, and so much more. The notion that mobile devices would be used only for quick and simple tasks has been challenged by research showing that a growing portion of the population—especially low-income and minority mobile users—use their phones as the primary means of accessing the web (Smith 2010). This growth in the usage of mobile devices in all aspects of people's lives has led educators to look to it as an ideal mechanism for delivering content and improving interactivity in learning. In 2011, mobile learning was named a top trend with an adoption horizon of less than a year in K–12 and in higher education in the *NMC Horizon Reports* (Johnson et al. 2011;

Johnson, Adams, and Haywood 2011). Mobile phones and other handheld devices have become valuable learning tools that can be capitalized on inside and outside of the classroom.

MOBILE LEARNING

Mobile learning is more than just providing content that is accessible on a mobile device. Just like the social technologies that made the web a more participatory medium, mobile devices and technologies can have a tremendous impact on teaching and learning. The large-scale adoption of mobile devices has opened up new pedagogical possibilities for making learning more seamless, contextual, and individualized.

Many scholars have written about the growing disconnect between how people learn in the classroom and in the world around them (Pence 2011; Squire 2010). The divisions between learning, work, and recreation have become increasingly blurred as seamless, open, networked, web-based learning has become the new norm. In order to prepare students for the world in which they will continue to learn once they are finished with school, it is critical that we build bridges between formal and informal learning activities.

Mobile learning has the potential to transform the experiences of both learning and teaching, merging formal and informal learning seamlessly. Because people can take their mobile devices anywhere, instructors can provide just-in-time information for users in modular pieces rather than providing all of the information students might need from the outset. It gives students more autonomy, enabling them to direct their own learning at their point of need. Increased learner autonomy has been shown to improve student achievement by encouraging students to take responsibility for their own learning (Mcloughlin and Lee 2008).

When information is meant to be accessed at the point of need, according to Traxler, "finding information rather than possessing it or knowing it becomes the defining characteristic of learning" (Traxler 2007, 3). Students can individualize their learning by seeking out the information that meets their unique learning needs. A student who needs additional help in a specific area can spend more time on that topic than one who already feels confident in her or his knowledge of that topic. This shift towards student autonomy is consistent with a constructivist pedagogy, which sees students as active participants in learning. The instructor is more of a facilitator than a "sage on the stage," creating a positive environment for individualized learning (Barnes and Tynan 2007).

Mobile technologies can help to engage students at multiple levels, providing a richer and more contextualized learning experience. Learning does not happen in a vacuum; context and application are critical elements of learning. Building experiences using mobile devices that allow students to apply their learning in real or realistic contexts can lead to better learning outcomes (Liestøl 2011). Mobile technologies can connect users to additional information in a variety of formats, appealing to multiple learning styles and diverse student needs. They are also useful for both gathering data and providing feedback, enabling a more seamless information flow between learner and environment, and learner and instructor.

Tools like QR codes can provide a bridge between the physical and virtual worlds. QR codes tie physical and web-based content together much in the way that hyperlinks connect web pages. The great benefit of electronic content is that users can easily move from what they are reading to find additional information on a topic they want to know more about. Many e-book readers allow users to easily query Wikipedia or other reference works to get the definition of a term with which they are unfamiliar. Given that interest in the adoption of e-books in education is decidedly mixed, QR codes may be the perfect tool to provide similar functionality for physical books. Rather than reading a book and then walking to one's computer to look something up, QR codes enable professors to provide additional information on a topic that the students can access simply by scanning a QR code with their phones.

A number of studies have been conducted on the use of QR codes to connect physical learning materials to virtual ones, and all have found it to be an effective method of providing seamless access (Chen, Teng, and Lee 2011; Ozcelik and Acarturk 2011; Law and So 2010). Professors have provided suggestions of individual readings on topics for years. With QR codes, however, they can provide these materials to students within the required texts, accessible at the click of a button. This is an excellent way both to scaffold learning for students and provide an individualized experience. It can also be helpful in connecting texts to supporting multimedia, such as videos or 3D learning objects. Ozcelik and Acarturk (2011) compared students who read a text and accessed complementary resources from a computer to those who accessed the resources through a mobile device using QR codes embedded in the text. They found that "reducing the spatial distance between disparate sources of information reduces extraneous cognitive load, thus leading to an enhanced learning" (Ozcelik and Acarturk 2011, 2083).

Because most mobile devices contain global positioning systems (GPS), location-aware mobile learning software can be designed to provide information to the user in relevant geographical spaces. This takes point-of-need learning to the next level, providing context-specific information to individuals rather than expecting the user to seek it. In the United Kingdom, Durham University is using location-aware technology to provide campus information to students based on where they are (Walsh 2010a).

In addition to providing location-based information, location-aware learning software could be a powerful tool for authentic learning. Authentic learning is focused on engagement and information seeking in real or realistic settings (Traxler 2007). Connecting digital information to real-world experiences can provide valuable context that is missing when students simply digest information in their dorm rooms. One interesting example of this is the game *Sick at South Beach*, a mobile learning game that requires students to play the roles of chemists, doctors, and ecologists engaged in uncovering the cause of a mysterious illness. Participants in the game go into the field armed with personal digital assistants (PDAs) that provide useful data when the participants reach specific sites (Squire 2010). This closely simulates what experts investigating a real public health crisis would do. Problem-based learning has long been shown to provide a more authentic and lasting learning experience, and marrying problem-based activities with location-aware mobile learning will only make it more authentic.

GreenHat is a mobile learning application developed at the University of California at Berkeley with the goal of helping students to think like experts. Ryokai, Oehlberg, Manoochehri, and Agogino (2011) designed GreenHat to enable "students [to] learn about biodiversity and sustainability issues in their surroundings from experts' points of view, before participating in unfamiliar debates about their familiar surroundings" (Ryokai et al. 2011, 2149). Rather than simply reading expert views on a particular topic, students in the GreenHat research watched videos where experts discussed their perspectives on a particular ecosystem on the Berkeley campus while the students were touring that ecosystem. When students would come to a particular place in that ecosystem, a relevant video would play on their mobile device, providing additional context to what they were observing. The researchers hoped that students would look at this familiar landscape through new eyes, gaining perspective from the diverse views of the experts.

Ryokai et al. (2011) compared a group accessing this expert content in the field to a group of students accessing the content on a computer inside of a building. Students using mobile devices in the field gave answers to follow-up questions about the ecosystem that melded both their own personal views and those of the experts. The students on the computers tended to simply regurgitate what the experts said. The students using mobile devices also stated that the assignment felt more personal because they were experiencing it as they were learning. Providing students with context-specific information while in the field can be a valuable tool for helping students develop the critical inquiry skills and personal views necessary to think like an expert in their field (Ryokai et al. 2011).

Another way of providing location-based instruction is through augmented reality. Augmented reality overlays content (data, images, and information most commonly) over reality. For example, the Yelp application allows people to view ratings and reviews of the shops, restaurants, and bars in their local area. The Monocle augmented reality part of the application places those ratings in an individual's field of vision as they look through the phone's camera. Augmented reality brings the virtual and physical even closer than QR codes by actually placing both in the same frame of view. Right now, most people access augmented reality applications through a handheld device with GPS and compass and a phone, but in the future, people might use glasses that provide the same functionality but do not require the user to walk around with a device held in front of their face.

When it comes to learning about places and events in history, augmented reality can provide additional context to student learning. Reading about a Greek temple can't compare to actually seeing an image of that Greek temple superimposed over the ruin itself. iTacitus (Intelligent Tourism and Cultural Information through Ubiquitous Services) is an augmented-reality application that overlays images, audio clips, events, and other information over the views at cultural heritage sites in order to provide additional context for tourists (Pence 2011). The Bavarian State Library developed Ludwig II: Walking in the Footsteps of a Fairytale King, an augmented-reality application that layers photographs, audio, and 3D recreations of buildings over locations in modern Bavaria. It allows individuals to see buildings specific to Ludwig II's history that no longer exist and to get a sense of what life was like there while actually in the field (Die Bayerische Staatsbibliothek 2011). Augmented reality can make history come to life, providing additional context that is impossible to gain from reading a book or simply walking around a historical site. This sort of "ambient learning" brings information to users through an exciting visual medium by virtue of their being at a specific location (Fletcher 2010).

One university that has embraced mobile technologies in a big way is Abilene Christian University in Texas. In 2008, the university began offering each incoming student a choice of either an iPhone or iPod Touch (Woodbury 2009). Other universities have experimented with giving students mobile devices, but none have also made research into mobile technologies for learning such an integral part of the university's mission. The university has aggressively funded research into mobile learning and mobile-learning application development and has pushed faculty in every department to make pedagogical use of mobile technologies in the classroom. From podcast lectures in Chemistry, to augmented-reality apps in Art, to blogging via mobile devices in Musicology, faculty members are truly embracing the challenge of incorporating mobile technologies into their teaching. A fall 2010 faculty survey found that 84 percent of faculty regularly use mobile devices in class (Abilene Christian University 2011).

In Abilene's 2010–2011 Mobile Learning Report (2011), the director of educational innovation, Dr. William Rankin, assesses their progress:

Our efforts are increasingly breaking down the walls of the classroom, removing barriers so teachers and students can engage more fully with and take their learning more easily into the world around them. We're discovering that the power of mobility comes not only from the ability to access information, but also from the ability to create it, and the creative opportunities during this third year of our initiative have been staggering. (3)

Figure 4.1
Ludwig II: Walking in the Footsteps of a Fairytale King augmented reality app.

In addition to being a model for other universities exploring mobile learning, Abilene is doing a tremendous service to its students by preparing them for an increasingly mobile world where point-of-need inquiry will be the key to success. The vast majority of students at Abilene (approximately 85%) feel that mobile technologies in the academic experience have increased collaboration, improved communication with teachers, and increased their sense of control over their learning environment (Abilene Christian University 2011).

LIBRARY APPLICATIONS OF MOBILE TECHNOLOGIES FOR LEARNING

The majority of libraries are still in the infancy of their efforts to provide services to patrons with mobile devices. In most cases, libraries have, at best, a mobile website that provides access to the library's hours, catalog, reference help, and other basic services. It is not surprising that the examples of libraries providing instructional services for mobile users are not nearly as common as mobile website examples. However, there are plenty of libraries that have developed innovative mobile technologies and services to improve student learning. In addition, there are plenty of possible applications of mobile technologies for instruction that no library has yet attempted. The possibilities discussed in this part of the chapter range from the free and easy-to-implement to projects that require a great deal of time and technical expertise. It's important that librarians consider which applications would be a good fit for their library, given the needs of patrons and the library's technological constraints.

Figure 4.2
Ludwig II: Walking in the Footsteps of a Fairytale King augmented reality app.

Orientations and Tours

Library orientation tours are almost always a source of stress and excitement for instruction and outreach librarians. Some libraries struggle with getting students in the library at all, while others have to find ways to cope with thousands of first-year students descending on the library over the course of a day or two. Whatever the challenge, planning for library orientations is also exciting as there are so many interesting ways libraries can approach this activity. Most libraries have moved away from the typical walking tour guided by a librarian, opting for strategies that require students to be actively engaged in the learning process.

Since iPods became the go-to accessory for most people in their teens and twenties by 2004, libraries have been developing audio-based instructional content. Museums often offer audio tours of their collections. These tours take the visitor through the museum, offering background information on items of interest. This offers visitors the opportunity to learn more about the collection than they would by simply looking at it. It is also meant to replace the traditional group tour, which forces each individual to go at the same pace as everyone else. Some libraries have similarly developed audio tours that introduce patrons to the layout of the library and the library's services and collections. These self-guided introductions to the library allow patrons to learn more about the library on their schedule and at their own pace.

While one might think that an audio tour provides an opportunity to go into greater detail about the collections and services, librarians developing audio tours should strive to provide only the most important information with the greatest relevance to students. The tours must be succinct and engaging in order to keep students interested. Also, because this is a self-guided tour, it is critical to ensure that library terminology users may be unfamiliar with is well-explained. The audio tour for the Bostock Library at Duke University[1] uses terms like "circulation," "open stacks," "reserve," and "interlibrary loan," which may not be familiar to first-year students. It may be worthwhile to test the terminology used in the library tour on library novices in order to ensure that the communication is effective. Librarians and even work-study students often have difficulty seeing things from the point-of-view of the novice user.

When the fifth-generation iPod was released with the capacity to play video, librarians not surprisingly started to think about ways to capitalize on this innovation. Many video tours created by libraries are not designed for use by someone simultaneously touring the physical library; these are usually more fast-paced and focused on promoting collections and services than on orienting users to the building. Those video tours that are specifically designed as walking tours are often broken up into sections or contain instructions to pause the video so that users can position themselves at the location relevant to the content being displayed.

The University of California–Merced Library developed a video tour[2] for students that introduced them to the physical building as well as the services housed within it. Staff loaded the tour onto 15 iPod Touches that could be checked out but also made the tour available for download onto the students' own devices. This sort of hardware support is vital when not all students on campus necessarily have the requisite technology. The librarians worked with the freshman writing program to embed the tour into those classes because they were a key place in the curriculum for students to be introduced to the library. For students who took the tour as part of the freshman writing program, they were also required to complete an online assignment tied to what they learned in the tour. This provided both acknowledgment to instructors that students completed the tour and valuable assessment data for the library regarding the efficacy of the tour as an instructional tool (Mikkelsen and Davidson 2011).

One benefit of audio or video tours is that the audio content can be translated into different languages, providing a valuable service for students whose first language may not be English. The Wells Library at Indiana University provides its audio tours[3] in 24 languages, including Korean, Swahili, Mandarin, Italian, and Farsi. Another benefit over a live tour is that students can always come back to parts of the library tour they didn't understand or are most interested in.

Game-based learning has become increasingly popular in libraries because of its huge potential to engage learners. One type of game-based orientation that takes advantage of the near ubiquity of mobile devices is the QR code scavenger hunt. Burns (2011), a librarian at Penn State Wilkes-Barre, developed a QR code hunt for her English 004 classes. She placed QR codes all over the library that linked users to either text or a web page that would help them answer the questions in the hunt. Burns stated that in addition to providing information literacy instruction, the activity "forced the students to pay attention to their surroundings, not only to look for the codes, but to look at the code in the context of the physical space of the library" (Burns 2011, 12). Other QR code scavenger hunts require users to take pictures of specific things, proving that students actually visited each location.

Public libraries have also jumped on the QR code scavenger hunt bandwagon. The Lake Forest Public Library in Illinois and the Contra Costa County Library in California offered scavenger hunts with QR codes scattered around each library. Both libraries

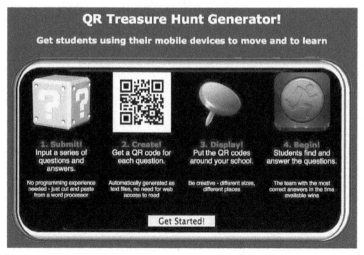

Figure 4.3
QR Code Treasure Hunt Generator from ClassTools.net.

offered incentives to get patrons to participate, ranging from tote bags to money and gift cards. Activities like this are not only useful for orienting users to the library but also can help improve patron awareness of QR codes—critically important if the library plans to use them for other services.

In K–12 libraries, where mobile devices are frequently banned, librarians wanting to do QR code scavenger hunts have either purchased iPod Touches for students to use or developed QR code scanning stations. A scanning station can be created with just a computer, webcam, and a webcam QR code reader such as dansl.[4] Using a system like that, students will need to be able to bring each of the QR codes to the scanning station. ClassTools.net offers a free QR Code Treasure Hunt Generator,[5] which requires teachers only to input their questions and answers, then print out the resulting QR codes.

The library could also use augmented reality for tours, providing video, audio, and information layered over specific, relevant locations in the library. While creating a much more immersive learning experience, this would require significantly more technological expertise and time to implement than any of the other options. It might also be a bit risky to have students rushing around the library with their phones held up to their faces.

Point-of-Need Instruction

Libraries around the world have created online learning objects designed to provide instruction to their patrons. Learning objects take various forms, from HTML content to screencasts—videos that show activity on the narrator's desktop—to pathfinders and research guides, to podcasts and videos. There are learning objects on using the library catalog, searching specific databases, using equipment and technologies around the library, and illustrating various aspects of the research process. Unfortunately, unless those objects are a required part of a specific course, they are infrequently used, as they are rarely provided at the patron's point of need (Hicks and Sinkinson 2011). Having an arsenal of instructional content living under the heading "tutorials" is going to attract only the most motivated library patrons. Mobile devices offer the possibility of providing instruction at the point of need. In addition to the greater likelihood of library learning objects being used, according to Ozcelik and Acarturk (2011, 2083), "prior research has shown that learning is enhanced when relevant information is immediately available."

QR codes have the potential for being fantastic tools for providing point-of-need instruction in libraries. A QR code in a specific location could link a user to a web page or a video that provides instruction on some aspect of that location. This would be ideal for equipment that users regularly need help from a librarian to use, such as microfilm scanners, copiers, and self-check machines. In places where people frequently get lost in the building, QR codes that link to maps of that area can be provided. For example, the Syracuse University Library has QR codes in the map room that link to the floor plan of the room and online map resources. QR codes can also link to research guides and pathfinders. At the Half Hollow Hills Community Library in New York, QR codes are placed in the stacks that link users to pathfinders related to the content on specific shelves.[6]

At the University of Colorado at Boulder, Hicks and Sinkinson (2011) looked at issues students commonly have around finding specific things and using specific technologies, and they developed posters with QR codes designed to link students to the answers. Those posters were placed in relevant locations in the library. Early results showed that stacks maps were the things most commonly scanned by their users. Given that so many patrons will not ask for help even when they need it, the best thing we can do is to make unmediated help available at their point of need.

The biggest barrier to QR code use is the general lack of QR code adoption in the West. In addition to providing the codes themselves, libraries could provide a shortened URL just under the QR code that the patron can easily enter into their mobile device. While it's easier to snap a QR code with a camera, a URL is certainly more recognizable to the general population.

In-Class Use

Instructors are frequently looking for ways to get students to play an active role during class. Active learning has been shown to have a positive impact on student learning outcomes and can help build a sense of community in the classroom (Markett et al. 2006; Aagard, Bowen, and Olesova 2011). However, incorporating active learning components can be difficult in large lecture classes where there are too many students to do the sort of activities possible with smaller groups. This is why classroom response systems have become a popular way to get students actively engaged in classroom discussions. Classroom response systems allow students to provide feedback via handheld devices. While traditionally this handheld device was a clicker that students or departments had to purchase, more and more often instructors are capitalizing on the handheld device that nearly all students have in their pockets.

History

Half Hollow Hills Community Library, 55 Vanderbilt Parkway, Dix hills, New York, 11746, 631/421-4530, hhhlibrary.org

Figure 4.4
QR code on an end stack at the Half Hollow Hills Community Library (design by Dan Epstein).

There are a variety of ways that classroom response systems have been implemented to allow students to use their mobile phones. The simplest is to use text messaging for students to provide feedback or answer polling questions. Given that a 2011 survey found that 18- to 24-year-olds send, on average, 1,914 text messages per month (Nielsen 2011), it seems like a seamless way to collect information from students during a classroom discussion. Some response systems have been designed to get feedback from students solely via text messaging (Cheung 2008; Markett et al. 2006), but others allow students to provide feedback via multiple modalities. Poll Everywhere[7] is an online polling tool that allows students to use text messaging or a web form to answer questions during class. The answers are then updated in real time on a PowerPoint slide or the website itself. Student responses are reported in aggregate in the class and cannot be attributed to a particular individual. Classroom polling can be useful as formative assessment, to get an idea of where students are pedagogically, so that instructors can tailor their lessons to immediate needs (Mandernach and Hackathorn 2010). Polling can also be useful as summative assessment at the end of class to see whether students have adequately absorbed the information. Librarians use classroom polling tools as icebreakers in one-shot sessions, for pre- and posttests, and to get feedback on the quality of their instruction (Sellar 2011). These tools provide valuable feedback for the instructor and wonderful opportunities for students to be active and share their thoughts during the session.

One potential drawback of using text messaging is that not everyone has unlimited text messaging on their phones and may have to pay for each text message sent

(Cheung 2008). However, it is certainly still cheaper than requiring students to purchase a clicker device. At schools where cell phones are banned, classroom response systems that require students to text their answers are not a viable option. That is why having a system with the flexibility of Poll Everywhere is valuable, because students can provide their feedback through a web browser instead of their phone.

Some instructors are using Twitter[8] as a classroom backchannel where students can comment on the lecture topic, ask questions, answer questions, and provide feedback. With Twitter, students can use a mobile device or a computer to provide their feedback, and the feedback can be easily collected together in one place by asking students to use a class hashtag in their tweets. Some conferences have displayed Twitter and other backchannels behind the instructor, which can be distracting or even offensive depending on the content of the tweets.

Twitter has a few major drawbacks for use as a classroom backchannel. First of all, what students tweet is visible not only to members of the class but to all of their followers and possibly the world if they do not have a private feed. Students who use Twitter in their personal life may not want to also use it academically. Because ach tweet can be traced back to an individual user, students may not feel as comfortable asking questions and providing feedback as they would if they were anonymous. Ebner (2009) has experimented with anonymous microblogging (using a private non-Twitter application) in the classroom to promote more interactivity in lectures and found that students enjoyed the ability to comment and felt more engaged in the classroom.

Wiffiti[9] is another technology for capturing the classroom backchannel. Wiffiti essentially creates a digital pinboard to which people can add comments. People can comment via Twitter with a hashtag, anonymously via a web form, or anonymously via text message. All of the messages show up on the board, which can be embedded on any website or on a digital display. Wiffiti can be used as a backchannel for feedback about the lecture throughout the class, or individual screens can be used for getting feedback on specific discussion questions (Mandernach and Hackathorn 2010). Like displaying a Twitter backchannel, displaying Wiffiti behind the instructor can be a major distraction for students. Therefore, displaying it at key moments—like when a question is being asked—or having the instructor or teaching assistant view it from their own computer makes more sense than having it up throughout the class.

A robust and exciting classroom response system is HotSeat,[10] a "micro-discussion" tool created by and used at Purdue University. In HotSeat, a faculty member can ask a question or provide a framework for student discussion. Students can then respond in 140 characters or less via a web application, Twitter (using a hashtag), a Facebook application, or their mobile device. Students can vote on the responses from their classmates so that the most interesting or insightful responses float to the top, and they can respond to other individual student questions or responses (Aagard, Bowen, and Olesova 2011). This encourages peer-to-peer learning and engages students in a collaborative discussion much more than if they were only providing their own response. HotSeat could be a useful tool for asking questions, providing feedback, having discussions, or conducting formative or summative assessment. While Hotseat is currently available only at Purdue, it is possible that they will release the source code in the future. Regardless, it is an interesting model for other universities or companies to emulate.

Classroom response systems are not only useful in large lecture classes but also can encourage more discussion in classes of any size. Many students feel uncomfortable asking questions and taking part in classroom discussions. Many classroom response systems allow students to share their thoughts or questions anonymously. This may be especially useful in classes that discuss sensitive or controversial topics (Ebner 2009; Markett et al. 2006). Classroom response systems also allow students to ask questions throughout the class time, and even after. One instructor at Purdue used HotSeat as a tool for students to ask questions that his graduate assistants would collect for him to periodically answer during the lecture (Aagard, Bowen, and Olesova 2011).

With all of the potential benefits of mobile classroom response systems, there are also potential drawbacks. Having students use a web-enabled mobile device in class may lead them to also use it for purposes unrelated to class. A quick check of their email or a text message to a friend can become a serious distraction in the classroom. Also, while anonymity can encourage shy students to share their thoughts, it can also encourage people to write things that are offensive and inappropriate (Aagard, Bowen, and Olesova 2011). Even students providing feedback that is critical of the instructor or their lecture can undermine the instructor. Instructors need to consider how they will handle such uses of the classroom response system, much as they need to consider how they would handle any disruptive classroom behavior.

Figure 4.5

With HotSeat, students can add their own thoughts and vote for or reply to those of their classmates.

Instructional Outreach

Point-of-need instruction is certainly vital to providing effective instructional outreach, but it's also important to put instructional content where our users are, which is not always in the library. Libraries should consider where in their communities patrons have information needs and how libraries can make their instructional content accessible from there. Libraries could create topical posters with a QR code and/or a shortened URL that takes the user to relevant instructional content. Libraries with guides to finding grants or for small businesses could create posters to place in other local organizations dedicated to supporting businesses. Subject liaison librarians could create posters for academic departmental offices that link users to relevant subject guides. In computer labs across campus, libraries could provide posters that link patrons to information about citing sources or citation management tools like Zotero and Mendeley. Patrons' library-related needs do not end when they leave the library, and neither should our outreach efforts.

There are a variety of additional ways that libraries have been providing instructional outreach to patrons via mobile devices with varying levels of success. Walsh (2010b) describes a service at the University of Huddersfield where students can choose to receive research tips via text message from the library. In the first semester it was offered, 60 students signed up for the weekly SMS tip and link to related instructional content, but on average only two students actually clicked on the provided link each week. Services of this kind must be opt-in, both because of the charges associated with receiving text messages and the potential annoyance factor of receiving unwanted texts from the library.

Another way that libraries have been providing mobile-friendly instructional outreach is through podcasting and vodcasting, episodic audio and video respectively, that users can subscribe to and have downloaded automatically to their mobile device. One excellent example of this approach to instructional outreach is Arizona State University's *Library Minute* series,[11] which provides slick and engaging video instruction on library collections, services, and more, all in around one minute. The videos are uploaded to YouTube, where patrons can easily subscribe to and access them via mobile devices. While the *Library Minute* is an extreme example, audio and video segments should always be short, ideally under three minutes but certainly no more than five.

CONSIDERATIONS FOR THE USE OF MOBILE DEVICES IN LIBRARY INSTRUCTION

For libraries considering providing instruction to mobile users, there are many things to consider before getting started. It helps to know what devices the majority of patrons have and what they use those devices for. While research on mobile trends is valuable, it is not a substitute for getting to know the needs of your unique population. Web analytics tools like Google Analytics and AWStats can give you a sense of what mobile operating systems are accessing your library website, but that will only give you statistics on those that choose to access your website through a mobile device, which is likely a very small subset of your population. Surveys can give you a useful baseline response, but the information will quickly become dated as many individuals update frequently.

It is also important to determine what your patrons' instructional needs are. If your library keeps track of questions asked by patrons at the reference desk, this can be amazing data to mine to determine priorities. Otherwise, librarians who frequently work at the reference desk likely have useful insights regarding the things that patrons have trouble with most often.

When working with existing instructional content, the first major consideration is how that content should be adapted for mobile use. There needs to be recognition that there is more of a difference between mobile devices and desktop or laptop computers than just the smaller screen. Libraries need to design mobile interfaces based on how people actually use those devices rather than just thinking about how to shrink down their existing content to fit the form factor. Educational content needs to be bite-sized and modular, allowing people to easily jump to the information they need rather than forcing them through a specific progression (Motiwalla 2007).

There also needs to be some consideration of the great variety of mobile devices students have, from smartphones to iPads to feature phones. It is critical that applications and interfaces are tested with a wide variety of devices to make sure that students can interact with the content at least on the most common devices (Fox 2010). This becomes even more complicated when developing educational mobile apps because an app is designed for a specific mobile platform. Unless the vast majority of patrons are using one specific platform—which seems unlikely given Android's growth in market share—libraries will need to develop applications for multiple platforms.

In synchronous instruction sessions, whether a tour or a classroom situation, WiFi and cell-phone signals may be a concern. Students will not be able to text their answers if their phone does not get a signal and will not be able to access a web form if the wireless signal is poor. This is just another reason why it is valuable to offer multiple methods for providing classroom feedback. Even then, it is a good idea to test signal strength throughout the classroom with various devices.

Libraries are developing learning objects with varying levels of mobile-friendliness. Some systems, such as LibGuides,[12] can serve up a mobile-friendly version of each guide and tutorial created. Other tutorials may not render well on a mobile device, requiring horizontal scrolling or resizing of the text. When libraries are creating tutorials, it's important to consider how they will display on mobile devices and to create separate mobile versions or a mobile style sheet if necessary. When designing video tutorials, it is essential they are filmed and exported in such a way that allows for viewing on a mobile device. If a video can be uploaded to YouTube, students should be able to easily view it on their smartphones or tablets.

While they have so many exciting potential uses in education, QR codes suffer from several major flaws. The first is the lack of awareness of QR codes in North America and Europe. While lots of people have seen them around on magazine ads and billboards, the majority of the population has never scanned one and does not really know what they are. After a QR code awareness campaign at the University of Huddersfield, Walsh (2010a) found that awareness increased from 8 percent to 22 percent of survey respondents, but that still is a very small percentage of their population. Currently, QR code readers do not come preinstalled on most mobile phones in the United States, which means that users have to go through the effort of installing a QR code reader app on their phone before they can even start scanning codes. In some cases, this might provide enough of a barrier to use that people will not bother. Burns (2011) found that some students had trouble downloading the QR code reader app before the scavenger hunt she held, perhaps caused by slow WiFi or cell-phone provider network. The final issue is the diversity of cell-phone cameras. High-resolution cameras should have no trouble scanning the codes, but older and lower-resolution cameras sometimes have difficulty reading QR codes, especially if they are too small or do not have sufficient visual contrast.

This is an exciting time for rethinking teaching in light of the growth in mobile-device usage and mobile technologies. The reasons to provide mobile learning platforms go beyond the mere fact that most teens and adults carry a mobile device. Mobile learning provides opportunities for developing immersive, interactive, and individualized forms of instruction. Learners develop more autonomy with modular, on-demand instructional content that they can access at their point of need. Instruction can be tied to specific texts, contexts, and locations, helping students meld their personal observations with expert information. Even in large lecture classes, the "sage on the stage" model can be augmented by increased opportunities for student feedback and collaborative peer-to-peer learning. Libraries can take advantage of mobile learning in the classroom, the orientation tour, and at the user's point of need. Learning can be made more seamlessly available wherever the user happens to be.

NOTES

1. library.duke.edu/support/renovation/tours.html
2. ucmercedlibrary.info/about-the-library/ipod-touch-library-tour
3. podcast.iu.edu/Portal/PodcastPage.aspx?podid=5f1d6a9c-504b-44ba-8b54-bebe9002421d
4. dansl.net
5. classtools.net/QR/

6. hhhl.wordpress.com/tag/qr/
7. polleverywhere.com
8. twitter.com
9. wiffiti.com
10. purdue.edu/hotseat/
11. lib.asu.edu/librarychannel/?cat=87
12. springshare.com/libguides

REFERENCES

Aagard, Hans, Kyle Bowen, and Larisa Olesova. 2011. "Hotseat: Opening the Backchannel in Large Lectures." *EDUCAUSE Quarterly* 33 (3): 1–13.

Abilene Christian University. 2011. *Abilene Christian University 2010–11 Mobile-Learning Report*. http://issuu.com/abilenechristian/docs/acu_ml_report_2010-11.

Barnes, Cameron, and Belinda Tynan. 2007. "The Adventures of Miranda in the Brave New World: Learning in a Web 2.0 Millennium." *ALT-J* 15 (3): 189–200.

Burns, Erin M. 2011. "Remaking the Library Information Hunt Using QR Codes." *Pennsylvania Library Association Bulletin* (Jan/Feb/Mar): 11–13.

Chen, Nian-Shing, Daniel Chia-En Teng, and Cheng-Han Lee. 2011. "Augmenting Paper-Based Reading Activity with Direct Access to Digital Materials and Scaffolded Questioning." *Computers & Education* 57 (2): 1705–1715.

Cheung, Stephen L. 2008. "Using Mobile Phone Messaging as a Response Medium in Classroom Experiments." *Journal of Economic Education* 39 (1): 51–67.

Die Bayerische Staatsbibliothek. 2011. "Ludwig II—Walking in the Footsteps of a Fairytale King." http://www.bsb-muenchen.de/Ludwig-II-Auf-den-Spuren-des-Maerchenkoenigs.ludwig-app.0.html?L=3.

Ebner, Martin. 2009. "Interactive Lecturing by Integrating Mobile Devices and Microblogging in Higher Education." *Journal of Computing and Information Technology* 4: 371–381.

Ericsson Corporate Public & Media Relations. 2010. "Mobile Subscriptions Hit 5 Billion Mark." http://hugin.info/1061/R/1430616/377332.pdf.

Fletcher, Jon. 2010. "Mobile Learning: What Exactly Is It? *Multimedia Information & Teachnology* 36 (1): 22–24.

Fox, Robert. 2010. "Library to Go." *OCLC Systems & Services* 26 (1): 8–13.

Hicks, Alison, and Caroline Sinkinson. 2011. "Situated Questions and Answers." *Reference & User Services Quarterly* 51 (1): 60–69.

Ingram, Matthew. 2010. "Mary Meeker: Mobile Internet Will Soon Overtake Fixed Internet." *GigaOM*. http://gigaom.com/2010/04/12/mary-meeker-mobile-internet-will-soon-overtake-fixed-internet/.

Johnson, Larry, Samantha Adams, and Keene Haywood. 2011. *The NMC Horizon Report: 2011 K–12 Edition*. Austin, TX: The New Media Consortium.

Johnson, Larry, Rachel S. Smith, Holly Willis, Alan Levine, and Keene Haywood. 2011. *The 2011 Horizon Report*. Austin, TX: The New Media Consortium.

Law, Ching-yin, and Simon So. 2010. "QR Codes in Education." *Journal of Educational Technology Development and Exchange* 3 (1): 85–100.

Liestøl, Gunnar. 2011. "Learning through Situated Simulations: Exploring Mobile Augmented Reality." *ECAR Research Bulletin* 1: 1–14.

Mandernach, B. Jean, and Jana Hackathorn. 2010. "Embracing Texting during Class." *Teaching Professor* 24 (10): 1–7.

Markett, C., I. Arnedillo Sánchez, S. Weber, and B. Tangney. 2006. "Using Short Message Service to Encourage Interactivity in the Classroom." *Computers & Education* 46 (3): 280–293.

Mcloughlin, Catherine, and Mark J. W. Lee. 2008. "The Three P's of Pedagogy for the Networked Society: Personalization, Participation, and Productivity." *International Journal of Teaching and Learning in Higher Education* 20 (1): 10–27.

Mikkelsen, Susan, and Sara Davidson. 2011. "Inside the iPod, Outside the Classroom." *Reference Services Review* 39 (1): 66–80.

Motiwalla, Luvai F. 2007. "Mobile Learning: A Framework and Evaluation." *Computers & Education* 49 (3): 581–596.

Nielsen Company. 2011. "New Mobile Obsession: U.S. Teens Triple Data Usage." *Nielsenwire* (December 15). http://blog.nielsen.com/nielsenwire/online_mobile/new-mobile-obsession-u-s-teens-triple-data-usage/.

Ozcelik, Erol, and Cengiz Acarturk. 2011. "Reducing the Spatial Distance between Printed and Online Information Sources by Means of Mobile Technology Enhances Learning: Using 2D Barcodes." *Computers & Education* 57 (3): 2077–2085.

Pence, Harry. 2011. "Smartphones, Smart Objects, and Augmented Reality." *The Reference Librarian* 52 (1): 136–145.

Ryokai, Kimiko, Lora Oehlberg, Michael Manoochehri, and Alice Agogino. 2011. "GreenHat: Exploring the Natural Environment through Experts' Perspectives." *Proceedings of the 29th international Conference on Human Factors in Computing Systems*, Vancouver, Canada, May 7–12: 2149–2152.

Sellar, Melanie. 2011. "Poll Everywhere." *Charleston Advisor* 12 (3): 57–60.

Smith, Aaron. 2010. "Mobile Access 2010." *Pew Internet and American Life Project*. http://www.pewinternet.org/~/media//Files/Reports/2010/PIP_Mobile_Access_2010.pdf.

Squire, Kurt. 2010. "From Information to Experience: Place-based Augmented Reality Games as a Model for Learning in a Globally Networked Society." *Teachers College Record* 112 (10): 9–10.

Traxler, John. 2007. "Defining, Discussing and Evaluating Mobile Learning: The Moving Finger Writes and Having Writ. . . ." *International Review of Research in Open and Distance Learning* 8 (2). http://www.irrodl.org/index.php/irrodl/article/viewArticle/346.

Walsh, Andrew. 2010a. "QR Codes—Using Mobile Phones to Deliver Library Instruction and Help at the Point of Need." *Journal of Information Literacy* 4 (1): 55–63.

Walsh, Andrew. 2010b. "Supplementing Inductions with Text Messages, an SMS 'Tips and Tricks' Service." *ALISS Quarterly* 5 (3): 23–25.

Woodbury, David N. 2009. "A Survey of Undergraduates' Use and Attitudes of Cell Phones for Instruction, Learning, and Collaboration." Master's Thesis, University of North Carolina, Chapel Hill.

5

Going Mobile: Reaching the Younger Generations

Bonnie Roalsen

Key Points

- In our children's world, knowledge is mobile, global, social, and forever interconnecting in new ways. Libraries need to modernize, mobilize, and operate across a multitude of platforms to engage and serve this generation.
- To be effective, mobile technology and services need to be integrated into every aspect of collections, programs, and services. A new model for youth services needs to be developed that blends the best of traditional library services with constantly evolving, innovative tech environments.
- Children need access to "always open" digital learning environments where they can practice and build their digital literacy in community with others.

Today's children are growing up in an era in which the United States is transitioning from a paper society to a digital society. The very nature of knowledge, scholarship, cultural objects, and community is in rapid flux. The fundamental cornerstones of our society have shifted. Freedom of access to information, freedom of assembly, freedom of inquiry, as well as core concerns like privacy and identity have been altered by the mass adoption of mobile technology. Our children's world is mobile, global, fast-paced, and forever interconnecting in new ways.

Over the past several years, the Dover Town Library in Massachusetts has transformed itself to meet the needs of families in this rapidly evolving mobile and digital age. The transformation has excited the community, and the library has rapidly become an inspiration for libraries across the country.

The library adopted a new and simple mission statement: "To provide our patrons with free, open access to the world's knowledge, information, and culture" and established the goal of being a leader in helping the public learn how to build and manage effective knowledge networks, develop and craft digital identities, and acquire the digital skills needed to fully participate in a globally networked and interconnected world.

Unlike many public libraries, our children's and adult services departments share the same philosophies of service and practice. When we implement a service or practice, it is implemented for the entire library and for the entire community we serve. We do not place artificial age restrictions or filters on any materials, devices, or technologies.

In 2011 the library renovated its interior spaces and integrated mobile technology into its collections and service model, simply and powerfully, to enable users to experience knowledge, information, and cultural objects in new and compelling ways.

As head of Children's Services, I am responsible for serving children from birth through age 12 and their families, and implementing our mission. When we integrated mobile technology into every aspect of our library collections and service model, we made a commitment to continued mobile innovation and a specific commitment to providing children with

- greater access to technology they could check out and explore for extended periods of time
- engaging digital learning environments to aid them in building the digital skills they will need to participate fully in a digital world.

TECHNOLOGY ACCESS AND DIGITAL LITERACY

When we renovated the library, we placed a tech bar at the center of the library, establishing that technology is the heart of what we do and is our future—and we threw out the old "fortress-style" reference desk. We do not have a designated "tech person" but rather have made technology, media assistance, and content creation a regular part of everyone's position. The library has a very open, collaborative, and energetic work culture, and staff members are on top of tech trends, tools, platforms, and innovations that impact our profession and the lives of our users.

We implemented the following to provide greater technology access to children and help them build digital literacy:

- We created a large, very visible Tech Board in the Children's Department to inform children what technology is available for them to check out and play with at any given time.
- We began to offer tablet computing and removed the "grandpa boxes" from the Children's Department, making it entirely mobile. For those who do not yet have smartphones, we offer fully loaded iPod Touches that children can check out or use in the library to scan codes, discover apps, and play with augmented realities (ARs).
- We mapped our children's collection using Google Earth to enable children to browse our collection with a global perspective via touch screen. The touch screen is mounted low so it is perfect for our youngest users, and it has become a fun and engaging part of the library for many families.
- We purchased a full collection of Kindles, Nooks, iPads, and iPod Touches and made them ready for checkout to children, preloaded with a wealth of materials and apps. We will offer other mobile devices as they evolve and become available.
- We built "always open" digital learning environments throughout the library, which children and families can explore and use to practice their digital skills.

- We built two gaming environments, which are available to children all the time. One area is equipped with a Wii, a Playstation3, an Xbox 360 and our entire gaming collection. The other area is set up with a big screen and Xbox 360 with Kinect for people to experiment with gesture computing. These gaming environments are always very busy and have been very well received by all users.
- We circulate gaming consoles to children—Wii, PlayStation3 with PlayStation Move, Xbox 360 with Kinect, Nintendo3DSs, as well as Blu-ray and DVD players. We add new gaming devices to this collection as they become available, keeping current.
- We circulate i-devices like iPhone and iPod Touch remote-controlled helicopters, Ferraris, and AR.Drones. We are closely watching the evolution of gesture computing, AR, and mobile devices and their intersections to be able to bring these meshed tech experiences to children to explore. The circulation of these devices gives children and their families a chance to explore technologies and devices that they would not be able to experience otherwise.
- We offer a wide range of events and programs that utilize mobile technology, engaging children and families and providing new ways for them to practice their digital skills, as well as new ways to explore and interact with knowledge, information, and cultural objects. For example, we took a scaled-down map of the solar system and overlaid it on the town to create a walking tour of the planets for children. Planets were created to scale, placed across town, and QR coded, linking mobile tourists to video, text, games, and the library's space collection.

MOBILE INNOVATIONS AND THE FUTURE

As a library, we recognize that mobile devices offer perhaps the best platform for content delivery, information retrieval, creative exchange, and location-based services for the future. Mobile technology offers us many opportunities to make knowledge, information, and cultural objects come alive for our users, as well as giving us the ability to deliver knowledge and information to mobile users at the point of need or greatest physical relevance.

We continue to integrate mobile technology into Children's Services at the Dover Town Library in the following ways:

- Music collections: We ripped our entire music collection and made it available on an iTunes server for all, plus we offer Sanza Fuze MP3 players with preloaded music collections for checkout.
- App collections: We are growing and managing app collections for our mobile devices, just as we would any other library collection. As with any other collection, children are encouraged to suggest titles for purchase and readily share apps of interest.
- A knowledge platform utilizing QR codes and AR: We implemented B3OK, a new open organization of knowledge that connects the digital, physical, and mobile worlds, and removed the Dewey system of classification for our materials.

We are QR coding our entire collection, meshing together physical materials with digital assets and resources. Children scan QR codes on materials and receive useful or fun streaming video or supplemental textual information, and they can explore subjects and topics to whatever depth they wish across a mobile platform. They can share or weave together the content we have created or curated with that in their networks, as well as share their own. We are active participants and content creators and curators on most major social platforms.

We hope in the future to deliver the following to mobile users in our community via QR codes:

- Recipes and food information at the local grocery market
- Local history information on location
- Music or audio books at the local gas stations
- Children's books at the playground

AUGMENTED REALITY

AR enables children to experience, engage, and interact with knowledge and physical objects in new ways. We are building two marker-based AR environments within the library and also adding markerless AR using natural feature tracking to our children's materials and displays.

One AR environment will be situated at the entrance to the Children's Department and will enable children to interact and play with all manner of subjects and will highlight our nonfiction holdings. We see this being a rotating experience, that is, swim with sharks this week, next week experience a medieval castle or dance the flamenco with a flamenco dancer, and so on.

The other AR environment will be situated on the main level of the library and will enable people to share and experience local history and local stories.

We are also building a creative space to encourage children to create augments for our materials for different subject areas and to create their own AR fairy tales, to be added to the permanent collection and accessed via QR code.

Looking a bit further into the future, we believe public libraries need a mobile, global knowledge platform in order to engage and effectively serve the younger generations. Building on the foundations we laid, we are transforming our service model yet again. We are expanding beyond our walls, tagging and augmenting physical objects and spaces to deliver relevant digital knowledge to mobile users out in the world.

As we build a mobile organization of knowledge, we keep in mind five considerations:

1. How can we enable children's participation and interaction with a library, object, place, or a topic to be more significant?
2. How can we increase community knowledge, trigger communication between people, and allow for playful interaction?
3. Can we enable children's participation within their own communities—be they digital, physical, or both—to be more significant?
4. Can we keep a knowledge platform open as it weaves through a multitude of social networks, media formats, and apps?
5. What is hidden here that can be made visible? What stories or knowledge are hidden in this area or object that can be made visible?

We hope to collaborate extensively with other knowledge institutions and tech organizations to bring this project to fruition and bring the best the world has to offer to our youngest, wherever they might be.

6

Bricks and Mortar and Wireless: The Impact of the Mobile Revolution on the Use of Physical Libraries

Thomas A. Peters

Key Points

- The number of users bringing mobile devices into physical libraries and connecting to the library's wireless network is increasing, as are their demands for bandwidth and wireless-related services.
- Library users expect and deserve to have good, seamless mobile experiences while in physical libraries.
- Many library users use multiple portable devices while in the library to communicate with others, seek and use information, be entertained, and create content. These four fundamental mobile activities are not necessarily tied closely to the content and services provided by the library in which the user is sitting.
- The quality of the library's wireless network has become a key performance indicator for successful libraries of all types.
- Space demands, furniture configurations, and tech support for mobile in-library users will be considerably different than they were for library users during the print era.

INTRODUCTION

Approximately 20 years ago there was much discussion about the development of libraries without walls. The basic idea and vision was that increasingly patrons would access library content, services, and systems from remote locations without coming into physical libraries. In this historical context, the recent mobile revolution appears to be the apotheosis of the "libraries without walls" movement. It is appealing to know that the library is available from just about anywhere at any time. Back then, the idea of actually coming to a physical library seemed destined to become passé.

The libraries-without-walls movement, however, has not turned libraries with walls into ghost towns. Libraries with walls continue to exist, and people continue to visit and use them. In many libraries, average daily gate counts are increasing. This chapter explores how the mobile revolution, with its plethora of rapidly evolving gadgets and increasing demand for wireless access, is affecting brick-and-mortar libraries. Wireless access to library content, services, and systems certainly means that the library has gone mobile, but the wireless revolution is also changing how the physical library is understood and used as a wireless network space in its own right. Many libraries, perhaps particularly academic libraries during these early years of the mobile revolution, are experiencing increasing and heavy demand on their wireless networks. The future of the library with walls now seems assured, if not downright bright.

Wireless access to the Internet is a heavily used service provided by most libraries within brick-and-mortar buildings. Table 1154 of the *Statistical Abstract of the United States* notes that, as of 2010, 85.7 percent of public libraries in the United States had wireless access currently available, and another 5.9 percent planned to make wireless connectivity possible within a year (http://www.census.gov/compendia/statab/2012/tables/12s1154.pdf). As a network service, it is not much different than similar services offered in many buildings and open spaces. In fact, people increasingly expect to find free (i.e., no direct out-of-pocket expense) wireless access in restaurants, hotels, public buildings, and other places. How can libraries excel at this service? How important is a good wireless network to the current and future success of libraries? Many libraries can and do provide free public access to their wireless network, but McDonald's, Starbucks, and many other retail establishments, organizations, and service providers do that, too, although there is a tacit expectation that users will purchase something while using wireless connectivity in a retail outlet.

People use mobile devices to undertake many tasks and to experience various things while on the go. This multitude of tasks and experiences can be organized into four basic experiential categories:

1. Communicating with others (via voice, text messaging, etc.)
2. Seeking and using information (often via the web)
3. Being entertained (games, music, videos, etc.)
4. Creating content (photos, videos, tweets, etc.)

Some types of mobile devices privilege some of the essential four activities more than others. The Kindle Fire, for example, seems to encourage seeking information and being entertained more than it does communicating and creating content. However, when librarians consider all of the patrons who are bringing mobile electronic devices into the library, we can safely assume that all four basic activities are being pursued within the friendly confines of the brick-and-mortar library. The question then becomes: How well does the wireless network, the library's service palette, and the library's stable of content foster and facilitate these four core functions as pursued on mobile devices?

THE EFFECTS OF THE MOBILE REVOLUTION
ON THE DESIGN AND USE OF PHYSICAL LIBRARIES

The mobile revolution is having, and will continue to have, a profound influence on how brick-and-mortar libraries are used. While people use their mobile devices to access library content and services from points beyond the library, they also bring their personal, portable electronic devices into the library. Every information medium (print, microformats, magnetic media, etc.) has its own space demands, and buildings have been designed to meet the demands for various information media in terms both of storage and use. For example, the fusion library/student center building at the combined campus of Ohio State University—Newark and Central Ohio Technical College was designed and constructed so that one bay of the upper floor could hold books and other printed materials housed in compact shelving, even though the current configuration is traditional wide-aisle, open-access shelving. The library space demands and affordances of the age of mobile information appliances (smartphones, tablet computers, etc.) will be quite different than the space demands and affordances of the era when print dominated. How to reconfigure the spaces within existing libraries to accommodate information seekers, users, and creators in the mobile era is not straightforward and self-evident. Librarians need to try different space configurations, observe user behavior patterns (which will evolve as the mobile era matures), and modify their space configurations accordingly. Space demands, furniture configurations, and tech support for mobile in-library users will be considerably different than they were for library users during the print era.

In the mobile era, the library's wireless network has become a key component of brick-and-mortar libraries. Most library users, if not also members of the general population, have come to prefer and expect wireless connectivity for most computer-related activities. The idea of carrying an Ethernet cable and connecting to a library-supplied network jack seems increasingly unattractive to users, especially members of the younger generation. They feel needlessly tethered.

In a little over 13 years, the 802.11 family of wireless standards has developed and become more robust. Caluori (2011, 29) notes that the IEEE 802.11b standard was released in 1999 and states, "The patron wireless network is an essential component of the modern public library." Patrons may feel more comfortable using their own devices connected to a wireless network, as opposed to a library-supplied computer. "Allowing people to bring in and use their own device also adds a level of comfort to the library. Sometimes people are reluctant to use library PCs to access websites that may expose their personal information" (Caluori 2011, 29). Also, the downloading of apps and software has become almost an everyday occurrence, which is much easier to do on a personally owned device.

In Milner Library at Illinois State University, there is a university computing lab (PCs and some Macs), several classrooms equipped with computers for instructors and students, and many public-access workstations. All of these traditional, wired computers receive lots of use. The library also has circulated laptops for years and iPads beginning in the fall of 2011, with circulatable Kindles and Nooks on tap for a 2012 service rollout. Although thousands of personal, portable electronic gadgets are brought into this particular academic library each day, and most of these devices connect to the library's wireless network at some point each day, the demand for library-supplied computing devices, from desktop PCs to iPads, continues to be strong.

A wireless network within a library building is not a simple plug-and-use system. It requires some calibration and tweaking. Caluori suggests that the most basic and important questions regarding any wireless network are, "How many simultaneous users will this network need to support at its peak usage, and where are these users located when they are using it?" (Caluori 2011, 30). A third key question to ask: What are these users doing with these portable devices when they are connected to the library's wireless network? The answer to this question can be understood and expressed in terms of bandwidth demands. Checking email and streaming media are radically different bandwidth propositions, which will affect the overall performance of your wireless network. Barker (2011) quotes Joseph Harrington, president of the Association for Information Communications Technology Professionals in Higher Education, as observing, "It's not so much the number of devices, it's the video-based content they're going after." Most mobile users of library-supplied wireless networks seem to pay little or no attention to their bandwidth usage.

The boundaries between the walled library and the library without walls are not distinct and fixed. The reach of the building's wireless network does not necessarily stop at the exterior walls of the building. If you have courtyards, gardens, seating areas, and parking lots near the library building, some use of the wireless network will originate from these local environs beyond the actual library walls. Evidently there is no way to confidently identify this "external" use of your library's internal wireless network. Some public libraries report the emergence of "parking lot patrons"—users who pull into the parking lot close enough to the physical library to get a good wireless signal, then sit in their cars using their portable devices on the library's wireless network without ever actually entering the library.

Wang (2011) explores how parks and other leafy public places could be optimized for wireless Internet users. Based on observations made in parks, coffee shops, and libraries in the United States and Australia, Wang (2011, 8–11) identifies four basic types of wireless mobile users in these "third places" (after home and work):

1. True mobiles: These people use the wireless networks in these public third places "as a backdrop for their primary activities such as reading or working at their computers. They seek a change of place of work without losing the convenience and functionality of undeterred access to the Internet" (Wang 2011, 8). True mobiles often spend hours in these wireless public third places.
2. Socializers: "These individuals freely engage in social interactions with casual acquaintances and primarily seek to connect with other patrons" (Wang 2011, 9). Socializers also tend to spend long periods of time in these wireless public third places, and Wang speculates that they may comprise the largest of these four user groups.
3. Passers-by: This group may be unique to open-air wireless third places. "The cell phone is the main portable device they use to kill time or contact people they plan to meet" (Wang 2011, 10).
4. Economically disadvantaged: "Especially for the low-income community, the public library and the wireless park are the only places for them to update job information and submit resumes" (Wang 2011, 11).

Librarians also need to consider how open and easy to access they want their wireless networks to be. Access to the wireless network is a separate issue than is access to specific content sources, such as e-books and subscription databases. Security and authentication are key components of the service. Caluori (2011) asserts, "All patron wireless networks should have some level of authentication." This is debatable and ultimately is a library or institutional policy decision, based upon a risk assessment and assumption of risk. For instance, the ISUpublic subnetwork of the Milner Library wireless network does not require any sign-in or authentication. Users are limited to what resources and services they can access while connected to ISUpublic, but the daily usage stats confirm that there is demand for this type of free-and-easy access to the library's wireless network.

How will wireless networks within brick-and-mortar libraries affect the future design and use of physical libraries? If you reconfigure the space in your library in any major way, such as adding seating, moving shelving ranges, or moving service points, you will want to consider how that could alter the performance of the wireless network in the space, as well as the demands for wireless connectivity in various zones within your built library space.

Portable electronic devices also can be used offline—without being connected to any wired or wireless network. Just because a user brings a portable device into a physical library does not necessarily mean that he or she intends to and indeed will connect to the library's wireless network. On the other hand, some portable devices automatically attempt to connect to any open wireless network they detect, regardless of the user's desire to connect to a wireless network at that moment in time. The ability of portable devices to search for available wireless networks within range and then connect to one without immediate, overt volition on the part of the user of the portable device could be called unwitting connections. If, for instance, you set up your smartphone to look for available WiFi connections, it will do so with dogged determination, even when you are oblivious or even asleep.

Peripheral services may experience increased demand as the mobile revolution continues to unfold. For example, we receive increasing requests to offer jump drives for purchase from the vending machines located on the first floor of Milner Library. Earbuds also are frequently requested. Most importantly, the demand for access to electrical outlets is substantial and intense. Some users will unplug library equipment to gain access to an electrical outlet. Other users bring their own power strips.

CHALLENGES OF MAKING A PHYSICAL LIBRARY VERY USEFUL FOR MOBILE USERS

All mobile use happens somewhere in the physical world, including brick-and-mortar libraries. If you think about a library space not only as so much bricks, mortar, and poured concrete, nor as so many printed volumes sitting on shelves, but also as a defined cluster of access points in a wireless network, then the library can be understood as a digital information zone containing many possible information experiences, including communication, entertainment, and content creation.

For decades, technology analysts and pundits have noted that one indicator of a successful technology is when it becomes so embedded in our lives that it recedes from consciousness. When a technology recedes from our collective consciousness, it succeeds. Wireless networks may take the concept of a self-effacing technology to a new level. For younger generations and their use of wireless networks, the network technology never really seems to rise to the level of conscious thought. They just expect to be connected without much effort, without many authentication challenges, and without much buffering. Downtime is not even an assumption or contingency for most wireless network users of academic libraries.

Libraries promote conversations and self-actualization, not just information and knowledge transfers. Are users of mobile devices in libraries primarily amusing themselves to death? Should we worry that users in the library may not be using the wireless network primarily to access library content and library services? I suggest that we not become too interested in or agitated by this question (other than as a professional research interest). I would strongly advise against encouraging or requiring users of your wireless network to access library content and services because this violates the expectation and spirit of personal, portable electronic devices—that they can be used for many purposes, depending on the needs and interests of the individual at that moment. The user decides when, where, and what to access. McEwen and Scheaffer (2012, 92) note, "As users participate in these [library] spaces, they are confronted with rules, policies, and guidelines that are antithetical to their domesticated mobile-phone practices."

The rapid growth in use of the wireless network in Milner Library and across the campus of Illinois State University is not atypical. Many institutions of higher education are reporting remarkable increases in the number of personal portable devices being used on campus and a concomitant increase in bandwidth demands. Barker (2011) reports that the University of Missouri—Columbia saw a dramatic rise—from 900 in 2010 to 8,000 early into the fall semester of 2011—in the peak number of devices connecting to their wireless network. During the fall semester of 2011, on many days during the latter half of the semester (particularly Mondays, Tuesdays, and Wednesday, the peak days for classes and people on the Illinois State University campus), it was not unusual to have over 18,000 unique devices connect to the campus wireless network in a given 24-hour period. At the same time, in Milner Library it was not unusual to see over 3,000 unique devices connect to the wireless network, meaning that approximately one in six devices that connected to the campus network did so from the library at some point during the day.

With so many personal, portable devices coming into the library, the demand for electricity can be substantial. Early in the fall semester of 2011, when we invited student representatives from the Student Government Association to meet with the library administrative team, we asked them what the library could do to improve the student experience in the library. We had imagined they would respond with requests for longer hours, new services, or even a café in the library. Their immediate, emphatic response, however, was, "More outlets." Brown-Sica's research (2012, 225) at the Auraria Library in Colorado supports this anecdotal observation that demand for electrical outlets is a high priority for current academic library users. As a short-term solution, rather than drill into the floor or add unsightly electrical poles in the middle of large rooms, Milner Library at Illinois State University added more electrical outlets around the perimeter of the areas of the library with large public seating capacities. One potential long-term solution is wireless electricity (energy transfer).

Although the library (or the parent organization) has some control over the configuration, size, and capacity of the wireless network, in other respects the users are in control. They decide which personal, portable electronic devices they are going to bring into the library, and they decide when and how they are going to use them.

A wireless network does not become saturated in predictable ways. For example, 35 people who are connected to a wireless access node and are basically checking email with some occasional web surfing may not experience any saturation, while at another time 25 people connected to same wireless access node who are all streaming media (movies, videos, audio, etc.) may experience some network saturation.

People also want to connect their personal, portable electronic devices with library hardware. For instance, in Milner Library we offer publicly available collaboration stations. These are tables with large monitors bolted at one end. Beneath the table is a controller box with 15-pin VGA cables running up through the table surface. If the user brings a device with a 15-pin VGA output port, all she or he needs to do is plug in the device in order to display his or her screen onto the large monitor. Four to seven different devices can be connected at a single table at any given time, depending on the size and design of the collaboration station. To change which device's screen is being displayed on the large monitor, the user need only press a button. For people with devices with 15-pin video ports, the collaboration stations are very intuitive and easy to use. Owners of Mac laptops, iPads, and other Apple personal, portable devices, however, face additional challenges and hurdles. Apple devices have an amazing variety of video output ports. Although Steve Jobs should be lauded in general for making computing easier and more intuitive for the rest of us, he and his team fell short when it comes to video output design and consistency. Also, some Apple personal, portable devices are set by default to not operate in dual-screen mode. The user, then, has to go into preferences and check a box to enable the device's video display to project also on the large monitor at the collaboration station.

CASE STUDY: WIRELESS NETWORK USAGE IN MILNER LIBRARY AT ILLINOIS STATE UNIVERSITY

Wireless access has been available in Milner Library at Illinois State University since October 2000 (http://my.ilstu.edu/~sagenung/telco/wireless.html). More recently, Illinois State University has undertaken an ambitious, three-year project to bring wireless connectivity to the entire campus, including all open spaces on campus and university-owned locations near the main campus. As part of the first-year phase of that project, the number of wireless access points in the library was increased to 55. The wireless coverage area within the six-floor library building is now virtually complete. Once coverage is complete, the focus of attention switches to capacity. Based on a wireless audit conducted early in 2012, three additional wireless access points were installed to meet observed capacity demands, bringing the total number of wireless access points within the library to 58.

To measure the use of the wireless network in Milner Library, we analyzed the data provided nightly by University Telecommunications and Networking. The usage reporting software treated each 24-hour period (midnight to midnight) as a new reporting period. Each portable electronic device has its own unique identifier. Whenever a new device connects to the wireless network, it gets counted as a unique device. Each wireless access point keeps track of how many unique devices connect to it during each 24-hour period. The cluster of 55 wireless access points is also treated as a unified network. The nightly wireless usage report de-dupes the reports coming in from each wireless access point and presents the total, de-duped number of unique devices that actually connected during that 24-hour period. Then at midnight the software resets to zero and begins the counting and de-duping process all over again.

Generally, this is quite informative and useful information, but, as with any data set, it has its limitations and drawbacks. For example, during most days of the week during most weeks of the semester, the library is open from 7:00 a.m. until 1:00 a.m. Thus the service day does not coincide with the 24-hour period used by the wireless-network-usage monitoring software.

For this specific research project, data about usage of the wireless network in Milner Library were collected for four months, from September 1, 2011, through December 31,

2011. That year, the fall semester at Illinois State University began on August 22, 2011, and concluded on December 16, 2011. No classes were held during the week of Thanksgiving. October was the only complete and "pristine" month of the fall semester with no major holidays, breaks, or other lulls in the life of the university.

The wireless-network daily usage reports provided by ISU Telecommunications and Networking indicate the total number of unique devices that connected to each of the 55 access points, the maximum number of simultaneous users of each access point, the daily bandwidth usage at each access point, the specific subnetwork used (e.g., ISUnet, ISUpublic, ISUguest, etc.), the distribution of 802.11 protocols across all the devices that connected to the network that day, and hourly use of the entire wireless network in terms of maximum simultaneously connected devices and bandwidth usage.

The wireless network usage patterns in Milner Library, Illinois State University (September—December 2011) were as follows:

- By floor and zone within the library building: The third floor of the six-floor building received the most wireless use, even though the second floor of the library has the main entrance and is generally considered the "main" floor of the library. During the summer of 2011, several ranges of books were relocated from the third floor to the first floor of the library, and additional tables and seating were added to the south side of the third floor. During the fall semester it became one of the most popular areas within the library to study, especially for small-group work. During a typical day, approximately 70 to 75 percent of all devices that connected to the library's wireless network did so from the third floor at some point during the day. The sixth floor of the library was the second most heavily used floor of the library during the fall semester of 2011.

- By time of day: Although numerical data about how many unique portable electronic devices had connected to the wireless network each hour of the day were not available, a daily chart over time of the total number of concurrently connected portable devices was part of the nightly report. By visually examining these line charts over a period of days, we came to the conclusion, corroborated by anecdotal observations from the evening staff, that peak use of the wireless network usually occurred between 8:00 and 10:00 p.m. Usage typically rose throughout the morning and afternoon hours, often plateauing during the late afternoon (4:00 to 6:00) hours, then rising again in the evening before reaching a peak sometime between 8:00 and 10:00, followed by a decline until the building closed at 1:00 a.m.

- By day of week: When analyzed in terms of days of the week, Saturday is the lowest-demand day, and Tuesday and Wednesday typically are the highest-demand days for wireless access within the library. When usage patterns are studied over the course of a semester, demand typically builds throughout the semester, often peaking during midterms and the final week of classes. The really interesting and important time study, however, may be the semester-to-semester analysis of trends. Unfortunately, we have not yet collected sufficient data to be able to perform this type of time analysis.

- By week and month of the fall semester: The first Monday, Tuesday, and Wednesday in December (the final week of classes) was a period of high use, averaging 3,619 unique devices per day over the three-day period. Usage of the wireless network during finals week actually declined a little as most students reviewed printed textbooks and written notes as they prepared to take their final exams.

- Uses of wireless devices within the library by library faculty and staff: We made no effort to differentiate use of the wireless network by patrons and staff. The fact that library staff members are also using the building's wireless network may be perceived by some as polluting or contaminating the wireless network usage data. It is difficult or impossible to identify and sequester or purge staff use of the wireless network. Nevertheless, with less than a hundred library staff members and often thousands of visitors to the library each day, the need to differentiate the two users groups is not essential.

At this point (early 2012) we know with confidence that several thousand mobile devices are being used in the library building, day in and day out. Casual observation suggests that laptops and mobile phones are the dominant mobile devices brought into the library and used while in the library. Tablet computers probably will gain local market share over the next few years. The adoption of the iPad on this particular campus seems to be primarily "top down" in the sense that most administrators and some faculty and staff members currently carry and use iPads and other tablets, but few students do so. The introduction of the lower-priced Amazon Fire and other lower-priced tablet computers beginning in late 2011 and moving into 2012 may have a significant impact on the local mix of actively carried and used mobile devices.

The campus use of the Internet and wireless devices also has been steadily growing. For example, between January and December 2010 the average amount of inbound Internet traffic doubled (Genung 2011). The average number of unique devices connecting to the campus wireless network increased from approximately 12,000 per day in May 2011 to nearly 17,000 devices in October 2011. The total traffic on the wireless network, measured in megabytes, also doubled between April 2011 and May 2011 (Genung 2011). There were over 1,100 wireless access points on campus in October 2011, with plans to add 300 more wireless access points by August 2012. When the current phase of the wireless network infrastructure upgrade is complete in 2013, nearly 2,000 wireless access points will be available (Genung 2011).

CONCLUSIONS AND RECOMMENDATIONS

Based upon this preliminary examination and analysis of the configuration and usage of a wireless network in one academic library, we offer the following tentative conclusions and recommendations:

- Give your wireless network the respect and attention it deserves. Wireless has become a key performance indicator for libraries. Usage of the wireless network in your brick-and-mortar library is becoming an increasingly important measure of the use and value of your library as a whole. Librarians should pay attention to and continuously monitor wireless network activities and developments.
- Plan for growth. The mobile revolution shows no signs of plateauing or abating. User needs, expectations, and behavior patterns continue to expand and evolve as the mobile era unfolds.
- Reconfigure your space. The use of mobile devices connected to a wireless network within a brick-and-mortar library almost certainly will alter space demands, furniture configurations, in-building traffic patterns, and so forth.
- Create professional performance measures and best practices for wireless. We need to develop national standards for mobile network services in libraries. Perhaps we should develop capacity targets for specific population groups, just as standards were developed in years past for seating capacities in various types of libraries. Collectively the library profession is still at the beginning stages of developing reliable measures and best practices for evaluating the wireless network services we offer within physical libraries.

- Support wireless content creators. Personal, portable electronic devices also are powerful engines for creating content—photos, videos, messages, tweets, and so forth. Sometimes library users want to be able to easily contribute their created content to library-managed websites, catalogs, blogs, wikis, archives, and institutional repositories. These "mobile content creation havens" within brick-and-mortar libraries should be designed so that mobile content creators can easily create, edit, and submit their content for consideration.
- Wired is withering. Reassess the deployment and use of your wired Internet connections, especially any public-access wired connections you may offer. Illinois State University is currently reexamining the configuration of its computing labs. While some of the labs offer wireless access, most of the university-supplied computers have wired connectivity.
- Instruct library users and library workers about safe, responsible use of wireless networks. Using a wireless network in a public place such as a library is not all cakes and ale. As Goldsborough (2012) notes, "Accessing the Internet at a free public hotspot, in a worst-case scenario, can allow identity thieves to steal your Social Security number, bank long-in [sic] name and password, and other personal information." Makaya and Pierre (2012, v) write from the network-administrative perspective that the challenging issues attendant to the explosive growth of types and usage of wireless networks include "security, mobility management, architectures, quality of service (QoS) provisioning, and resources allocation." Kern and Phetteplace (2012) describes how anyone can "harden your browser" against unwanted snooping and attacks via wireless networks through choosing a browser designed for security, selecting the best settings, and enhancing your browser's security via extensions.
- Spikes happen. Plan for spikes in demand on your wireless network. Sometimes social and communal events make unusual demands on a wireless network. When "Occupy Blo-No" (that is, Occupy Bloomington-Normal, the local branch of the Occupy Wall Street movement) was forming during the fall of 2011, it held an organizational meeting in the library. On the night of the meeting, there was a spike in usage of the wireless network.
- Electrical capacity fuels wireless activity. Check the configuration of outlets and other power sources in your public areas. Although many wireless devices claim to hold a charge during normal use for an entire day, many users of wireless devices will want to plug them into a power source. Most users do not like to be tethered, but when their batteries are low, they will expect to recharge in the library or wherever they happen to be.
- Keep everyone in the loop. Keep the librarians and library staff members informed about the growth and patterns of use of wireless services in your library building. They often will be the first people to hear of wireless problems in your library building.
- Work with the larger organization. If your wireless network is operated and maintained by some group external to the library but within the larger parent organization (e.g., university, city, county, corporation), make sure they are aware that the library is very interested in providing top-notch wireless access within the library building or library space, and that you are watching the growth in and patterns of use. Because most libraries are organizationally nestled within a larger parent organization, most library wireless networks tie into some larger organizational network before they reach the wide Internet. Capacities and problems with the parental network can affect the library's wireless network.
- Tweak your wireless network. If some wireless access points within the library are consistently underutilized, consider redeploying them elsewhere in the building. Consult with the wireless engineers in your parent organization or externally to get the most from your wireless network infrastructure.
- Plan for the expected and unexpected. Wireless networks, like any type of system, can experience emergency situations (e.g., unplanned downtime), planned short-term situations (e.g., planned

downtime), and long-range growth and upgrade needs. Each library with a wireless network needs to plan for each type of situation.

• Do not neglect immobile information technologies. It is important to note that, while mobile devices and services are the focus of this chapter and of this book, and while mobile, networked services and content are very popular with this community of users, immobile information technologies continue to generate high interest and use. For instance, five collaboration stations constructed and deployed in Milner Library in late summer of 2011 have received much use and high praise from small groups working on class projects. Demand was so strong that two additional collaboration stations were added during the winter of 2011/2012.

FINAL THOUGHTS

While the impact and importance of traditional measures of the patron's user experience in the library may be waning, the importance of wireless connectivity in relation to the overall user experience almost certainly is increasing. Unfortunately, a bad wireless experience for a user in a library may have more negative impact than a positive user experience has, in terms of a sustained sense of gestalt feelings toward the library. It would be really interesting to study, for example, the "halo effect" of a bad wireless experience on the patron's overall sense of the value of the library in meeting his or her information needs. This halo effect could be studied over time. For instance, if a patron cannot get connected to the wireless network in the library, he or she may immediately think something like "stupid library," but that negative response may or may not persist over the subsequent days, weeks, or months following that negative experience. The affective impact of a user's wireless experience needs more research.

Libraries typically have had certain key indicators of use, demand, and success. Gate counts and the circulation of library materials are traditional key indicators. In the mobile era, as long as the library remains a strong, viable gathering place for information seeking and information experiences, the use of the library's wireless network also will be a key indicator of success.

The library without walls is a growing phenomenon, but walled libraries still matter, and people continue to flock to them, their portable gadgets in tow. The quality and consistency of the wireless connectivity within those walls is of increasing importance to a rising percentage of library users. High demand for wireless access within a physical library is a good problem to have. We need to continue to promote the availability of wireless access in libraries. It is a service that library users need, expect, and appreciate.

REFERENCES

Barker, Tim. 2011. "College Struggle with Students' Data Demand." STLtoday.com. http://www .stltoday.com/news/local/education/article_77e313e4-480f-5942-8161-cf1e015f2c3b.html.

Brown-Sica, Margaret S. 2012. "Library Spaces for Urban, Diverse Commuter Students: A Participatory Action Research Project." *College & Research Libraries* 73 (3): 217–231.

Caluori, Robert A., Jr. 2011. "Successfully Planning a Scalable and Effective Patron Wireless Network." *Library Technology Reports* 47 (6): 29–32.

Genung, Scott. 2011. "Wireless and Internet Trends Report for Illinois State University." Presentation made at the November 9, 2011 General Session of the T-Tech Technology User Group (TTUG), Illinois State University, Normal, Illinois.

Goldsborough, Reid. 2012. "The Highs and Lows of Wi-Fi." *Teacher Librarian* 39 (3): 66.

Kern, M. Kathleen, and Eric Phetteplace. 2012. "Hardening the Browser: Protecting Patron Privacy on the Internet." *Reference & User Services Quarterly* 51 (3): 210–214.

Makaya, Christian, and Samuel Pierre, eds. 2012. *Emerging Wireless Networks: Concepts, Techniques, and Applications.* New York: CRC Press.

McEwen, Rhonda, and Kathleen Scheaffer. 2012. "Orality in the Library: How Mobile Phones Challenge Our Understandings of Collaboration in Hybridized Information Centers." *Library & Information Science Research* 34: 92–98.

Wang, Guangyan. 2011. *Guidelines for Outdoors WiFi Space Design.* Master's Thesis, University of Illinois at Urbana-Champaign. https://www.ideals.illinois.edu/handle/2142/29647.

FURTHER READING

Crow, Barbara, Michael Longford, and Kim Sawchuk, eds. 2010. *The Wireless Spectrum: The Politics, Practices, and Poetics of Mobile Media.* Toronto: University of Toronto Press.

Webb, William. 2010. *Being Mobile: Future Wireless Technologies and Applications.* New York: Cambridge University Press.

7

Snap & Go: The Delivery and Marketing of Library Services through QR Codes and a Mobile Website

Susan Kantor-Horning

Key Points

- QR codes make it easy to push new and existing library content and services—literally—into the hands of mobile phone users through a service called Snap & Go.
- A mobile-patron support system allows the creation and management of QR codes and the delivery and maintenance of available resources.
- Outreach involves creating library-service access points anywhere you can stick a two-inch QR code.
- With QR codes you can extend library services and information deeper into the community and to people on the go.

EXTENDING LIBRARY SERVICES TO PEOPLE ON THE GO

Imagine that you are traveling on a commuter bus heading into San Francisco and need a good read for the 40-minute ride. You spot a poster overhead depicting a man wearing headphones with books balanced on each side of his ears. A funny-looking barcode is also displayed on the poster along with instructions to download a reader to your camera phone so you can scan the code, select a title, and enjoy a book. Curious, you follow these instructions and immediately download an e-book to your mobile phone via your library account. This scenario played out on Tri Delta Transit[1] and WestCAT[2] buses in early 2011, where riders benefited from Contra Costa County (California) Library's Snap & Go project.[3] The service came courtesy of a $60,000 grant the library received to research the potential of quick-response (QR) code technology for changing the way libraries do business.

Figure 7.1
Westcat poster.

As budgets are trimmed and operating hours for community library buildings are shrinking, Contra Costa County Library's Virtual Library Team embraces the idea of finding technological solutions such as QR codes to extend the library's reach and to eliminate barriers to service. Seeking innovative uses of technologies to provide new models of self-service delivery and to extend and deploy library services outside of set points, the team scans the horizon for technologies that can be put to use in the library environment to improve service. This approach to innovation has given rise to a number of new services that are firsts of their kind for libraries: the eCard with real-time patron verification providing immediate access to resources and services even when the library is closed; Library-a-Go-Go, a fully automated touchscreen materials-lending machine providing stand-alone library services in nonlibrary environments; Discover & Go, an online museum pass-reservation program; and Snap & Go, a mobile application for smartphones utilizing QR code technology.

With an understanding that the mobile market was already widespread, would continue to expand, and that the public was becoming savvier about mobile, Contra Costa County Library's Virtual Library and Automation staff outlined the requirements for a mobile platform project to support the use of QR codes. Working with Quipu Group, a library-application consulting firm that had successfully partnered with the library in the past, staff felt confident that the project would take shape and applied for and received an innovative technology grant for the Snap & Go project from the Bay Area Library Information System (BALIS).

Contra Costa County residents are above the national average for owning a wireless email device, use of wireless Internet, owning a cellular phone, and owning a smart cellular phone, according to market profile information gathered from the *Lifestyle Market Analyst*.[4] Sixty-seven percent of the population of the county is between the ages of 15 and 64, landing this population in the "sweet spot" for mobile cellular usage.[5]

QR codes are two-dimensional codes that are readable by dedicated barcode readers and camera phones. While the technology was created in Japan decades ago for the manufacturing environment, marketers and other groups are adding the codes to just about any media to direct users to sites where they can learn more. The codes came onto the Virtual Library Team's radar in 2009, at about the same time Google decided to send window stickers with QR codes to top local businesses across the country. During this time, the codes were becoming more visible in marketing campaigns and began popping up on product labels, magazine covers, billboards, and buildings, inviting tech-savvy recipients to pull out their mobile phones, scan the QR code, and uncover the encoded information.[6] In addition to these uses, the codes were being recognized within the library and educational community, with a few organizations testing their effectiveness. As libraries can only fit so much information on a flyer or postcard, QR codes offer the interested user access to more information or can lead a user to more action.

ABOUT CONTRA COSTA COUNTY LIBRARY

With the rapid advancement in the use of mobile devices for accessing information, libraries everywhere are responding to the shift towards anytime, anywhere access by building mobile tools and platforms to offer their services and information to current and future patrons who are on the go. For Contra Costa County Library, a large suburban library located within the greater San Francisco Bay Area, its patrons are undeniably on the go.

After a 2001 article published in the *Contra Costa Times*[7] stated that Contra Costa County workers have the 10th worst commute in the nation and the longest commute time west of the Mississippi River, as well as the longest in the Bay Area, the library began working on a plan to better serve this peripatetic group. Propelled by its mission statement, "bringing people and ideas together," Contra Costa County Library has actively and successfully implemented and marketed library services to commuters over the past several years. A 2006 *Contra Costa Times*[8] article reaffirmed that 40 percent of Contra Costa County residents—compared to 30 percent of all Bay Area residents—work in one of the eight other Bay Area counties or outside the region. The commuter population accounts for approximately 402,600 workers.

Contra Costa County Library has 455,000 cardholders and serves a population of over one million with residents in urban, suburban, and rural communities covering 716 square miles through 23 community libraries, three outlets, three Library-a-Go-Go book-lending machines with locations in metro stations and a shopping mall, and a Virtual Library with online services available 24/7.[9] The library circulates 7.4 million items annually with over 3 million virtual visits to the library website each year. Contra Costa County Library patrons are ethnically, culturally, and intellectually diverse residents of California's ninth largest county.

The library's Strategic Plan identifies county residents as looking for a library experience that is fast, available at convenient hours, welcoming, easy to use, and customer-focused. A primary goal of the library's Strategic Plan is to change the way the library operates, including focusing outward toward target audiences, changing techniques of library service delivery, providing services relevant to the community when and where they are needed and not just within the confines of local branches, and expanding technology use, availability, and complexity. The grant for Snap & Go supported all four of the key initiatives identified in the Contra Costa County Library's Strategic Plan: reading, information for lifelong learning, branding, and collaboration. With the innovation grant, library staff could envision and successfully bring to fruition a system designed to use QR codes as a launching pad to demonstrate how a robust mobile platform can bring the library to mobile users and those mobile users to the library.[10]

The library's newest and most exciting services were created with the intention of providing patrons with self-service options that extend the library's reach outside of brick-and-mortar buildings to access points when and where the patron needs them. The connotation of movement is incorporated into the names of these services: Library-a-Go-Go, Discover & Go, and Snap & Go. As a result of its novel innovations and public relations efforts, Contra Costa County Library is recognized both locally and internationally as a leader in the application of innovative technologies for service delivery, especially in terms of library self-service implementations.

The Snap & Go project has attracted attention in the library world, and Contra Costa County Library staff members have been recognized for their work with national and local honors. Contra Costa County Library is one of four winners chosen from a total of 44 applicants for the American Library Association's (ALA) Cutting Edge Technology in Library Services Award for 2012. The award, given for Snap and Go, recognizes best library practices using cutting-edge technology and showcases libraries that are serving their communities with novel and innovative methods. This is the second time that Contra Costa County Library has been honored by ALA. The library received a 2009 Cutting Edge Service Award for its Library-a-Go-Go service.

The California State Association of Counties (CSAC) recognized Contra Costa County Library with a Merit Award for Snap & Go: QReative Mobile Library Services. CSAC received nearly 250 entries, and an independent panel of judges with expertise in county programs and challenges selected the award recipients. Snap & Go! Contra Costa County Library's Mobile Service Campaign received first place for the 2011 PR Excellence Award by the California Library Association. The article, *Snap & Go: A QReative Case in Point*[11] (MacKinnon and Sanford 2010), was chosen by the Emerald Literati Network Awards for their Excellence for Highly Commended Paper Award.

Contra Costa County Library pursues innovations that leverage and build upon its existing services, attracting new audiences, raising the library's profile in the community, and delivering excellent, convenient, needs-based services.[12] Through support from awards such as the BALIS innovation grant, the library continues to deliver leading-edge services such as Snap & Go and fulfill areas identified by the Strategic Plan.

With Snap & Go, the Virtual Library Team could embrace the opportunities for libraries inherent in QR code technology, visualize a new delivery model for existing services such as downloadable e-books and readers' advisory, and build a new system for its use. The team understood that with very little risk and investment of time, QR technology could be tested as a method for delivering service where it previously did not exist and also support self-directed use of the library. The decision to build a mobile platform instead of purchasing or developing an app made Snap & Go available to anyone with a mobile phone and not limited to only those users with a particular operating system such as Android or iOS.

With the grant money funding a mobile-patron support system, library staff and Quipu began working on designing and developing a service that extended beyond library walls and personal computers. Through the development of a mobile platform and the utilization of QR codes, the team found both opportunities and solutions for bridging the physical, digital, and mobile worlds. The platform was customized to meet users' needs at a time when no off-the-shelf, vendor-developed solution existed. The Snap & Go project required the development of new web applications and took full advantage of standard protocols and open-source technologies wherever possible.[13]

The platform can be deployed on any library system and can maximize available content for use on mobile devices with the notion that many users will land on the site via QR codes located on library books and on posters both inside and outside the library. Several small initiatives were initially developed to test the Snap & Go concept. These initiatives included a "Contact Us" QR code on the library's website that scans in the My Info Quest[14] text-a-librarian number and a QR code on the library's Summer Reading Festival event posters that provided more information and functionality surrounding the event wherever the posters were available.

CREATING A MOBILE-PATRON SUPPORT SYSTEM

More than simply a replication of the library website or a mobile public-access catalog for cell phone access, the mobile platform serves as a landing place for QR codes that launch web pages or catalog searches. The site provides real-time access to patron account functions, mobile access to catalog searching, and value-added content developed by staff to support QR code links. Patrons with cell phones are linked to library services and information through QR codes attached to library materials such as books, flyers, and posters. By taking a picture of the barcode, the phone launches the library's mobile site and provides access to three functional areas: detailed, dynamically generated information on titles scanned including reviews, first chapters, and read-alike information; links to library mobile web pages including hours and location information; and links to patron-account functions.

Regardless of how a link to a particular section of the site is initiated—whether it is a QR code launching a text-message session with library staff or one that provides direct access to downloadable audiobooks—the users can complete the interaction they are initially interested in and continue browsing other resources and services they may not have known were available by phone. This functionality allows the library to provide awareness of other resources and services that may be of interest to the user—either at that moment or in the future.

To support the use of QR codes for Snap & Go and to provide mobile web pages developed to maximize available content for use on mobile devices for the library's catalog that can be viewed by any smartphone browser, a mobile-patron support system needed to be created. Quipu's Mobile Patron Support System includes three parts: Mobile Tagger, a 2D barcode generator for staff workstations; MobileBridge, a manager application to allow library staff to configure the system; and a server to receive and respond to catalog and patron-account requests from mobile devices. The web-based server administration application allows library staff to configure and manage the mobile website including the location of resources like Amazon book jacket images, book reviews, summaries, and other enhanced content associated with individual titles; to manage pickup locations; and to use a what-you-see-is-what-you-get editor for adding new or editing existing content on the mobile website. This application adds a layer of security and opens up access to staff members who may not have experience editing PHP, XML, or HTML web pages.

MobileBridge takes full advantage of standard protocols and runs on any Linux or UNIX server with an Apache web server, MySQL, and PHP (LAMP). All of the web pages created with the application can be accessed using a QR code, and MobileBridge provides links for the immediate download of audiobooks or e-books to a patron's smartphone and also a mobile-accessible web space for other library web pages such as all of the community library locations and hours.

MobileBridge communicates with the library catalog through a Z39.50 server to provide patrons with the ability to search the catalog and view full records, including enhanced content.[15] Library customers also have access to their patron records and can update their email address

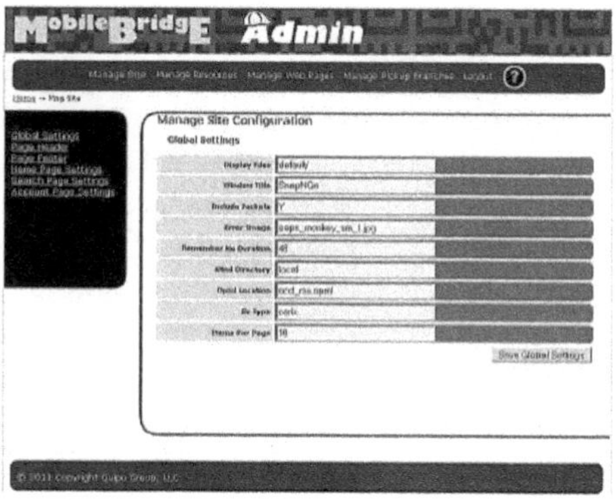

Figure 7.2
Mobile Bridge.

Figure 7.3
Top10 QR Codes.

or phone number from their mobile phone. Patron-account functionality was accomplished through the NISO Circulation Interchange Protocol (NCIP) standard for the exchange of borrower and circulation data between the Mobile Patron Support System server and the library system. At the time of the grant application, The Library Corporation (TLC), the library's ILS vendor, did not offer a mobile version for patron functions like placing holds, viewing account information, and updating selected account information.

Through the creation of function-specific QR codes, other value-added services were explored but not necessarily implemented, such as QR codes that enable patron self-service checkout of library materials. While the technology was successfully developed to allow for a "Snap & Checkout" service using QR codes, library staff decided that the service was not worth pursuing because it would require retagging materials with new barcodes and desensitizing items so that existing security systems would recognize that the items were successfully checked out.

Snap & Go serves as an innovative delivery mechanism for traditional library services such as readers' advisory. With Snap & Go Contra Costa County Library staff gave this traditional service a slight twist by tagging over 80 popular "seed" titles with QR codes linking directly to their read-alike recommendations. The read-alike booklists[16] were created as RSS feeds by public-services staff using the library's visual catalog, TLC's LS2PAC.

To tag and catalog the popular titles with QR codes for the read-alike lists, Virtual Library staff worked with the collection development and technical services manager to develop and implement best practices for the library's cataloging and processing staff. Mobile Tagger was installed on the processing staffs' computers so they could create a unique QR code for an associated booklist generated by each seed title. These codes were applied to the bottom right corner of the cover on the seed books.

Cataloging staff were able to associate each title with an 856 tag added to the machine-readable cataloging (MARC) record. The 856 MARC tag has two subfields. Subfield $u contains the Uniform Resource Identifier (URI) and provides electronic access data in a standard syntax, and Subfield $y can be utilized to record the link text, such as, "If you liked this, try these. ..." The text can be used in an online display instead of the uniform resource locater (URL) and acts as a hyperlink into the library catalog, supplanting the $u content in the display.

The Mobile Tagger barcode generator uses Adobe AIR and the Google Chart API to create and manage the QR code images. The application allows for the creation of a single code or a batch of QR codes that perform a specific function such as launching any web page or plain text message; opening up an SMS text message with the phone number; linking to a specific patron's account; linking to a specific item in the catalog; or linking to a series of related items, reviews, summaries, and first chapters. QR codes can be prepared and automatically stored for any number of purposes including for web, advertising, or marketing materials. The codes can print to various label sizes, business cards, or images of any size. Preferences can be set for margin size, any additional text to display on the code such as a URL for those who have an Internet-accessible computer but do not have a cell phone with a QR scanner, and the level of error correction desired for each code.

UBIQUITOUS READERS' ADVISORY AND REFERENCE

Thinking that early adopters, such as teens, could spread the word about Snap & Go and also show that QR codes can be fun while allowing people to learn something through using them, the library targeted this demographic for two activities. A scavenger hunt called Ready, Set, Snap & Go[17] was organized during Teen Read Week to promote the library's participation in My Info Quest, the nationwide text-a-librarian service, to raise awareness of the library's secure mobile website and to provide a simple tour of library resources and materials.

During the time of the Snap & Go project, participants in the teen advisory groups for two community libraries were asked to share their thoughts on My Info Quest. The participants responded that they loved the QR code on the library's contact page as it allows people to easily scan the code that prefills all of the identifying information and telephone num-

Figure 7.4
Mobile Tagger.

ber so all that is needed from the user is typing in his or her question and pressing send to get an answer from a librarian within minutes. Texting was a communication venue the participants were already familiar with, and the teens found this format a less intimidating way to ask for information than calling or talking to a librarian face to face.

Despite having information about the text-a-librarian service posted to the library website and on signs displayed in each of the community libraries, the participants believed that the service was not well known by their peers and by adults. Some of the teen advisory members were unclear on why people would use a text-a-librarian service, and their suggestions were given to help the library clarify this service to potential users. These suggestions included providing examples of the types of questions that users may ask such as help for school-related information needs, recommendations on resources, guidance on search strategies, ready reference help for assignments, and answers to library-related questions. Emphasis could also be made on the convenient and anonymous nature of the service along with the instantaneous access to a live person who remotely provides authoritative and trustworthy information.

For the scavenger hunt, a poster displayed a QR code and information encouraging participants to text a librarian if they needed help with a clue. The reference providers staffing My Info Quest were given access to the details about the scavenger hunt to help players decipher the clues. Several Contra Costa County community libraries hosted the indoor scavenger hunt using QR codes for unlocking clues and requiring interactive answers from program participants. All of the QR codes were printed with URLs underneath the image so people without cell phones could use a computer to get the clue information. Teens who did not have cell phones or data plans could also play the game as the codes brought up text instead of directing players to a website. The final code in the hunt initiated an SMS message to a number in Google Voice. Players could either email or text their library card number to Virtual Library staff so they could be entered into a prize drawing.

The other activity targeting teens included placing QR codes on copies of the Young Adult Library Services Association's (YALSA) Top Ten nominations.[18] The codes linked readers to an interactive website where they could access reviews, see other nominees, place holds, and directly participate in picking the winners by casting their vote for their

Figure 7.5
Ready, Snap, Go Poster.

favorites. All of these activities could be accomplished by snapping the QR code on the front cover of the book they just read without having to ask a question, visit the library, get on a computer, or type a URL. This exercise gave staff an innovative, reproducible way to strengthen their ability to provide readers' advisory and provide opportunities for participation in the creation of book-lists that are placed directly into the hands of young readers through QR code labeling.

ADVERTISING AS OUTREACH

The Virtual Library Team set out to explore the infinite possibilities for creating library-service access points anywhere they could stick a two-inch QR code—on bus posters, on books, in metro stations, on flyers, in newspaper ads, in library stacks, and on billboards in public spaces where people gather. The marketing campaign for Snap & Go developed around the use of QR codes to give the library a deeper reach into the community and to provide services offsite. Contra Costa County Library staff helped to design advertising with customized QR codes directing users to the library service most relevant to them based on their current location. As the QR code generators used in the campaign were freely available and not the more in-depth, paid versions, the codes did not provide the analytics necessary for tracking usage and measuring return on investment.

For the launch of Snap & Go, a QR code was attached to the 2010 Summer Reading Festival poster offering quick access to mobile web pages supporting this programming. Impressed by both the library's use of QR codes as a gateway to the festival and as a method for providing a preconfigured SMS message to an on-call librarian who answers questions within a few minutes, an editor for a local community paper wrote in his blog, "You just have to love a library system that lunges for the future with technology firmly in hand."[19]

As part of the educational campaign to inform patrons and the greater community about QR technology and the Snap & Go project, Virtual Library staff created a subject guide[20] using LibGuides by Springshare. During the first year of the project, the guide received 7,900 views.

SPECIFIC CONTENT IN SPECIFIC CONTEXTS

One of the most highly successful applications of the Snap & Go project was the partnership between the library and two regional transit authorities, Tri Delta Transit and WestCAT. Immediately recognizing the symbiotic relationship between reading and commuting, the marketing personnel for the transit authorities were quick in responding to library staff's requests for creating a partnership. Advertising promoting

Figure 7.6
Westcat audiobooks poster.

"enroute entertainment" and the transformation of peoples' commutes was soon developed after initial meetings between partners.

A QR code attached to advertisements onboard local buses became a service point where patrons were not only taken to the library's downloadable e-book service but were directly linked to only those formats compatible with mobile phones. From January through May 2011, a new fleet of hundreds of "digital bookmobiles" contributed to the 1,547 e-books that were wirelessly downloaded directly to library cardholders' mobile devices by customers scanning a QR code via posters providing instant access to the library's collection of e-books for immediate enjoyment during their commute.

A visually appealing billboard consisting of a QR code surrounded by a colorful word cloud was placed along BART stations during spring 2011. Commuters traveling along the lines within Contra Costa County were invited to interact with the message depicting library services available to them while they are on the go. The advertisement went beyond describing digital downloads to featuring other relevant services available from the library's mobile site, most notably Discover & Go, Contra Costa County Library's new virtual museum pass-reservation system, another product codeveloped with Quipu Group. By scanning the QR code on the billboard with a reader on their mobile phone, library users were directed to virtual museum passes; patron-account and catalog search functions; information on book titles, including reviews, first chapters, and read-alike information; library hours and locations; and more. Usage of the library's mobile site bumped up 11 percent the first month of the campaign, and awareness of the library services led to a sustained increase in usage of 16 percent.

CHALLENGES TO THE SNAP & GO PROJECT

Some of the challenges in delivering the Snap & Go service included the unfamiliarity people have with QR code technology and the need for patrons to have both web access and a mobile phone. When Snap & Go was first introduced on regional transit buses, only those titles in the MP3 format could be wirelessly downloaded from the Library's mobile eBook platform, limiting the number of items people could access. Shortly into the Snap & Go campaign, the library's e-book vendor, OverDrive, introduced a free app allowing wireless access to EPUB eBooks, opening up a significantly larger number of titles available to commuters on the bus. The mobile user still faced the challenge of finding an available title to download due to limitations in the search capability on the vendor's mobile application and the popularity of the e-book service.

Another challenge the library, and anyone using QR codes to connect people to services faces, is that as the physical distance between the code and the reader increases, the size of the code displayed needs to increase to compensate. For the marketing campaign targeting county residents commuting on BART, billboards were displayed at track level. It was important to increase the size of the code on the billboard to ensure that it would be successfully scanned from a distance of eight feet or more; however, it was difficult to increase the size without compromising the aesthetic quality of the design.

For the read-alike lists accessible to the public via QR codes placed on the covers of popular titles, the challenge for staff lay in the time it takes to create QR codes and attach them to books. Having a popular title out of circulation as processing staff brings the items back into the library was a challenge to following the usual protocol for getting books into the hands of customers as efficiently as possible.

Figure 7.7
Discover and Go Pass.

Creating new partnerships using cutting edge technologies can also be a challenge. Thinking that the Department of Motor Vehicles (DMV) would be a great fit for Snap & Go because people often find themselves with long waiting periods, the agency was one of the first contacts staff made regarding a partnership. The DMV was unresponsive to multiple requests.

By serving as a bridge from print to online content, QR codes can be used for future collaborations with other local entities such as coffee houses and medical offices. Where anyone is looking for a good read or quick access to timely information, QR codes have the potential for mutually beneficial collaborative efforts.

A NEW MOBILE SERVICE

Contra Costa County Library continues to develop its mobile services and look for ways to promote the usage of QR codes. Discover & Go is unlike existing library service models that circulate physical museum passes. Patrons using Discover & Go are not required to come into a library to pick up or return their passes. All transactions for the service take place online using a technology that requires minimal to no staff involvement. Participating museums have the option to accept mobile tickets on smartphones or to require the printed downloadable pass that utilizes QR code technology. The QR code provides a measure of security on the downloadable passes as the patron name and date of use are encoded and can be scanned by museum staff to ensure validity.

NOTES

1. Tri Delta Transit. 2011. "Download Free Audiobooks on All Tri Delta Transit Buses." Accessed December 19, 2011. http://trideltatransit.com/promo_free_books.aspx.

2. WestCAT Transit. 2011. "Transform Your Commute, Download Free Audiobooks on WestCAT Buses." Accessed December 19, 2011. http://www.westcat.org/booksforbusses.html.

3. Contra Costa County Library. 2011. "SnapNGo." Accessed December 19, 2011. https://snapngo.ccclib.org/.

4. *Lifestyle Market Analyst*. 2008. Wilmette, IL: Standard Rate & Data Service, p. 571.

5. Contra Costa County Library. 2011. "More Information on *Snap & Go!*" Accessed December 19, 2011. http://ccclib.org/press_releases/snapngo.html.

6. Educause Learning Initiative. 2009. "7 Things You Should Know about QR Codes." Accessed December 19, 2011. http://net.educause.edu/ir/library/pdf/ELI7046.pdf.

7. Simerman, John, and Lisa Vorderbrueggen. 2001. "No. 1 and Not Cheering—Contra Costa, Solano and Alameda have the Longest Average Commute Time of Large Counties West of Texas, Says the U. S. Census." *Contra Costa Times*, November 20,, final edition. NewsBank Access World News (2001324512).

8. Tribble, Sarah Jane. 2006. "Taking Their Work Home—Some Solve Roadway Crises from Living Room Supervisor's Plan May Allow County Employees to Telecommute." *Contra Costa Times*, January 26, final edition. NewsBank Access World News (2006026731).

9. Contra Costa County Library. 2011. "Contra Costa County Library." Accessed December 19, 2011. http://ccclib.org.

10. Contra Costa County Library. 2011. "More Information on *Snap & Go!*" Accessed December 19, 2011. http://ccclib.org/press_releases/snapngo.html.

11. MacKinnon, Paula, and Cathy Sanford. 2010. "Snap & Go: A QReative Case in Point." *Library Hi Tech News* 27, (4/5): 5–8.

12. Contra Costa County Library. 2011. "More Information on *Snap & Go!*" Accessed December 19, 2011. http://ccclib.org/press_releases/snapngo.html.

13. Contra Costa County Library. 2011. "More Information on *Snap & Go!*" Accessed December 19, 2011. http://ccclib.org/press_releases/snapngo.html.

14. My Info Quest. 2009. "My Info Quest." Accessed December 19, 2011. http://myinfoquest.info.

15. Quipu Group. 2010. "What Is MobileBridge?" Accessed December 19, 2011. http://quipugroup.com/index.php/Products/mobilebridge.html.

16. Contra Costa County Library. 2011. "If You Like . . . ," Accessed December 19, 2011. http://guides.ccclib.org/ifyoulike.

17. Contra Costa County Library. n.d. "Ready, Set, Snap & Go." Accessed December 19, 2011. http://guides.ccclib.org/hunt.

18. Contra Costa County Library. 2011. "Teens' Top Ten," Accessed December 19, 2011. http://guides.ccclib.org/top10.

19. Gensburger, André. 2010. "No Funding but the Library System Has Loads of QR and It Is Good," *MisterWriter's Extelligence* [blog]. May 6. http://www.misterwriter.info/2010/05/no-funding-but-library-system-has-loads.html.

20. Contra Costa County Library. 2011. "Snap & Go." Accessed December 19, 2011. http://guides.ccclib.org/qr.

REFERENCES AND FURTHER READING

Ekart, Donna F. 2011. "Codify Your Collection." *Computers in Libraries*, April: 38–39.

Farkas, Meredith. 2010. "Guided by Barcodes: QR Codes Link Patrons to the Library." *American Libraries*, August: 26.

Hadro, Josh. 2010. "QR Codes to Extend Library's Reach in Contra Costa, CA." *Library Journal*, January: 22–25.

MacKinnon, Paula, and Cathy Sanford. 2010. "Snap & Go: A QReative Case in Point." *Library Hi Tech News* 27, no. (4/5): 5–8.

8

Mobile Tours for the Library with Historic Photos and Podcasts

Lori Bell

Key Points

- Repurposing digitized historical photographs for mobile, interactive experiences is possible and effective.
- The ATLAS Project is examined as a case study.
- Historypin is explored as a newer platform for interacting with historical materials and locations using mobile devices and augmented reality.
- Examples of innovative audio and video tours are summarized.
- Tips for audio tour creation are offered.

PROVIDING ACCESS TO HISTORICAL PHOTOGRAPHS AND TOURS ON MOBILE DEVICES

Many libraries have been working on digitizing and providing access to historical photographs in their libraries, content not readily available except in the community where it originated. In addition to providing access to the flat images themselves, libraries must take advantage of opportunities to repurpose these images using new technologies and mobile devices to create interactive and innovative experiences. This chapter features a project by Alliance Library System (ALS), LearningTimes, and the Cullom-Davis Library at Bradley University to make historical images available on mobile devices, discusses other tools that can be used to do this, and examines projects utilizing these tools.

CASE STUDY OF A PROJECT

In 2009 and 2010, the Alliance Library System (ALS), which is now Reaching Across Illinois Library System (RAILS), embarked on a project with LearningTimes and the Cullom-Davis Library at Bradley University. Since 1997 ALS and Bradley had collaborated on a number of digital imaging projects to scan and make historical photographs available. Since these images had been first scanned, they had been used for several repurposing projects since 1997. There was a project to provide audio description to make the photos accessible to the visually impaired and a project to use the photographs to create multimedia electronic books to bring the history to life. In 2009, ALS applied for a Library Services and Technology Act (LSTA) grant from the Illinois State Library to repurpose the images yet again to provide access to selected images on mobile devices and to use social media tools to promote the photographs and encourage interaction. The ATLAS Alliance's Trail to Learning-Casts and Syndicated Sites (ATLAS) was born (http://www.atlaspodcasts.org).

ALS, LearningTimes, and Bradley University wanted to create a new, innovative method for enhancing and presenting existing historical digital images and information in an interactive manner that enabled visitors to add value to the resource. ATLAS used podmaps (that is, an interactive map of Illinois that users can use to find podcasts, images, and other historical information) and other Web 2.0 tools to bring historical information to life for all citizens of Illinois. The goal of the ATLAS project was to take existing digital images and information, expand and repurpose them, and deliver them in a more intuitive, interactive environment wherein librarians and the citizens of Illinois can add comments and tags, create playlists, and add additional content to the resource. The project repurposed and revitalized proven popular historical digital images of Illinois places and people by creating a new modular model for collaborative digital image collections.

Another goal of the ATLAS project was to help librarians and library staff members at ALS member libraries to become more comfortable, knowledgeable, and adept at creating and delivering great podcasts. To that end, Jonathan Finkelstein from LearningTimes created and delivered an online course consisting of three online sessions lasting about one hour each, with homework between sessions on how to use Audacity to create podcasts.

Two existing collections of historical digital images and information were used as the basis for the ATLAS project. "Early Illinois Women and Other Unsung Heroes: The First One Hundred Years 1818–1918" (http://www.alliancelibrarysystem.com/IllinoisWomen/index.cfm) was created in 1997–1998 from the collections of several different sizes and types of libraries in west-central Illinois. The purpose of "Early Illinois Women" was to capture and convey digitally the experiences of Illinois women during the nineteenth century. Images and text from participating libraries were grouped generally according to topic: women pioneers, public life, religion, work, medicine, education, arts and entertainment, and war. Project librarians selected images, scanned them, and wrote accompanying text. More than 10 years later, this collection is still heavily used, even though the website is primarily static (there are a few reenactment videos) and not very interactive. It was cutting edge at the time, but not now.

The second baseline collection was developed in the following year. In 1998, ALS was awarded an Institute of Museum and Library Services (IMLS) grant to build

"Illinois Alive! The Heritage and Texture of a Pivotal State during the First Century of Statehood 1818–1918." Twenty-eight multitype libraries participated in this project to build on the "Early Illinois Women" project. Categories for this project were expanded from agriculture and business, early Illinois authors, the Civil War, the African American experience, and emigration/immigration.

By the end of June 2009, 10 items had been created via a collaborative effort between ALS and LearningTimes and added to the podmap online resource (http://www.atlaspodcasts.org/). Users of the podmap can explore the content via the interactive map of Illinois, with each podcast pinpointed on the map as a beacon of sound, or they can explore predefined themes to the collection (e.g., Illinois River, Mississippi River, the Underground Railroad, higher education, and many more themes), follow guided tours, or consult an index. Users may also create their own playlists and subscribe to the RSS feed for the online resource so they can be notified when new content is added.

Once the digitization leap has been made from analog to digital resources, some libraries and other cultural institutions may pause and consider their work complete. However, the ATLAS project has proven that if existing digital resources are refreshed and reenvisioned approximately every decade or so, their overall usefulness and sense of worth to the general public can continue unabated, if not enhanced.

The ATLAS project provided one realizable method for repurposing existing historical digital content so that it becomes more interactive using the Web 2.0 tools that have become so popular in the last few years. Libraries, museums, historical societies, and other cultural institutions in Illinois, nationwide, and worldwide with existing historical digital collections could replicate the ATLAS model to refresh and revitalize their digital assets.

One of the unique aspects of the project was the creation of a podmap of Illinois. Visitors to the project website can click on a map of Illinois and see "hotspots" of locations where there are materials to view and listen to. If they click a hotspot, they can then see a collection about a certain topic like Peoria distilleries; Lydia Moss Bradley, who founded Bradley University; Peoria; Abraham Lincoln; Quincy; and others. After selecting a hotspot and topic, the user can see historical photos, read text, or listen to a podcast about the topic—on his or her computer or mobile device. Users then can subscribe to a series of podcasts about the topic, take a guided tour of podcasts and videos on the topic, or see similar productions around themes such as slavery, higher education, and medicine. For some topics, videos in Windows video format were created for viewing on a computer or a mobile device.

LearningTimes staff taught ALS staff, and Bradley staff how to create high-quality podcasts. Staff used historical materials to write scripts about selected topics and then recorded them using Audacity. The scripts were made available as text on the website or mobile devices, as a podcast for audio access and as video with images.

The goal of the project was to create a model and a framework through which ALS libraries could make their photographs available, create podcasts about them, and allow the community to interact with them. Unfortunately, in 2010, ALS lost much of its funding and staff, and the project could not continue. Since 2010, a variety of options for sharing historical photos and information via mobile device have become available, affordable, and feasible for libraries.

HISTORYPIN

Historypin (http://www.historypin.com) launched in November 2011. Historypin allows you to pin photos, video, and audio to a specific location. After that, users can search for them in a map view. It comes with Android and iOS applications that can be used with augmented reality to take you to a photo at a location. Libraries can set up channels like they can with YouTube. There is bulk uploading and also manual uploading, which has a great deal of detail (title, description, tags, and so forth). Historypin has a partnership with Google, so photographs can be put into Google Street View and searched via location in Google Maps. Libraries also have the ability to create tours with embedded sound and video. Users can interact with the photos by sharing a "story." A number of libraries and museums are already using Historypin (http://www.historypin.com/community/lams-involved), including the New York Public Library and the Library of Congress. The mobile application allows the user to browse collections, search the map, and post a photograph. Nick Stanhope, cofounder and executive director of Historypin, stated, "But, really, it's not about the tech. It's about those conversations—little ones, across families and streets, and big ones, involving millions of citizen historians. Through all of these conversations, we can create a place to explore history in amazing ways and help families and neighborhoods come together around what we all share: history." (Stanhope 2011)

OFFERING MOBILE AUDIO AND VIDEO TOURS OF YOUR LIBRARY

The mobile revolution is transforming tours and other place-based orientation and information-sharing options offered by libraries, museums, and other cultural institutions. Many libraries and museums have provided mobile audio and video tours for years, if not decades. There are now a variety of ways to offer this service, and users are enjoying the benefits of these for a number of reasons. Tours can be audio with menu generation; for instance, a user can call a specified phone number and listen to a menu of options for audio tours or information. QR codes can be located around the physical space to serve as cues for the playback of specific audio or video clips. Audio tours can also be available via an audio file for a podcast that can be played on an MP3 player, a phone with MP3 capability, or a desktop computer, thus enabling the user to have a mobile tour experience without getting up. Video tours that are available on YouTube can be accessed on the iPhone through the YouTube app. These types of tours were more expensive for libraries to produce and deliver before library users began purchasing their own devices in droves and the cost of producing videos of acceptable quality and overall production values dropped significantly.

There are a number of advantages to offering mobile audio and video tours in the library. No staff needs to be scheduled for these. Library users can access them at any time at their convenience. This can make these tours more reasonably priced than having to schedule staff. These types of tours can be provided on technology library users already have—their phone or MP3 player. Because of this, library users do not have to learn how to use a new technology to take advantage of these services. Tours can be self-guided at the interest and convenience of the user. Library users can download these tours before they visit the library, saving time. They can experience the tour on their own schedule when they have time and it is convenient for them. Asynchronous tours can save staff time. Although many staff and students are comfortable with their own mobile devices, developing these tours can introduce staff and students to new technologies as well.

One of the disadvantages of these types of tours is the possible large sizes of audio and video files. Because the files are large, it may take awhile to download the audio and video files from a computer to the device, depending on the Internet connection speed of the user. There may also be varying volume and quality levels of audio and video.

SOME EXAMPLES OF LIBRARY TOURS

Below are some examples of mobile tours of libraries.

- Wolfwalk, by the North Carolina State University Libraries, is a photographic guide to the history of NCSU for mobile devices. The tour can be taken using the location-aware campus map. Users can browse photos by decade (pre-1900s to the present) or by theme. There are over 1,000 photographs available (http://www.lib.ncsu.edu/wolfwalk/).
- Duke University Libraries offer a video virtual tour of the Perkins and Bostock Libraries. The library has also compiled a downloadable audio tour of the new Bostock facility. The tour is in MP3 format and can be used with any digital audio player. There are 10 parts to the tour, and it takes about 25 minutes. Users can download individual files of interest or all 10 in a zip file (http://library.duke.edu/support/renovation/tours.html).
- Simmons College offers a four-minute video tour of the library with Stormy the Shark (http://www.simmons.edu/library/).
- Arizona State University's Hayden Library has a video tour of the library; the Library Channel, which produces podcasts and videos; and the award-winning The Library Minute, which keeps the campus up to date on library services and programs (The Library Channel: http://lib.asu.edu/librarychannel/; The Library Minute: http://lib.asu.edu/librarychannel/category/library-minute/).
- The C.V. Starr East Asian Library at Columbia Universities offers "enhanced" podcasts in MP4 format, which includes images and audio. These can only be played on the web using Quick-Time or iTunes or on a video-capable iPod. Tours are offered in English, Chinese, Japanese, Korean and Tibetan (http://library.columbia.edu/content/libraryweb/indiv/eastasian/tours.html).
- The University of California—Merced Library developed an iPod video tour that can be accessed by scanning a QR code that links to the video in YouTube or iTunesU. It can also be downloaded from the website to the user's computer and then his or her phone. The tour can also be downloaded to other types of devices such as Android. This iPod Touch Video Library Tour was developed to replace in-person instruction for freshman library orientations (http://library.ucmerced.edu/about-the-library/ipod-touch-library-tour).
- The Sheridan Libraries at Johns Hopkins University have developed a series of podcasts so users can learn about library collections, services, people, and making the most of the library. Podcasts are approximately 6 to 20 minutes in length and include "How to Make Maps," "Who's Citing Whom?" and others. (http://www.library.jhu.edu/podcasts/).
- The Hood Museum and Dartmouth College Library collaborated to create an audio tour as a new way to experience part of their collections. Library users can borrow an iPod at the reserve desk or download the audio files to their device (http://hoodmuseum.dartmouth.edu/collections/overview/americas/mesoamerica/murals/).

- Guide by Cell (http://guidebycell.com/) enables users to dial a toll-free number from their cell phone to access a guided tour of library. They can specify items they want to learn about from a menu—going at their own pace and leaving feedback for the library. The Folger Shakespeare Library used this technology to create an audio tour of and highlights of the Shakespearean Sisters exhibition that is available on the web, cellular phones, and other mobile devices. Library users can visit the exhibition and hear the tour by dialing a telephone number and following menu prompts (http://www.folger.edu/template.cfm?cid=4036).
- The Library of Congress has created an iTunes app that can be downloaded and used on iPhone and iPad and video tours of the Main Reading Room, the Great Hall, the Bible Collection, Exploring the Early Americas, and others (http://www.loc.gov/loc/lcib/1009/app.html).

TIPS FOR AUDIO TOUR CREATION

Listed below are some tips and tricks for mobile-tour podcast creation.

1. Create an outline for your project.
2. Get buy-in from staff, administrators, and faculty.
3. Collaborate with other departments. Has someone else already done something similar?
4. Apply for a technology grant from your institution or other funding agencies.
5. Investigate audio and video production units on campus or within the parent organization and collaborate if possible. Also consider using students or volunteers.
6. Create a detailed script.
7. Give yourself a reasonable amount of time to complete the project.
8. Keep it simple.
9. Use a quality microphone. Often the audio quality is the weakest link in many videos created by libraries, museums, and other cultural organizations.
10. Keep things moving—keep it short and sweet.
11. Script writing—keep it for the ears, not the eyes.
12. Build a connection with the audience as if you are speaking directly to the person.
13. Sound natural.
14. Vary the voices; make it sound lively and exciting.
15. Listen, check, and recheck your "final" production.
16. Evaluate the production.
17. Provide audio in languages other than English that are appropriate for the community you serve.
18. Provide a written transcription of the audio tour to make the information accessible to users who have hearing impairments.

Equipment needed for audio production includes a computer, high-quality microphone, sound recording and editing software like Audacity (free), and an MP3 encoder.

FURTHER READING

Buczynski, J. A. 2008. "Libraries Begin to Engage Their Menacing Mobile Phone Hordes without Shhhhh!" *Internet Reference Services Quarterly* 13 (2/3): 261–269. doi:10.1080/10875300802103916.

Dempsey, Megan. 2011. "QR Codes for a Library Audio Tour." *Scan Me! QR Codes in Libraries* [blog] April 19. http://qrinlibs.blogspot.com/2011/04/qr-codes-for-library-audio-tour.html.

Hao, Shuang. 2011. "Development of an Interactive Virtual Library Tour." Master's Thesis, Western Illinois University.

Kroski, Ellyssa. 2008. "Library Mobile Initiatives." *Library Technology Reports* 44(5): 33–38.

Library of Congress. 2010. "There's an App for That." *Library of Congress Information Bulletin* 69(9): 184. http://www.loc.gov/loc/lcib/1009/app.html.

Mikkelsen, Susan, and Sara Davidson. 2011. "Inside the iPod, Outside the Classroom." *Reference Services Review* 39(1): 66–80.

Stanhope, Nick. 2011. "Let Historypin Be Your Guide." *Google Lat Long Blog* (July 11). http://google-latlong.blogspot.com/2011/07/let-historypin-be-your-guide.html

Part 3

Mobile Access to Content

9

Practical Mobile Web Design

Chad Mairn

Key Points

- Begin by understanding how your full website is being used.
- Determine who will design the mobile-optimized website and what to include.
- The differences between native apps and mobile-optimized websites are summarized.
- An overview of using jQuery Mobile to design a mobile-optimized website is provided.
- Various ways to test and validate a mobile-optimized website are covered.
- The future of responsive web design is explored.

INTRODUCTION

According to the International Telecommunication Union, in 2010 the United States had nearly 279 million mobile subscriptions—a 64.62 percent increase in just 10 years. At that time, it was estimated that by the end of 2011 there would be 5 billion mobile subscriptions in a world with 6.8 billion people (Whitney 2010). These are impressive numbers, and now that information is available literally at everyone's fingertips, the time is fitting for librarians to plan accordingly for this growth in order to place vital library resources and services into their users' hands. For those who may feel intimidated by the task, there is good news. It is not necessary to spend a lot of money or to be a computer scientist in order to create a successful mobile web presence for libraries.

Being able to fit a library's vital resources and services into a smaller, more mobile package is important because many mobile library users expect to obtain information easily via their mobile devices. If a library's website does not display well on their devices, then these mobile users will go to another resource that does display well while providing them with the information that they need. More than likely, these users will not look back and wait for libraries to get caught up. This unfortunate outcome can be prevented easily with some planning, however.

FIRST STEPS IN PLANNING A LIBRARY'S MOBILE PRESENCE

In order to get one's library ready for the mobile experience, a good first step is to study how the full website is being used. Most full websites include Google Analytics or some other web analytic software to help them determine how the site is being used. Although Google Analytics is discussed in more detail later, the key is to find the essential components from the full website and include them in the mobile-optimized version. Throughout this chapter the words "mobile-optimized" will be referred to often; the phrase basically means that the website is designed to fit within the constraints of smaller screens, usually called the viewport, which are usually 320 pixels wide by 480 pixels high. (These dimensions will be increasing as more and more tablet computers and other mobile devices are introduced to the market.)

As in any project, creating a mobile-optimized website requires some consideration. First, determine who will design the website. If no one on the library staff has elementary web design experience, then reach out and find a volunteer who does, or hire an outside expert to do the work for you. There are many resources that can help librarians follow best practices for mobile web design; some of these can be found in the Suggested Readings section later in this chapter. Another consideration is to determine what to include on the website. It is important to note that not every feature that is included on a library's full website will work on a mobile-optimized version, primarily because technologies like Adobe's Flash and other third-party browser plug-ins will not work on most mobile browsers. It is also a good idea to eliminate large graphics files and other unnecessary "bells and whistles" because a faster-loading mobile web page is one of the major goals when designing a mobile-optimized site.

Most users use mobile technologies while they are on the go. Going further, mobile users are probably not using sophisticated research tools or conducting rigorous studies using their mobile devices. Instead, they are searching for resources and then sharing them via email or their social networks; in-depth reading will occur, for now at least, when they are using their desktop or laptop computers or, increasingly, when using more sophisticated tablet computers. When designing a mobile-optimized website, it is important to remember, as Ballard states, that "*mobile* refers to the user, not the device or application" (2007, 3).

Another way to help determine what to include and perhaps what *not* to include on a mobile-optimized website is to use Google Analytics or some other web analytic tool. After creating a Google Analytics account, a web developer would copy some JavaScript tracking code and paste it into every library webpage just before the closing </head> tag. The tracking code looks like this:

```
<script type="text/javascript">
var _gaq = _gaq || [];
_gaq.push(['_setAccount', 'UA-account#']);
_gaq.push(['_trackPageview']);
(function() {
var ga = document.createElement('script'); ga.type = 'text/javascript'; ga.async = true;
ga.src = ('https:' == document.location.protocol ? 'https://ssl' : 'http://www') +
'.google-analytics.com/ga.js';
```

```
var s = document.getElementsByTagName('script')[ 0] ; s.parentNode.insertBefore(ga, s);
} ) ();
</script>
```

After collecting website usage data for a while in order to gain some insight into what resources and services are being used the most, the developer would then try to include those in the mobile-optimized version. Google Analytics has a feature called In-Page Analytics that will overlay clicking statistics on top of hyperlinks, which show percentages of links clicked; this is valuable information to consider when developing for the mobile web. If, for example, users click more than 80 percent of the time on a map to your library locations, then a developer would obviously want to include this within the mobile-optimized site. More recently, Google Analytics has introduced a real-time feature so a developer can see who and what is using a site in real time when they are actually on the site. Google Analytics also reveals what types of devices are accessing one's website; this, too, is extremely valuable when designing for mobile devices and also if a developer is contemplating designing a native application. For more information about Google Analytics, visit http://analytics.google.com. Finally, it's a good idea to ask your users what they expect in a mobile experience. Using that input, be sure to work diligently to get those features built into your mobile-optimized website.

Once some preliminary work has been done to determine what to include in the mobile-optimized website, the next task is to determine the look and feel. It is important to determine what type of device or devices to design for. Some designers choose to design for the lowest common denominator, meaning that the mobile-optimized website will display well on all mobile devices including legacy flip phones. Others choose to create a mobile-optimized site that will work primarily on smartphones or mobile devices with touch screens. Still others will design more than one mobile-optimized website so that they can reach all their mobile users. Responsive web design, however, is starting to become more popular; its fluid design and adaptive layouts may eliminate the need to design multiple versions of a site because the pages are responsive and change when the screen dimensions change. Responsive web design is the future of web development and is discussed later in this chapter.

With tablets and other mobile devices utilizing touch screens becoming more popular, the design considerations should change. Forcing a mobile-optimized website to display automatically for tablet users, for example, may not be an ideal practice because most of the tablet's built-in web browsers have the pinch-and-zoom function where users can adjust the web page to fit within the constraints of their screens. In addition, many users are accustomed to navigating the web this way, and forcing an interface onto them is generally not a good idea. Nonetheless, if a web page is coded to automatically redirect a mobile user to a mobile-optimized website, then it is a good idea to include an option so that the user can opt to go to the full website if they wish.

NATIVE APPLICATIONS VERSUS WEB APPLICATIONS/ MOBILE-OPTIMIZED WEB SITES

It is frequently argued whether or not a native application, a web-based application, or both should be developed. This depends on one's budget and the institution's technical expertise. Developing a mobile-optimized website requires little to no money and some web design expertise to develop; however, developing a native application requires programming experience for specific mobile operating systems (e.g., iOS, Android, Windows Mobile). The primary differences are as follows.

Native Applications	Web Applications/Mobile-optimized Websites
Internet access is not required.	Internet access is required; however, HTML5 has offline capabilities.
Can share content via social media if it is built into the application.	Web links can be shared easily via social application programming interfaces that allow one-click posting.
Have access to hardware sensors (e.g., camera, gyroscope, microphone, compass, accelerometer, GPS).	Access to hardware sensors via a web browser at this time is limited. Geolocation works.
Developers must build the application to work on target platforms (e.g., Android, iOS). Updates must be downloaded and reinstalled.	Developers can write once, publish once, and view it on most any device. Updates happen seamlessly.
Before distributing an application it must be approved by the target platform's app store.	It can be distributed everywhere via the open web.

Going further, a native application must be downloaded and then installed on the supported device; in contrast, a mobile-optimized website should work on most modern Internet-enabled devices and does not require a user to download, install, or upgrade the application in order to use it. To clarify, a mobile-optimized website is basically a website that fits within the constraints of smaller screens. A web application, on the other hand, includes sophisticated features like offline storage and is discussed in more detail later. A native application must be coded to work on a specific device's operating system (e.g., Apple iOS, Android, Microsoft Windows, Research in Motion, Symbian.)

It seems that if a library wants to reach as many mobile users as possible, the goal would be to design a web-based application or a simple mobile-optimized website instead of a native application that would only work on one type of mobile device. It is important, again, to look at the web analytics for all pages (i.e., full, mobile, etc.) to determine what devices are already accessing the library's website. If a significantly large percentage of mobile users were using, for example, an iPhone to gain access to a library's full website, then perhaps a native iOS application would be the way to go. This, however, is probably an unlikely scenario; realistically, a web application or a mobile-optimized website may get the most use on multiple devices.

SIMPLE MOBILE DESIGN USING HTML

One option is to use Hypertext Markup Language (HTML) and design a simple text-based website that will display well on all mobile devices. Alternatively, free tools such as jQTouch or jQuery Mobile can provide a framework to help one design more sophisticated mobile-optimized websites that resemble the way native applications work. Information on jQTouch and jQuery Mobile can be found at jqtouch.com and at jquerymobile.com. The Suggested Readings section includes links to other mobile frameworks and tools.

When designing a mobile-optimized website for the lowest common denominator (i.e., to include legacy phones such as a Nokia flip phone), it is good practice to include minimal content and to include few images so that users do not have to wait a long time in order to view the site. Although more and more people are acquiring cell phones with touch screens, some people may still use devices without a touch screen, so it is important to also include access keys so that numeric keypads can be used to select hyperlinks. For example, `<a class="call" href=" tel:17273417177" accesskey="6">Call the Library</a> | (727) 341-7177/>` allows the user to touch the 6 on the phone's keypad to select the telephone-number link and subsequently make a phone call directly to, in this case, a library's reference desk. The screenshots throughout this chapter were created using Cowemo's mobile emulator (http://www.mobilephoneemulator. com) and are discussed later in this chapter.

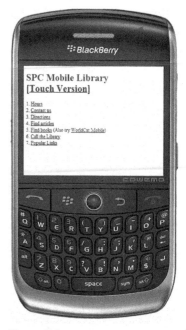

Figure 9.1
The user would tap 6 on the keypad to automatically dial the library.

MOBILE WEB DESIGN USING JQUERY MOBILE

One popular mobile web design option is the jQuery Mobile framework. Its included templates make it fairly easy to create a mobile-optimized website or application that responds to user interaction (i.e., touch) similar to the way a native application would work on a supported mobile device such as an iPhone, Microsoft Windows phone, or Android phone. jQuery Mobile has recently moved from beta to a 1.0 version and has excellent documentation. This chapter cannot get into much detail on this or any other mobile framework, but getting started with jQuery Mobile is not as intimidating as one may think. To start using jQuery Mobile, visit http://jquerymobile.com/ and download the latest stable version, which at the time of this writing is 1.0.1. Downloading the "jquery.mobile-1.1.0.zip" file from the jQuery Mobile website includes all the JavaScript, Cascading Style Sheets (CSS), HTML, and image files that are needed to get started designing a mobile-optimized website or application. In all, there are 280 files in the complete archive file; these include the CSS and JavaScript files, which initiate the look and feel (i.e., user interactions) of the mobile-optimized website or application.

If using jQuery Mobile, anyone who has basic HTML and some CSS experience can create a mobile-optimized website fairly easily and without a lot of coding from scratch. And with tools like Codiqa, a developer can drag and drop jQuery components into a blank canvas and in a short period of time, depending on the scale of the website, have a jQuery Mobile prototype almost ready to deploy. More information regarding Codiqa can be found at http://www.codiqa.com/; to see a screencast demo, visit http:// bit.ly/UsingCodiqa. If one desires more theme customization, ThemeRoller is an excellent web-based drag-and-drop tool where up to 26 theme swatches can be built

Figure 9.2
jQuery Mobile prototype built using Codiqa.

and later imported into Codiqa. More information on ThemeRoller can be found at jquerymobile.com/themeroller/.

ADDING MOBILE-OPTIMIZED CONTENT

After creating a mobile-optimized website or at least a prototype, it is a good idea to explore what library vendors already have mobile-optimized versions of their resources and services and be sure to include hyperlinks to those resources within the library's mobile-optimized site. A good practice to remember is to include only hyperlinks that link to content that is also mobile-optimized. It is a shame when everything fits well into the constraints of a mobile display and then a hyperlink directs a user to a full website. The usability of the mobile-optimized site becomes inconsistent and can confuse the mobile user. Including hyperlinks to a vendor's non-mobile-optimized resource or service is permissible as long as there is a brief mention that this link opens in a new tab or window and that the linked to item will not be mobile-optimized.

ADDING DYNAMIC CONTENT

Many options are available when it comes to including dynamic content within a mobile-optimized website. One simple example is Feed2JS, which is a free web tool that will take an RSS feed and automatically create JavaScript code to be inserted into the page or pages where dynamic content is desired. Once an RSS feed URL is input into the appropriate field, there are several ways to change the look and feel of the output feed (e.g., show/hide the title or description, show how much of the description to display, number of posts to display, show/hide dates). In addition, a developer can style the feed's output using a variety of style selectors. Feed2JS also automatically creates CSS code. Now, the developer copies the JavaScript and CSS code and pastes it into the page or pages where the dynamic feed content should display. In the example shown, every time a new blog post is added to novarelibrary.com/news it automatically displays in the mobile-optimized website. To see the feed, visit m.novarelibrary.com/ and select the "News" button in the Navigation bar. For more information on Feed2JS, visit http://feed2js.org/. There are many other examples for adding dynamic content within the jQuery Mobile archive file. It is recommended to explore the jQuery Mobile demo files and to see what can be done with regards to adding dynamic content as well as to linking to external data sources like maps, weather information, and more.

TO REDIRECT OR NOT REDIRECT, THAT IS THE QUESTION

Many methods are available for redirecting mobile users to specific websites. JavaScript, CSS, or PHP code is commonly used to detect the type of device or the size of the screen that is being used to access the website. The code then directs the user to, in some cases, a simple web page that provides options for choosing which version to use (e.g., full website, simple text-based version, "touch" mobile-optimized version), or the code automatically sends the user to the mobile-optimized version of the developer's choosing. Automatically directing mobile users to certain websites, however, can annoy some people, so it is a good idea to provide an option or provide a way to turn off the mobile-optimized version.

In the future, when mobile browsers become better at rendering full website functionality, then the question will be raised as to whether or not it will even be necessary to develop mobile-optimized websites and applications. Nonetheless, at the time of this writing, it is important to have a mobile-optimized presence and to seriously consider whether or not it is desirable to automatically direct users to specific web pages. The Suggested Readings section at the end of this chapter provides some resources regarding redirecting users to mobile-optimized sites.

TESTING AND VALIDATION

Before releasing a mobile-optimized website to the public, it is important to confirm that the new site is mobile-compliant to ensure that everything will load quickly and display well on a variety of mobile devices and browsers. Although mobile device emulators are excellent tools to use when designing mobile-optimized web pages, testing a new mobile-optimized website should be done on as many different mobile devices as possible. Web Developer 1.1.9, developed by Chris Pederick, is a free extension for the Firefox

Figure 9.3
Feed2JS.org RSS feed on mobile.

and Chrome browsers that provides an amazing set of tools for web developers and includes a small-screen rendering option. This option displays any web page viewed on a desktop computer as if rendered in an emulated mobile format. Going further, the World Wide Web Consortium (W3C) has a mobileOK Basic Tests document (http://www.w3.org/TR/mobileOK-basic10-tests/) that has extensive documentation to help design a mobile web page that is compliant (i.e., mobileOK) according to industry best practices and standards. To reiterate, a developer who is planning to include library research databases or a library catalog should be sure to include only mobile-optimized versions

so that the look and feel remain consistent with the overall design of the mobile-optimized version.

Entire books have been written to showcase different markup languages and web authoring tools that are available to web developers, but the bottom line is to make sure the web pages are tested on actual mobile devices and that they validate via the W3C's mobileOK checker or via ready.mobi's mobile checker system. Ready.mobi and the W3C Mobile Web Initiative sites have great resources worth exploring if a library is planning to design a mobile website. The W3C's mobileOK checker can be found at validator.w3.org/mobile/, and mobiReady's dotMobi compliance checker can be found at ready.mobi/.

PROMOTING MOBILE-OPTIMIZED WEBSITES

Even if there is code to redirect mobile users to a mobile-optimized website, it is a good idea to promote the fact that the library has a mobile-optimized website just in

Don't have a QR code reader?

case a user has JavaScript disabled or some other issue prohibiting the redirect code to function properly. The easiest method is for the full library website to provide a clearly visible link to the mobile site. Also, posting something regarding the newly designed mobile-optimized site via a blog or on a variety of other social media outlets is another good idea. Finally, creating informative print flyers with quick-response (QR) codes is useful because users will not have to type a URL on a small keyboard; instead, they can scan the QR code and be automatically directed to the mobile site. Under the QR code, it is a good idea to also include a shortened URL so that users who do not have a QR code reader installed on their phones can type a shorter URL and still gain access to the site. For more information on QR codes, visit http://en.wikipedia.org/wiki/QR_code or simply scan the QR code reproduced here.

FUTURE OF MOBILE WEB DEVELOPMENT

Although HTML version 5 (also written HTML5) will take a couple more years before it becomes an official W3C specification, it is still becoming widely used and is positively changing how we use the traditional web as well as the mobile web. With HTML5 it is now possible to do things like play multimedia files within a compatible web browser without the need to install a third-party plugin like Adobe's Flash. Also with HTML5, it is possible to utilize offline storage (e.g., localStorage, IndexedDB, and Web SQL), meaning it is now possible to store data within a user's web browser so that the information can be accessed even when the device is not connected to the Internet. Cookies were used before HTML5's offline storage came into play, but they had limited storage capabilities and had to be sent from a server to be stored on the user's computer. Cookies were useful for many years, but now most everything can be handled locally within the user's mobile web browser. For example, the Florida Library Association had a mobile-optimized program for its 2012 conference that was built using the jQuery Mobile framework. It utilized Web SQL so that users could add favorite speaking sessions and store them within their web browser until they selected the "MyFavs" button in the footer to display all their favorite conference sessions that they would like to attend.

This writer has plans to include a similar feature for an updated version of his library's mobile-optimized website that will allow library users to add their favorite library resources and services to their own "MyFavs" section. Finally, there has been a lot of speculation that HTML5 coupled with CSS version 3 (CSS3) will eliminate the need to create native applications; instead, everything will be written to work on the web and developers will not need to develop for multiple operating systems. This would change everything on the mobile web if applications became device agnostic and essentially worked on any device with an Internet connection.

"Responsive architecture" is an interesting discipline where walls and art installations can "bend, flex, and expand as crowds approach them" (Marcotte 2010). Responsive web design is similar in that it makes it possible to design a single website that responds to

Figure 9.4
Mobile web app using Web SQL.

a variety of screen dimensions. Although responsive web design is starting to gain traction, it can be fairly complex to write pages using its design principles; however, tools will more than likely be developed to make designing websites easier. Consequently, designing multiple websites for multiple screen displays will become a thing of the past when developers begin to work more with responsive web design principles, because only one website needs to be created as that one website will respond and adapt to whichever screen is displaying it.

A good example of a library website that uses responsive web design is Nova Southeastern University's Alvin Sherman Library. The site can be viewed at www.nova.edu/library/main/ and looks great on any device. The responsive part comes into play because a user can view the site on a full desktop browser like Chrome, Firefox, Internet Explorer, or Safari, but if one makes the browser window smaller and smaller, the site responds to those changes and looks fine no matter what size the display becomes.

Whatever the future brings, it seems likely that the world will continue to move toward mobile computing. As noted earlier, it has been estimated that by the end of 2011 there would be 5 billion mobile subscriptions in a world with 6.8 billion people. Of course, the world's population gets larger each year, but as the technology gets more sophisticated and less expensive, almost everyone on earth, even those who live in the most remote villages, will have access to a mobile device. Because of this, libraries of all kinds should have a mobile presence so that people will continue to use authoritative resources and services available from their libraries. Providing an easy way for users to gain mobile access to their library's resources and services will go a long way to ensure the continued relevance of libraries.

Figure 9.5
Mobile web app using Web SQL.

REFERENCES

Ballard, Barbara. 2007. *Designing the Mobile User Experience*. Chichester, England: Wiley.

International Telecommunication Union. 2010. "ITU Estimates Two Billion People Online by End 2010." [Press release]. October 19. Accessed November 2, 2010. http://www.itu.int/net/pressoffice/press_releases/2010/39.aspx.

Marcotte, Ethan. 2010. "Responsive Web Design." *A List Apart Magazine* (May 25). Accessed April 11, 2012 from http://www.alistapart.com/articles/responsive-web-design/.

Whitney, Lance. 2010. "Cell Phone Subscriptions to Hit 5 Billion Globally." *CNET*. February 16. Accessed February 13, 2012. http://reviews.cnet.com/8301-13970_7-10454065-78.html.

FURTHER READING AND RESOURCES

Best Practices

World Wide Web Consortium (W3C). *Mobile Web Best Practices: Basic Guidelines*. http://www.w3.org/TR/mobile-bp/.

World Wide Web Consortium (W3C). *Mobile Web Application Best Practices Cards*. http://www.w3.org/2010/09/MWABP/.

World Wide Web Consortium (W3C). *MobileOK Basic Tests Document* http://www.w3.org/TR/mobileOK-basic10-tests/.

Mobile Frameworks

DHTMLX Touch: http://www.dhtmlx.com/touch/
iUi: http://code.google.com/p/iui/wiki/Introduction
jQuery Mobile: http://jquerymobile.com/
jQTouch: http://jqtouch.com/
Sencha: http://www.sencha.com/
WebApp.net: http://webapp-net.com/
Wink Toolkit: http://www.winktoolkit.org/
Zepto.js: http://zeptojs.com/

Mobile Redirect

Design Your Way.net. "Detecting and Redirecting Mobile Users." http://www.designyourway
.net/blog/resources/detecting-and-redirecting-mobile-users/.

10

Mobile Catalogs

Chad Haefele

Key Points

- Readers will learn how a mobile catalog is technically built.
- We will explore how a mobile catalog should be designed.
- We will discuss a key decision: building an app for one or more specific mobile operating systems and/or designing a webapp—a website designed and formatted for use on all web-capable mobile devices.
- Due to hardware-oriented and practical reasons, currently webapps provide a better way to build mobile catalogs from scratch.
- Consider use cases for the mobile catalog. What will users want to accomplish?
- Best practices for mobile catalog interface design are presented.
- Various third-party mobile catalog options are summarized.
- Several locally built mobile catalogs are presented.
- A development case study from the University of North Carolina—Chapel Hill is presented.

INTRODUCTION

Why build a mobile catalog? A mobile-optimized library catalog offers a unique opportunity for your library's mobile site to engage users. Much of the content libraries can offer in a mobile format is relatively static—hours and locations don't change. A catalog instead offers an opportunity to provide an answer to a much broader swath of questions related to information retrieval, and it can meet users at their point of need. Imagine a user wandering the stacks, having forgotten to write down a call number.

Pulling the information up on a mobile device is much more convenient than tracking down a static desktop terminal.

Much has been written about designing for the mobile web, including elsewhere in this book. Large buttons are important in a finger-based, mouseless world. Single columns are better than double- or triple-column layouts, and disabling the zoom feature might be a good idea. All of this remains true in building a mobile catalog, but when dealing with a catalog it is just as important to optimize the data. What data are worth presenting to users in a mobile context, and what data would be superfluous and useless?

In this chapter we'll look at mobile library catalogs from two different perspectives. First, how is a mobile catalog technically built? Second, how should that catalog be designed? A number of best practices are addressed, and examples of mobile catalogs in action are covered. The chapter concludes with a practical overview of the development process of a mobile catalog at the University of North Carolina (UNC) at Chapel Hill.

HOW TO BUILD A MOBILE CATALOG

Online library catalogs are not a new concept, and libraries are by now rather familiar with the vendors, designs, and feature options available to us. Building a mobile catalog does not require that all of our accumulated knowledge and experience be thrown out, but instead builds on it in a slightly different direction. New possibilities inherent in mobile hardware simply add a few new considerations to the process.

Early mobile catalogs, even just three or four years ago, were highly experimental text-based affairs. Some simply used automated services that presented the existing desktop catalog with all images and formatting removed. Unfortunately, this also removed all possibility of custom design. The state of web browsing on mobile devices has since improved, thanks largely to the advent of the iPhone and other recent smartphones. Current mobile browsers and apps are much more functional and can handle more than text. This gives us more freedom in how a mobile catalog is designed and works, but that freedom also means more responsibility and potential for substandard interface decisions.

One of the first decisions a library must make when building a mobile catalog is whether to provide it in the form of an app or a webapp. An app represents an installable program written for smartphones and is usually distributed through and downloaded from a third-party service. Apple's App Store and the Android Market are two of the largest examples of app distribution platforms. A webapp is in some ways a simpler concept—it is a website designed and formatted for use on mobile devices.

Should a mobile library catalog be built as an application or a website? If you are purchasing a mobile catalog from a third party vendor, this question is somewhat irrelevant. In that case, push the vendor to provide both options. If you are building the mobile interface within the library, other concerns need to be taken into account. While apps have some inherent advantages, I believe a webapp provides a more realistic and useful option for many libraries and their available resources.

Apps provide two major advantages over webapps. They have easy access to a device's hardware and have better offline capabilities. Webapps can provide limited access to a mobile device's GPS data or camera (which I'll cover later in this chapter), but a mobile project requiring extensive use of device hardware would be better executed as an app. An app's easy offline storage means that a mobile project likely to be used in a low-signal area might also be appropriate for app development. A library catalog does not require use of a mobile device's special hardware, and the notion of an offline library catalog does not make a lot of inherent sense. A library catalog is most useful when accessed in an updated, realtime state. Cached offline data would go stale quickly, especially in regard to availability of individual items. Because it meets neither of these criteria, a library catalog is a strong candidate for construction as a webapp.

Putting these theoretical considerations aside, apps raise an additional complexity-based barrier if developed locally by a library. iPhone apps are written in the Objective C programming language, which requires the app coder to have a background in object-oriented programming. Not many librarians I've met have this kind of experience. Webapps, on the other hand, are built with the simpler technologies of HTML, CSS, Javascript, and scripting languages like PHP. These are the same tools libraries have used to build websites all along.

An iPhone app won't run on an Android or Blackberry phone, but a well-designed webapp will have cross-platform use. Due to this fact, a webapp will be available to a higher percentage of users than any one app would be. With a webapp, less duplication of effort is necessary to reach all platforms.

For both hardware-oriented and practical reasons, webapps provide a better way to build mobile library catalogs from scratch at this point. I will admit that webapps don't have the wow-factor of distributing something through an app store. The District of C Public Library got extensive publicity out of the launch of their catalog app for the iPhone.[1] They were fortunate enough to have developers available to build the app. But when building the catalog in-house, practicality will often win out over a public-relations coup. A webapp can be deployed faster and updated more often than an app, meets user needs more quickly, and requires less specialized technical knowledge. An app can come later, resources permitting, for promotional value and other bonuses.

This isn't to say that a library should ignore app development with respect to library catalogs. Again, the promotional value alone of having an app in an app store for users to find is significant. But if resources are only available for one of either a webapp or an app, a webapp should come first.

After deciding which of those approaches to take, it is crucial to consider use cases for your mobile catalog. What do you want users to be able to accomplish? This will greatly influence your choice of interfaces and product features. In my opinion, simple use cases are best suited for the mobile environment. I've never met anybody who enjoyed doing in-depth research on a tiny screen with no physical keyboard. Mobile users often want quick access to small bits of information. Mobile-suited use cases can be simple, like looking up a forgotten call number of a known item while lost in the stacks. This is a very traditional library task that maps well onto the way a mobile device is used. It frees users from the need to track down a stationary terminal and saves them time.

The use case could also be more complicated, as in searching via an ISBN barcode scan. This would take advantage of the mobile device's camera, a feature rarely present on a library's desktop machines. It also leverages the device's capability of leaving the building. Imagine if a user could scan an ISBN barcode at a book store, easily figuring out if the library owns a copy before making a purchase. To me, that's a compelling use case. QR barcodes could also be added to library books, linking to extended online content such as reviews or ratings formatted for a mobile screen. Either type of barcode provides an easy way of linking a physical object to relevant online information.

Regardless, these are just two examples. Replicating a desktop-centered catalog in mobile form could easily be overwhelming, so it is crucial to decide what your users will do with a mobile catalog. After identifying those use cases, a design can be built on top of them. Most use cases will lead to a simple search screen with fewer options than in the desktop catalog. If aiming for a known-item use case, for example, elaborate subject-heading searching likely won't be necessary. On the other hand, new options may appear too. Searching by barcode scan requires interface elements not seen in other catalog versions. Options and buttons friendly to the desired use case should be given prominence, while irrelevant ones can be hidden or removed entirely.

Item display pages need to be treated similarly. In a known item search, a user likely wants to know whether the item is available and where it is. If that's your use case, that information needs to be displayed prominently. Mentally sorting through extraneous data is much more difficult on a small screen than on a desktop monitor. It may be better to cut too much information out than to not cut enough. Mobile catalogs' item pages often include a link back to the nonmobile version of the page, allowing users to escape back to all the possible information about an item if need be. A well-thought-out mobile catalog with data that matches realistic use cases minimizes the need for those links, but as a last-resort option there's no reason not to include them.

As discussed earlier in the chapter, keeping a specific use case in mind for the catalog can help focus the design and keep it relevant to the tasks users wish to accomplish. Aiming for a user base who conducts known-item searches requires a focus on elements like title, availability, and cover images. A use case of conducting in-depth scholarly research in the catalog would require a different—and likely much more difficult—design tactic entirely. But these opposed cases ultimately come back to a small list of common best practices:

- Search-form elements and options in the catalog should be relatively large and easily selectable by the relatively imprecise touch of a finger.
- If the mobile catalog does not contain the full set of item information, include a link to the nonmobile version as a fallback option. Frustrated users who fall outside of an expected use case can still find their way to their desired information via this link, even if the ultimate formatting isn't ideal on a mobile screen.
- A mobile catalog may contain links to pages not formatted for a mobile device. They may be a nonmobile catalog page, request forms, or other pages. If so, make sure to indicate with an icon or text that the link leads to a nonmobile page. This sets user expectations and avoids unpleasant surprises. Oregon State's mobile catalog has a particularly good example of this in action, using an icon to indicate nonmobile links.[2]
- Some mobile web-design frameworks produce item pages that cannot be bookmarked. Test to make sure users can bookmark an item to call up later while in the stacks.

After use cases and basic design ideas are established, a mobile catalog is ready to be built. The catalog can be hand-coded from scratch, but that route isn't always possible given limited resources. There are two major approaches to getting around this problem. A number of third-party vendors have complete mobile catalog packages, and there are also frameworks that ease the burden of internal custom coding. Depending on your library environment and available resources, the best choice of a product or homegrown solution will of course vary. Neither of these options should exist in a vacuum but should instead inform each other. Design elements or ideas from a commercial solution might influence an in-house project, and custom-built examples may provide insights about which features are desirable from a vendor solution.

THIRD-PARTY SOLUTIONS

The simplest way to get a mobile library catalog up and running might be to contract the service out to a third party. Some traditional library ILS vendors now offer mobile catalog solutions, but new vendors have begun to build offerings as well. Screenshots displayed with these examples are how they display on an iPhone, but they all function well on Android devices and some Blackberries as well.

Innovative's Airpac service offers a mobile catalog to users of their Millennium traditional online public-access catalog (OPAC). It provides a relatively simple interface, perhaps designed to ensure functionality across the widest possible array of mobile devices. A sample implementation can be seen at the Virginia Tech University Libraries' mobile site. There is only one search option, allowing users to filter by location. Because Innovative themselves built this solution, it also provides easy access to My Account features. Users can view their checked-out books, renew titles, and do other functions along those lines. These features can be particularly difficult to replicate in a solution built by a library for the local community of users.

SirsiDynix's mobile catalog offering for libraries using their OPAC platforms is called Bookmyne. While Bookmyne is an app, not a webapp, it is still worth considering as a third-party option. They currently provide the app for iPhones only, though an Android option is in the works. As an app, Bookmyne has easy access to the mobile device's hardware elements. It makes interesting use of the camera by allowing users to search by barcode scan. We'll come back to this idea later in the chapter.

While Serials Solutions's Summon product in some ways covers broader material than a traditional library catalog does, the product's mobile interface can absolutely be used in the same way a mobile catalog would. Summon's mobile search options are extensive, allowing users to limit by publication, format, scholarly items, and much more. The item-display pages include cover images and a level of detailed information not reached by many other mobile offerings. This detail is in some ways commendable but is also perhaps too much for a mobile user to take in. Summon mobile is provided at no extra cost to libraries that have purchased Summon.

Library Anywhere is currently used by more than 200 libraries and works with a wide variety of OPACs. Their mobile catalog provides a web interface, iPhone app, and Android app. Search options are relatively basic here too, but Library Anywhere's integration with My Account functionality is unusual for a service not built by an OPAC vendor.

WorldCat Mobile is a mobile catalog option for any library with materials listed in WorldCat. It can be scoped to search one library's titles or broadened to the entire interlibrary holdings.

Boopsie for Libraries is like Library Anywhere in that it's a product provided by a vendor who isn't an OPAC provider. Boopsie sits on top of your OPAC, and it works with a variety of them. Boopsie provides a mobile catalog as a webapp but also as an installable app for iPhones, Android phones, and Blackberries.

BiblioCommons's BiblioMobile catalog product can be seen in action in the Daniel Boone Regional Library's mobile app. BiblioMobile provides both an installable app and a catalog for use in mobile browsers, which should reach a broader audience than either approach alone. This is all part of their BiblioCore "Complete OPAC Replacement" offering. BiblioMobile provides each library with its own independent listing in each platform's app store, which is a somewhat unique offering. Other services with

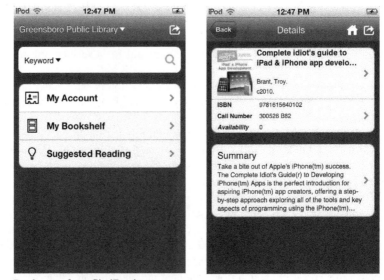

Airpac from Innovative Interfaces.

installable apps, like Library Anywhere, require the user to open a generic app and then select their library from a list. BiblioMobile lets users avoid that step.

There are likely other third-party mobile catalog options available for libraries, and probably others coming soon that don't quite exist yet as I write this. These are only meant to be a representative sample of the major options available today.

Beyond these options, some libraries have chosen to develop a mobile catalog in-house. This approach allows greater flexibility but also requires greater effort

Bookmyne from SirsiDynix.

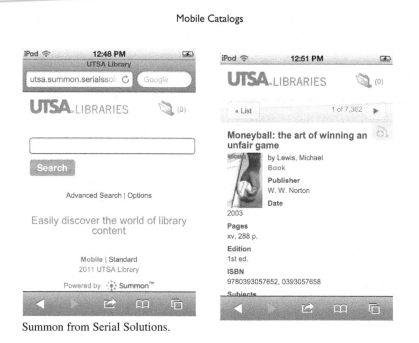

Summon from Serial Solutions.

and more library resources for long-term maintenance. The following are some examples.

MobileCat walks the line between being a third-party solution and being developed in-house by a library. It's an open-source project designed to provide a mobile interface to Innovative Interfaces, Inc. (III) catalogs. While technically not developed by your library, it would still require some coding experience and understanding to get it up and running. An example can be seen at the Bryn Mawr library's website, where their MobileCat implementation looks very similar to the Airpac example above.

The University of Rochester Library's catalog interface is built on the open-source jQuery Mobile code suite. It is particularly notable for its advanced search screen, which not all mobile catalogs offer. This one provides a long list of searchable facets along with location, item type, and format limiters. Users can also customize the number of results shown per page.

The University of Illinois Library's catalog was custom built from the ground up without using an external framework for interface elements. They have done a particularly nice job of integrating the request form for each item into the mobile-formatted pages. Many mobile library catalogs instead resort to linking to nonmobile versions of interactive form content, which produces a more frustrating user experience.

The University of North Carolina Libraries' mobile catalog interface was built in-house using the iUI framework for mobile interfaces combined with PHP scripting. Search options are limited, though it does provide a method of searching via barcode scan. Information for each individual item is likewise limited, pointing out only location and availability.

DEVELOPMENT CASE STUDY

As a librarian at the University of North Carolina, I was the primary developer on the UNC Libraries' mobile site and catalog. Because I was so involved in the development process, I want to take a deeper look at this catalog as a case study. I do not mean to

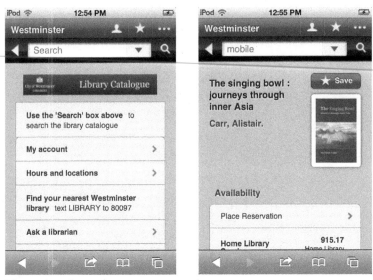

Library Anywhere.

present it as an ultimate paragon of what a mobile catalog can be—in fact, I am somewhat critical of my work and see many areas where it can be improved given development time. I simply want to discuss the development process as I went through it.

Building a Mobile Catalog at UNC Chapel Hill

The primary objective in building this mobile catalog was to provide an easy way for
users to access availability information on the go. The development team did not
believe that users wanted to do in-depth searches on a mobile device with a small
screen. Anecdotal evidence from interacting with users at the reference desk covered
occasional instances of users showing the librarian a catalog item on their phone and
asking questions like "Where is this book?" The library's nonmobile catalog did not
display properly on mobile browsers at the time, creating a frustrating user experience.
The team wanted to address this issue. The resulting mobile catalog can be viewed on a
mobile device at www.lib.unc.edu/m.

In order to build a custom mobile catalog, it is crucial to have access to catalog data
in some kind of machine-readable format. If a programmer can access data at this level,
the rest of the project comes down largely to simple interface design. There are three
common ways to get access to the catalog data in this fashion.

1. Direct application programming interface (API) access. Your OPAC or ILS may provide a
   formal programming API to the data contained in the catalog. This is ideal simply because
   the access methods are likely well documented and standardized. Vendor support may also
   be available if developers run into problems.
2. Screen scraping. It is possible to build software that loads a regular, nonmobile catalog page
   and "scrapes" through that data for relevant bits like Title, Author, and other bibliographic

WorldCat Mobile from OCLC.
© 2012 OCLC Online Computer
Library Center, Inc. Used with permission. "WorldCat", "Find in a
Library" and the WorldCat logo are
registered trademarks/service marks
of OCLC.

data. Further scripting can then reformat the data into something better suiting a mobile
screen. While this method can in theory be used to gain access to any library catalog's data,
it is likely to also be the most complicated and to be prone to breaking if the nonmobile catalog interface ever changes.

Boopsie.

BiblioMobile.

3. Feed access from a third-party product. If your library runs a discovery layer like Endeca to provide an interface to an underlying OPAC or ILS, that intermediate software may provide some kind of machine-readable data feed. This is how the UNC Libraries' mobile catalog works.

The UNC Libraries' discovery layer, viewable as the UNC Libraries nonmobile catalog at www.lib.unc.edu, is provided by software called Endeca. Endeca interfaces with the underlying OPAC and formats the data nicely for users to see. Beyond this,

Mobilecat.

Endeca also provides XML feeds of catalog results. By using a scripting language like PHP, a programmer can easily parse catalog data from that XML feed and reformat it for a mobile screen.

XML is a common data standard, so parsing it via PHP was not a difficult task. With data and a formatting tool in hand, the next task was to develop an interface.

Gaining data-level access to the catalog is simply an item to check off a list. It is either available or it isn't. For contrast, an interface for that data provides a much wider range for success or failure. As with any web-development project, interface designers have two broad tactics to choose from in approaching this issue. They can either write a custom design from scratch or rely on an existing framework. Frameworks are code templates built to handle basic user interface (UI) concerns such as buttons, backgrounds, and navigation links. My recommendation is to use a framework. Why reinvent the wheel if someone else has already done the work? Using a framework can also provide some level of standardization in a user experience, as users may encounter sites built with the same framework elsewhere. Standardized UI elements can provide a sense of familiarity to users. Some frameworks are even designed to copy the look and feel of standard iPhone application interfaces.

Two of the better-known mobile web frameworks available today are jQuery Mobile and iUI. Both are open source and freely available. For examples of each, look at some of the sample catalogs mentioned in this chapter. For example, the University of Rochester's catalog was built on jQuery mobile, and the UNC Libraries' catalog was built with iUI. At the time developers built the UNC mobile catalog, jQuery Mobile did not exist. The choice was made much simpler just because iUI was one of very few available options.

iUI is designed to evoke the look and feel of standard iPhone design elements. It was developed out of a desire to let web developers build app-like experiences without needing to learn Objective C and go through Apple's app store. Buttons, text boxes, and top-bar navigation are almost exact copies of their app-based iPhone counterparts.

University of Rochester Library.

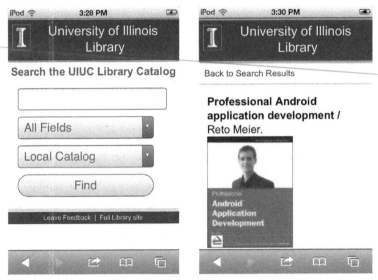

University of Illinois Library Mobile
Catalog.

UNC's developers downloaded the free iUI code, which consists of a set of JavaScript, CSS, and image files. Using a framework in this fashion makes it possible to get a skeleton site up and running in just a few minutes. The process is extensively documented on iUI's website, which includes help forums if developers run into trouble.

After choosing these two tools—XML feeds from Endeca and iUI's code framework —UNC's team was able to format the XML content in a customized fashion inside the interface provided by iUI. A skeleton iUI site is structured in a way that makes it very easy to insert content into the interface.

With these technical pieces in place, the next step was to design the interface. UNC's developers had a primary use case in mind, arising from the previously mentioned incidents of users approaching the reference desk with a catalog item displayed on their phone. Based on this, the catalog was designed to suit the primary task of assisting users who are wandering through the stacks and need a call number. Users are assumed to usually have a known author or title in mind for this type of query. As a result, complicated search options were eliminated in favor of a streamlined experience. Users can search by Keyword, Title, Journal Title, Author, or Subject. Additional facets could have been implemented but would have taken more development time. They may be added in the future after more dedicated user testing and feedback can be gathered.

An item page is displayed in a similarly stripped-down fashion. Availability is clearly indicated by both an icon and text. Location, Author, Title, and any notes about the specific copy or edition are displayed alongside a cover image, if available. Any other information remains hidden from the user as it is largely irrelevant to answering a known-item search. A link back to the full nonmobile page for that item is also displayed as a means of accessing that broader information if truly necessary. Users also have options to email or text the item's location information to themselves for later use.

Users can also search by barcode scan, a feature that takes advantage of the mobile context. The imagined use case for this feature is use by someone not inside the library at all. The user might be at a book store and want to check if the library owns a book before making a purchase. Scanning the ISBN barcode searches the library catalog for a match and saves the user the time and potential frustration of typing in a lengthy title on his or her device.

Scanning a barcode works on iPhones and Android devices but admittedly is not entirely smooth or intuitive. The scan is accomplished through the mobile device's camera, but webapps don't have any way to access the camera's information directly. To work around this fact, users must install a separate barcode-scanning app on their device: Barcode Scanner on Android, and pic2shop on iOS devices. A properly format-ted link, when selected on a catalog search screen, will trigger the appropriate third-party app. The app scans the barcode, then returns the scanned information to the web browser by loading a new URL. Here's an example of how the UNC Libraries' barcode-scanning link is constructed for Android devices:

```
http://zxing.appspot.com/scan?ret=http://www.lib.unc
.edu/m/isbnsearch.php%3FNtt
={CODE}
```

The portion in italics is what triggers the Barcode Scanner app. The bold portion tells the app what to do with the scanned barcode afterward. In this case it reopens the browser and loads the mobile catalog search page. The text {CODE} will automati-cally be replaced with the scanned ISBN number. URLs for the pic2shop app on iPhones are structured very similarly.[3] The Android Barcode Scanner link process is also more formally documented online.[4]

University of North Carolina Libraries.

As admitted above, this is not a smooth and intuitive process. It is, however, functional in a way that makes sense only in a mobile context. Users may not be inclined to scan barcodes at their desktop, but it fits a use case for times away from the desk and also makes use of mobile-specific hardware. For now, barcode scanning can most easily be accomplished inside an app instead of a webapp. But I am confident that in time mobile devices will gain easier ways to accomplish this kind of task via a webpage.

Continuing Development

As with any web project, it would be foolish to describe a mobile library catalog as "finished." The development process outlined in this chapter essentially covers the low-hanging fruit of mobile catalog development. A catalog formatted for a mobile screen that addresses obvious use cases is nice, but where should the catalog go from there?

While webapps and apps will likely add new functionality for catalogs to take advantage of in the future, the most important aspect of continuing development is simply asking your users what they want out of a mobile catalog. Most user populations will be well-served by the same set of basic catalog functions. But more advanced features can be tailored for a specific population. A dedicated mobile-user feedback campaign is necessary to shape future efforts.

CONCLUSION

Even the best-designed mobile catalog use will never replace a full desktop catalog. In-depth research makes much more sense, and is simply easier to do, on a larger screen where detailed options can be clearly laid out. But a catalog optimized for mobile devices provides a unique opportunity to literally go where the users are. They might be in a bookstore, hopelessly lost in the stacks, or simply looking to avoid jotting down call numbers. Whatever that use case may be or which future ones may arise, libraries can meet it with a little foresight and relatively low expenditure of time or funds. The mobile context for use of library resources is changing alongside the related technology, and libraries should be there to continue to serve users.

NOTES

1. https://itunes.apple.com/app/dcpl/id301077850?mt=8
2. http://m.library.oregonstate.edu/about.html
3. More information is at http://www.pic2shop.com/developers.html
4. http://code.google.com/p/zxing/wiki/ScanningFromWebPages

Reading Transformed by the Mobility of E-books

Andrew Revelle and Sue Polanka

Key Points

- Reading is being transformed by the combination of e-books and the mobile device revolution.
- The very concept of a book is being transformed.
- What separates e-books from other long-form texts is their source, not their format.
- Several factors are motivating most libraries to expand their e-book offerings.
- The bring-your-own-device (BYOD) aspect of the mobile revolution has advantages both for library users and for libraries, as well as some disadvantages.
- The advantages and disadvantages of smartphones, tablets, and dedicated e-readers are enumerated.
- Most portable devices are designed down to the operating-system (OS) level to be single-user devices, which makes institutional use difficult.

INTRODUCTION

Reading, like many other activities, has been transformed by the introduction of mobile devices capable of accessing the Internet. More and more people are using mobile devices like smartphones and tablets to read news, blogs, and other online sources. Library patrons are using their phones and tablets to search for library materials and conduct research. This trend has also expanded into the reading of books; more and more people are reading electronic books (e-books) on phones, tablets, and dedicated e-readers like the Kindle. Publishers, in their race to meet consumer demand for electronic content, have employed a number of techniques to preserve some of their traditional business models while exploring new revenue streams. The varying policies of publishers, coupled with the ever-expanding array of mobile devices owned by the American population, provide both opportunities and challenges for libraries. The purpose of this chapter is to explore these trends and provide some suggestions on how libraries of all types can best get their increasingly broad ranges of electronic book content onto their patrons' preferred devices.

LANDSCAPE OF E-BOOKS AND MOBILE READING

The effect of e-books in the publishing industry has been similar to that caused by the introduction of the MP3 to the music industry. In fact, this change has been so drastic that one could say that e-books have "caused the greatest transformation to the long-established publishing industry since Gutenberg and his printing press" (Carreiro 2010). In fact, e-books are changing the very concept of a "book" from a physical printed object to one that encompasses all types of texts, whether printed or electronic (Carlucci-Thomas 2012). What separates e-books from other types of lengthy electronic texts for librarians is their source, not their format; usually, e-books are produced by traditional publishing houses and are purchased from a vendor such as ebrary, Netlibrary, or directly from the publisher (Slater 2010). E-books typically have had a printed analog, but many academic publishers are exploring a move to a model where the e-book is the primary format.

E-books are a growing presence in American libraries; 95 percent of academic libraries and 82 percent of public libraries offer e-books to their patrons (Miller 2011). The reasons for the expansion of this format have been many. First of all, library users are demanding more e-books from their libraries; 94 percent of public libraries and 58 percent of academic libraries reported an increase in e-books requests between 2010 and 2011 (Miller 2011). Second, much as they have done with electronic journal content, many academic libraries have acquired large e-book collections via "big deals," where they get every title released by a publisher in a subject-area collection. For example, academic publisher Springer has provided an e-book option for every title they have released since 2005. For those who have a strong aversion to reading electronic media, Springer provides their MyCopy service, giving users who have access to a Springer e-book title through their library the option to purchase a printed copy on demand ("Springer Launches MyCopy Service for Ebook Users" 2009).

Many libraries are also experimenting with patron-driven acquisition models, where libraries load all holdings of a vendor in certain subject areas into their catalog. Purchases of individual titles are then triggered based on a set of criteria established beforehand (Breitbach and Lambert 2011). These criteria usually relate to the number of views and the length of each view. Additionally, increases in the number of titles being published are causing many libraries to face space constraints. E-books ease this problem by allowing libraries to add materials without taking up additional shelf space. Finally, an increasing number of library patrons are acquiring mobile devices that allow for e-reading, and they are demanding content for these devices.

One factor that has limited the growth of e-books has been problems related to extended periods of reading on a backlit computer screen. As the majority of e-book reading still takes place on desktop or laptop screens, this aspect of e-book reading has soured many library patrons on the format (Abdullah and Gibb 2008; Shrimplin, Revelle, Hurst, and Messner 2011). The issues cited by those who object to long periods of screen reading include eye fatigue, a lack of retention when reading on the screen, and the lack of portability of desktop and laptop computers when compared to print books. They also report the inability to take notes or highlight the text when screen reading as a drawback of reading on a computer screen (Shrimplin et al. 2011). Fortunately, some of these concerns may be addressed by making e-books available on the various mobile devices.

Over the past five years, mobile devices have become a ubiquitous part of American society. According to the Pew Internet and American Life Project, as of May 2011, 83 percent of American adults owned a mobile phone (Pew Research Center 2011). And these phones are increasingly being used for other tasks beyond making phone calls. Fifty percent of cell-phone owners report having apps on their phones. Thirty-nine percent of the cell phones in the United States operate on a smartphone platform such as Apple's iOS, Google's Android, or the Blackberry operating system (Smith 2011). Eighty-seven percent of smartphone owners use their devices to go online or read email.

Mobile device ownership is not limited to cell phones. Dedicated e-book readers, such as the Amazon Kindle, Barnes & Noble Nook, and Sony's e-book reader, are gaining a following among the American reading public. Ownership of these devices doubled from 6 percent to 12 percent between November 2010 and May 2011. Ownership of tablet computers, such as the Apple iPad, Motorola Xoom, and Samsung Galaxy Tab, is also growing. Between November 2010 and May 2011, the ownership of these devices doubled from 4 percent to 8 percent. Additionally, Pew Internet Research conducted studies of gadget ownership over the 2011 holiday season and found ownership jumped from 10 percent to 19 percent (Pew Research Center 2012). And Amazon touts its Kindle Fire tablet as "the most successful product [they've] ever launched" (Amazon.com, Inc. 2011).

PERSONAL DEVICES VERSUS DEVICE LENDING

As library patrons purchase an increasing array of mobile devices, they are requesting e-books and other electronic materials for them. The main advantages for libraries of allowing patrons to consume library material on their personal devices relate to convenience and cost, both for the owner of the device and for the library. First of all, because the patrons own the devices, the library does not have to purchase them. Relatedly, the library does not need to devote IT staff hours to manage and repair mobile devices. This is a rather significant point because these types of devices tend to require a high degree of maintenance due to their mobile nature.

As with most decisions made by libraries related to technology, there are some challenges with allowing patrons to access e-books on personal devices. With print books, librarians could be sure that the materials that they purchase for their collections would be readable long into the future. However, as devices and formats change, e-books may be rendered unreadable. Additionally, the library has to support a multitude of operating systems, formats, screen sizes, and apps. If the library purchases devices on which to consume e-books and other electronic resources, librarians can choose to purchase materials for them and as such can ensure that they are providing an optimal experience for their patrons. They can also make decisions related to e-book formats and vendors based on the devices on which they intend them to be consumed. If patrons use their own devices, libraries cannot control the compatibility and usability of their content.

In addition to supporting the devices their patrons own, many libraries have begun making electronic devices such as tablets and dedicated e-readers that can be used for e-reading available for checkout. In this way, librarians can be sure that their ever-increasing collections of electronic materials are accessible to the majority of their patrons. It is important that libraries do not make the ownership of an expensive piece of consumer electronics a prerequisite to accessing a significant portion of their collections. This point is clearly illustrated in the arguments against the Rockford (IL) Public Library. Members of a community initiative, Save Our Library, along with the Rockford National Association for the Advancement of Colored People (NAACP) are protesting the decision of the library to allocate 25.5 percent of its budget to e-books, stating difficult financial times and a high poverty rate in the area could leave behind patrons unable to afford the technology to read e-books (Lee 2012). Also, making mobile technology for reading available for checkout makes e-books more usable for patrons who dislike reading on a computer screen but do not own the technology to make the reading of electronic materials more palatable.

TYPES OF DEVICES FOR READING

There are a number of different types of mobile or portable devices that can be used for the consumption of electronic books. These devices include smartphones, tablets, and dedicated e-readers with e-ink screens. Each of these devices has different strengths and weaknesses.

Smartphones

The main advantage of smartphones is their abundant nature; many library patrons already have one. They are also the most portable of the widely available mobile devices that can be used to read e-books. Reading e-books on mobile phones requires either a browser or an e-reading application compatible with the phone. Many library patrons have one in their pockets at most times. However, it is that very portability that represents their biggest downside in this context; reading on a small screen for extended periods of time is unacceptable for most patrons. Also, they by nature have backlit liquid-crystal display (LCD) screens that have been shown to cause eye fatigue. But due to their omnipresence, libraries have to take mobile-phone reading into account when making collection-development decisions related to e-book formats.

Dedicated E-readers

Another major segment of the mobile technology market is devices dedicated to reading e-books. While there are currently over 30 different brands of e-readers in the United States alone, by far the most well-known and best-selling examples of these types of devices are the Amazon Kindle and Barnes & Noble Nook Wikipedia n.d.). Both of these popular electronic readers are manufactured and sold by book sellers and are designed to be used to consume material purchased from their online stores. There are some e-readers, Sony's eReader and the Kobo e-reader most notable among them, that have a more open platform that makes getting outside materials onto them easier, but these have not been as popular with consumers. E-readers' main strength in comparison with other mobile devices is their unlit, nonreflective e-ink screens, which mimic the look of a print book. This serves to reduce the eye fatigue that is a notable drawback to backlit LCD screens. Also, because the screen only uses power on page turns, the battery life is much longer than on other mobile devices.

However, there are some significant drawbacks to this type of device. First of all, because e-readers are designed around the primary task of reading e-books, they do not excel at other tasks users expect to be able to accomplish on current mobile devices. Although most e-readers allow their owners to listen to digital music, view pictures, play games, and surf the web using a rudimentary browser, none of them provide a satisfactory experience in any task except for reading. Many think that because of this fact, dedicated e-readers may be a stepping-stone to more powerful and feature-full multifunction devices. This is why dedicated e-readers are on the shortlist of technologies set for extinction. Some prognosticators have even gone as far comparing the role of dedicated e-readers in the transformation of reading in the electronic era to that of the 8-track player in the development of portable music players (Pelikan 2009). Also, the proprietary nature of the most popular e-readers makes putting PDFs and other documents onto them a complicated procedure. For example, to put a PDF onto an Amazon Kindle, a user must email the document to a specific email address, retrieve that email on the Kindle, and then open the file. The web browsers on dedicated e-readers are bare-bones at best. This makes it difficult to access library e-book collections that are limited to reading in the browser. Finally, these devices are designed to exist as a single-user device at the operating system level. This means that if libraries wish to check out e-readers to their patrons, they cannot create a single image with a set of materials and settings and push it to all managed devices. E-reader vendors have made some accommodations to make their devices more applicable to institutional environments. For example, Amazon and Barnes & Noble allow up to six devices to be registered to a single account. Users can then push the same content to all six devices. Additionally, Barnes & Noble offers a managed account where they will preload all the purchased content for institutional customers. This still does not address the usability of the devices in terms of electronic content purchased by libraries by other vendors.

Tablets

Although the concept of tablet computing long predates it, the release of the Apple iPad in 2010 brought about an explosion in this market segment. Much like smartphones, these touchscreen devices allow their users to read books, surf the web, read and send email, listen to music, watch videos and movies, play games, and use an ever-expanding wide variety of apps. As reading devices, their main advantage over smartphones is the screen size, which can be as large as 10 inches. This cuts down on much of the eyestrain endemic to reading on a smartphone. Also, these devices tend to have ways to get files on to them, so using them to consume e-books in PDF or epub formats is easier. Tablets are designed to browse the web, so library patrons may use them to search for and read e-books in the browser.

Tablets suffer from the same issues related to eyestrain caused by backlit screens as laptops and smartphones. Multitouch tablets like the iPad and the various Android models also have glass screens that are reflective. This can cause glare, making them difficult if not impossible to read in direct sunlight. The multifunctional nature of tablets, coupled with their bright backlit screens, also results in much lower battery life than a dedicated e-reader. Also, much like dedicated e-readers, tablets are designed to be single-user devices at the OS level, making them hard to manage in an institutional environment. For example, 127 iPads[1] can be synced to a standard image housed on a single Macintosh computer. One solution for this in a library setting is a cart with an

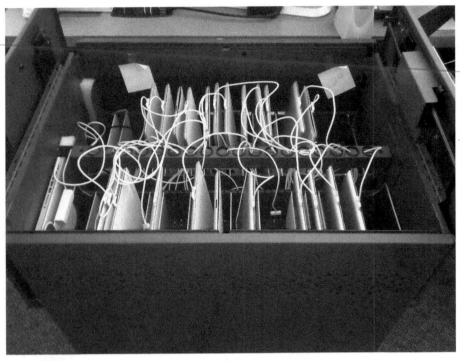

Figure 11.1
Cart for syncing and charging multiple iPads.

integrated USB hub and power management that allows for the syncing and charging of multiple iPads (Figure 11.1). Apple also has enterprise iTunes accounts that allow for bulk purchases of apps at a discount. However, unlike with public PCs or laptops, there is no way for users to log in, create individual accounts, and save work that is viewable only by them. Also, any changes made by one user to an iPad's settings are viewable by the next user. This is largely because Apple and other manufacturers see tablets as personal electronic devices more than computers.

VENDERS, PUBLISHERS, AND LICENSING ISSUES

E-books have been a disruptive technology to publishers, much like electronic music and digital video have been to their respective industries. Much like in the other creative content industries, as e-books have risen in popularity, so has the level of piracy (Rich 2009). E-books, in their raw form, can be used by any number of users at a time. They can also be copied and disseminated much like any other computer file, and online services like Scribd and file-sharing sites like Megaupload and Mediafire make finding a pirated e-book as simple as a Google search. In an attempt to combat piracy and preserve their traditional business models while still responding to increasing demand for e-books, publishers have employed a number of strategies related to digital rights management (DRM) and licensing that affect the use of their materials on mobile devices. In short, the publishing industry wasn't about to repeat the mistakes of the music industry; employing DRM from the outset has prevented the Kindle and the iPad from becoming the mobile device for the consumption of pirated material that the MP3 player was for music (Schiller 2010). Many question whether DRM does prevent piracy, and if piracy negatively affects sales. O'Reilly Media conducted a study on a title from a popular technical writer, Thomas Nelson. They found a net lift in sales of books that had been pirated (Webb 2011).

Licensing and DRM models with e-books stand in stark contrast to those presented with electronic academic journals. The vast majority of e-journals allow their readers to download full-text content as PDF files with no DRM restrictions. This is due to a number of factors. Most importantly, libraries do not have the leverage with e-books that they had with e-journals. Because academic libraries are the primary market for research journals, they had a great deal of collective sway in setting the norm for DRM in that industry. In the case of books, individual buyers and hardware manufacturers all provide alternative market strategies for publishers, so they do not have to bend to the wishes of libraries attempting to provide the best experience for their users. One notable exception to this trend is academic publishers; their primary market is academic libraries, so their DRM strategies have been much more library friendly.

One common aspect of e-book licensing is restrictions on the number of simultaneous users a single book can have. Most e-book vendors allow only a single simultaneous user per item in their default pricing scheme. Libraries can, if they wish, purchase additional licenses to allow for additional users for high-use items. This practice effectively mimics the print world, where libraries might purchase multiple copies of titles that circulate in large numbers. However, much like with print books, it is difficult for librarians to predict high-use titles, so these usage restrictions present another hurdle for potential e-book readers. Additionally, the idea of "waiting" for a digital copy to become available is frustrating and nonintuitive to many users, especially members of younger generations.

Many publishers' and vendors' DRM models restrict their items to on-screen use only. This means that mobile device users would have to read e-books from these platforms in the browser at suboptimal resolutions. On a device with a smaller screen such as a smartphone, users are often required to scroll side to side to view pages. Even in the case of the iPad and other tablets with a large screen, the interfaces of e-book platforms designed for reading on the desktop do not support the touch-enabled features of the proprietary e-book platforms designed specifically for the devices. For example, the Safari Tech Book Online collection allows for a full-screen view that reads and scrolls nicely on an iPad. However, to flip pages a user must press a small bar on the left- or right-hand side of the page that can be difficult to touch. This is in sharp contrast to books available through Apple's proprietary iBooks platform that allows users to change pages with a flip of their finger. At some point, the price advantages of using library materials will be outweighed by the convenience of proprietary optimized platforms. In this case, libraries will be bypassed altogether by patrons looking for electronic material to consume on their mobile devices.

Some e-book vendors allow library users to check out items for offline view. This model of e-book distribution is especially prevalent in public libraries, where patrons, vendors, and publishers wish to replicate the physical book world in the electronic environment. OverDrive and 3M are the primary public-library vendors for downloadable e-book formats. The public-library lending model is primarily based on purchasing a title for use by one user at a time—that is, the one-book/one-user model. While this solution allows library users the ability to borrow e-books instead of purchase them, it has several barriers. First, many users are unable to find titles they want. Some of this is due to publishers withholding content from public-library aggregated vendors. Simon & Schuster and Macmillan are in this category, while Penguin has suspended library lending of content due to security concerns (Kelley 2011). Second, libraries are unable to purchase enough copies of e-books to meet the demand. Best-selling titles may have hold lists and require patrons to wait for a copy to be returned. Publishers and aggregators are unwilling to sell titles for unlimited simultaneous use, which enhances the problem. Finally, many library patrons have technical difficulties during the download process. This process requires that one download software, register software, and manually move files from a computer to the device through a USB. The launch of the OverDrive/Kindle lending program made this process easier for Kindle owners by downloading the content through a user's Amazon account and wirelessly delivering it to any registered device. While the addition of Kindle devices to the library service was much awaited, it was met with resistance from some librarians who felt patron confidentiality was in jeopardy (Goldberg 2011). Speculations of barriers to e-book access were confirmed with a recent Library Journal Patron Profiles study indicating that 23 percent of library patrons experience technical difficulties with the download process, while 44 percent were unable to find the content they desired. Despite these setbacks, 74 percent of public-library e-book users want the library to purchase more e-book titles (Library Journal 2012).

In the fall of 2011, public libraries experienced another shock wave when Amazon announced its Kindle Lending Library. The Kindle lending program allows Amazon Prime subscribers the ability to borrow one e-book per month from a limited Amazon e-book collection with the annual $79.00 fee. This subscription service model has not been met with open arms from all publishers; however, in December 2011, the top ten KDP Select authors participating in the Kindle Owners Lending Library received unprecedented royalties (up 449 percent from November to December) from the program (Dilworth 2012).

Academic e-book vendors are also exploring checkout-based distribution systems. Ebrary has a system like this, where library users can "check out" an e-book. If they do not check the item back in, other patrons cannot use the item for a period for seven days. Because a lot of academic monograph usage, print or electronic, is short and partial, this means that often the usage rights to a book are being held by a patron who no longer needs it (although patrons have the ability to return the item early). This does mirror patterns with print books, but one of the major advantages of e-books is immediate remote access, and this model often negates that. In fact, the Library Journal Patron Profiles stated "Ebook patrons have a greater sense of immediacy than general patrons. They are less inclined to wait for library copies to become available and more likely to use alternate media versions. However, if a waiting list exists, they are willing to wait for an ebook to become available—at least for now" (Library Journal 2012). Navigating the differing licensing and DRM restrictions placed on electronic content almost requires library patrons to have a working knowledge of rights management, something which they should not need to use library materials. This runs counter to users' expectations of instant, barrier-free access and may make them not view the library as a place to obtain content for their mobile devices.

Some academic publishers have much more liberal DRM models, and some have no DRM on their titles. This may be because unlike trade publishers, who derive a substantial portion of their sales from the retail channel, academic publishers are largely reliant upon libraries for their revenues. Removing the DRM barriers makes e-book content very readable on a wide array of mobile platforms. One notable example of an academic publisher that makes its titles available to libraries free of DRM is Springer. Not only are Springer e-books DRM free, but users also may download individual chapters as PDF files. This affords library patrons the opportunity to use their preferred device to read Springer content. When readers download a Springer PDF chapter on an iPhone or iPad, for instance, they are given the option of importing that PDF into iBooks. From that point, they are able to read the content offline. They also have most of the features of iBooks, including flicking to turn pages and pinch zooming.

CONCLUSION

As this chapter has demonstrated, e-books present a number of challenges for libraries, some of which threaten to transform how we provide materials and services for our patrons. But as brick-and-mortar bookstores that trade in printed books see their business contract in the face of increased competition from online and e-book distribution, libraries have to be sure not to repeat their mistakes. Libraries need to assert their primary role in expanding the scope of the growing e-book landscape. It is important for libraries to become a place where mobile device owners can get content for their devices. And it is also important for libraries to maintain their role in helping to close the digital divide by making tablets and e-readers available to those who cannot afford them. Finally, libraries need to work with vendors and publishers to find licensing models that maximize access to e-books for their patrons while preserving the revenue streams of publishers and protecting the intellectual property rights of authors.

NOTE

1. This limit is the number of devices that can be connected to a single computer, not an additional limit introduced by Apple.

REFERENCES

Abdullah, Noorhidawati, and Forbes Gibb. 2008. "Students & Attitudes towards E-books in a Scottish Higher Education Institute: Part 1." *Library Review*, 57(8): 593–605.

Amazon.com, Inc. 2011. "Customers Purchasing Kindles at a Rate of More than 1 Million per Week for Third Straight Week." December 15. Accessed December 16, 2011. http://phx.corporate-ir.net/phoenix.zhtml?c=176060&p=irol-newsArticle&ID=1640193&highlight=.

Breitbach, William, & Joy E. Lambert. 2011. "Patron-driven Ebook Acquisition." *Computers in Libraries* 31(6): 17–20.

Carlucci-Thomas, Lisa. 2011. "Making Sense of Change: Ebooks, Access, and the Academic Library." In *No Shelf Required 2*, edited by Sue Polanka, 61–70. Chicago: American Library Association.

Carreiro, Erin. 2010. "Electronic Books: How Digital Devices and Supplementary New Technologies Are Changing the Face of the Publishing Industry." *Publishing Research Quarterly* 26(4): 219–235. doi:10.1007/s12109-010-9178-z.

Dilworth, Dianna. 2012. "Amazon Authors See 449% Royalty Growth from Library Lending." Accessed January 31, 2012. http://www.mediabistro.com/galleycat/amazon-authors-see-449-royalty-growth-from-library-lending_b45354.

Goldberg, Beverly. 2011. "Librarians Weigh Kindle Ebook Lending against Reader Privacy." *American Libraries*. Accessed January 31, 2012. http://americanlibrariesmagazine.org/e-content/librarians-weigh-kindle-ebook-lending-against-reader-privacy.

Kelley, Michael. 2011. "Librarians Face Patrons Unhappy with Penguin Policy Change; ALA Condemns Ebook Decision." Accessed January 31, 2012. http://www.thedigitalshift.com/2011/11/ebooks/librarians-face-patrons-unhappy-with-penguin-policy-change-ala-condemns-ebook-decision/.

Lee, Michelle. 2012. "In One Community, Residents Challenge Library Spending on Ebooks." Accessed January 26, 2012. http://www.thedigitalshift.com/2012/01/ebooks/in-one-community-residents-challenge-library-spending-on-ebooks/.

Library Journal. 2012. "Patron Profiles: Mobile Devices, Mobile Content and Library Apps." Library Journal's Patron Profiles 1(2): 17.

Miller, Rebecca. 2011. "Dramatic Growth." *Library Journal* 136(17): 32–34.

Pelikan, Michael P. 2009. "The Kindle Is the 8-track Tape Player of the eBook Age." *Against the Grain* 21(2), 48–49.

Pew Research Center. 2011. "Device Ownership." Accessed December 9, 2011. http://www.pewresearch.org/Static-Pages/Trend-Data/Device-Ownership.aspx.

Pew Research Center. 2012. "Tablet and E-book Reader Ownership Surge in the Holiday Gift-Giving Period." Accessed January 31, 2012. http://www.pewinternet.org.

Rich, Motoko. 2009. "Print Books Are Target of Pirates on the Web." *New York Times* (May 12). http://www.nytimes.com/2009/05/12/technology/internet/12digital.html.

Schiller, Kurt. 2010. "A Happy Medium: Ebooks, Licensing, and DRM." *Information Today* 27 (2): 1–44.

Shrimplin, Aaron K., Andy Revelle, Susan Hurst, and Kevin Messner. 2011. "Contradictions and Consensus—Clusters of Opinions on E-books." *College & Research Libraries* 72(2): 181–190.

Slater, Robert. 2010. "Why Aren't E-Books Gaining More Ground in Academic Libraries? E-Book Use and Perceptions: A Review of Published Literature and Research." *Journal of Web Librarianship* 4(4): 305–331. doi:10.1080/19322909.2010.525419.

Smith, Aaron. 2011. "Smartphone Adoption and Usage." Pew Research Center's Internet & American Life Project. Accessed December 9, 2011. http://www.pewinternet.org/Reports/2011/Smartphones.aspx.

"Springer Launches Mycopy Service for Ebook Users." 2009. *Advanced Technology Libraries* 38(8): 6.

Webb, Jenn. 2011. "Book Piracy: Less DRM, More Data." Accessed January 31, 2012. http://radar.oreilly.com/2011/01/book-piracy-drm-data.html.

Wikipedia. n.d. "Comparison of e-book readers." Accessed December 19, 2011. http://en.wikipedia.org/wiki/Comparison_of_e-book_readers.

12

Electronic Resources in Medical Libraries

Max Anderson

Key Points

- Readers will receive a brief overview of medical libraries and medical librarianship.
- The path from print to electronic resources to offering mobile access will be described.
- Readers will learn about platform determination for mobile resources.
- Selection criteria for mobile electronic resources will be provided.
- Gauging use of mobile electronic resources will be discussed.
- Conclusions and future trends will be shared.

OVERVIEW

Selecting electronic resources in libraries today is a lot like trying to hit a moving target. Beyond that, securing mobile access to electronic resources can be like trying to hit a moving target while riding on a Ferris wheel. Building a library collection today is more challenging than it used to be. The process for building a print collection changed slowly over the twentieth century, and standards were put in place gradually (Gregory and Hanson 2006). However, user needs have changed quickly, and the introduction of electronic resources has revolutionized the process of resource selection. The vendor-library negotiation process was turned upside-down with the introduction of electronic access to resources, and libraries also had software and hardware issues with which to contend. Electronic resources bring another layer of complexity because of access costs. The availability of electronic resources and access in libraries changes, often with budget reductions (or with rare dollar increases in budgets) as well as with needs from the stakeholders who use them. Another issue is the fluctuating prices given to libraries by vendors during the negotiation process. As we enter the second decade of the twenty-first century, yet another radical change has emerged that affects how information is delivered to the patron—the mobile device.

Before mobile devices became ubiquitous in our society, access to electronic resources might have only meant the ability to read a book or journal on a computer screen rather than using a print copy. This has been a boon for the library industry as well as a headache. The ability to increase the size of the collection and to not have to take up extra shelf space has enabled more access to information for today's patron. "Mobile devices now allow users to take the library with them wherever they go" (Hallerberg et al. 2011). However, negotiating with vendors can be a vexing experience for print subscriptions, let alone for access to electronic versions. While some database vendors have developed specific mobile interfaces, others have been slow to adopt mobile platforms. The author speculates that it might be related to difficulties with authentication of users. Institutions or individuals usually have to pay for access to electronic resources. Up to now, vendors and publishers have figured out ways to be gatekeepers of information. For example, libraries can pay a subscription fee that allows a limited number of accesses during a time period or a limited number of concurrent users. Mobile technology has brought some challenges to this model. It is challenging for publishers and libraries alike to figure out ways to keep track of who is accessing a resource and how they are doing it. It may also be simply a matter of finding the right developers to create either a mobile application (app) or website and to keep up with the quickly evolving world of mobile access.

Unlike print journals, electronic resources sometimes have a time limit—some contracts with vendors stipulate that if the library decides not to renew a journal, the library loses access to the electronic version of the journal. In other instances, the library can keep the years for which they have paid. Libraries can purchase both the electronic and the physical formats at the same time—and again it depends on the negotiation process with the vendor whether this is even an option. While budget reductions have hit academic health science libraries quite hard, hospital libraries are often the biggest losers. In 2010 the author visited a hospital library in central Wisconsin. The library had been essentially shut down and was staffed by the continuing medical education coordinator, who was not a degreed librarian. This staff member said that the budget for journals—physical or otherwise—was literally zero. She made the number zero with her hand to emphasize the point. In this particular hospital, the doctors use continuing medical education funds to purchase their own access to electronic resources like Up-ToDate. Mobile adds some challenges to the mix for librarians. "With rapid and continuous improvements in mobile technology, medical institutions and libraries are challenged to adapt and respond accordingly" (Burnette 2010). Librarians use their skills to investigate the best methods of access to the best resources for the people they serve and support.

This chapter attempts to summarize how medical librarians make electronic resources available to their patrons, whether it is an electronic book or journal, or if it concerns recommending particular mobile apps. The focus is on academic medical libraries and hospital libraries.

MEDICAL LIBRARIES AND HEALTH SCIENCES LIBRARIANSHIP

Health sciences librarians come from a wide variety of educational backgrounds that do not necessarily include the sciences. As with any library degree, it can be useful to have related subject-matter expertise. Also, health sciences librarians do not necessarily work for medical schools or hospitals. The field is as wide open as any other in librarianship. Medical libraries have a wide variety of settings that include academic institutions (and the library may be in a stand-alone building or may be a part of a particular school like medicine or nursing), hospitals, and also other types such as area health education centers (AHECs), Veterans Affairs medical libraries, patient education libraries, and so forth. Patrons in academic medical libraries might include doctors, nurses, and students in public health or pharmacy. Patrons in hospitals might include health professionals on staff or even the public if the library is open to nonstaff. Mobile devices are on the rise in the medical field. "The results of a 2009 survey by the American Academy of Nurse Practitioners [*sic*] further confirms that mobile device usage is rising among those in the health care field. The study shows that the majority of nurse practitioners use mobile devices to access drug resources, diagnostic studies, and reference books" (Havelka 2011). Students in a health sciences program are more likely to be expected to have a mobile device, which means that librarians will need to be able to teach information literacy skills to them. Some medical schools issue mobile devices to their first-year residents. Librarians are also somewhat more likely to have access to different mobile devices so they can test the resources they suggest to patrons. "To serve as an access point for mobile resources, the hospital library must keep these various devices and the programs and applications that are accessible on them in mind. Not all programs will work on all devices" (Klatt 2011). This need to stay current on mobile technology is the same for other types of libraries, not just hospital libraries.

ELECTRONIC RESOURCES

Electronic resources is a not a narrow topic area in and of itself. It includes a wide variety of materials including indexing and abstracting services, electronic books, serials and textbooks, electronic databases offered by information aggregators, document delivery services, and websites (Gregory and Hanson 2006). Due to the explosive growth in mobile technology, we can add mobile apps and websites to this list. Two sticking points with traditional electronic resources like e-journals and e-books are digital rights management (DRM) and intellectual property issues. Good resources for understanding these particular issues are the Association of Research Libraries DRM policies[1] and the Medical Library Association (MLA) Collection Development Section—Professional Resources for Librarians.[2] These two topics in particular merit their own examination and are not discussed in depth here. Some academic medical and hospital libraries offer downloadable e-books. Patrons can download these e-books and read them on their smartphone, tablet, or e-reader (Havelka 2011). Again, because of the capacity to serve multiple users, e-books are more readily available and accessible, and so more highly used. There are studies that indicate that e-books are more popular than the print version of the same title (Ugaz and Resnick 2008.) Ugaz and Resnick supply a table that shows total electronic and print use by package in 2005 and 2006. For example, using vendor-supplied data, AccessMedicine e-books were used 8,658 times compared to 76 for the same titles in print.

Academic health science libraries typically have to support many study areas of the institution. For example, the Charlotte Edwards Maguire Medical Library located at Florida State University supports nursing, psychology, human sciences, and biology as well as other life sciences (Shearer et al. 2009). Hospital libraries function similarly as they have to be able to support different departments of the hospital (or hospitals, if they support more than one physical location). As Havelka (2011) describes in her article, more and more health science practitioners are using mobile devices.

To access electronic resources, users should ideally be able to view them no matter where they are located. This leads to authentication issues. When a subscription is set up, the library typically provides some way for the vendor to authenticate its users. One way is via Internet Protocol (IP) address. The IP addresses are those from the library's computers or via some other authentication method. If a user is offsite and using their own technology for accessing the electronic resource, there are other ways to authenticate users. Some of these include authentication by user name and password, proxy servers (like EZproxy[3]), or via virtual private networks (VPNs). A problem with ever-popular mobile devices is that they do not have IP addresses. There are sometimes complex instructions on how to access a resource on a mobile device, whether access is made available via an app or a website.

Here is an example of how to obtain access to an electronic resource for a mobile device. DynaMed,[4] a clinical reference tool, is available as a mobile app for most of the predominant mobile platforms. A DynaMed serial number is required to download the app to a mobile device. In some cases, health science libraries that have subscribed to this resource are keeping track of these serial numbers and issuing them to patrons as needed. Otherwise, patrons can be directed to the vendor's technical support pages for DynaMed to obtain access.

Many libraries have created guides of electronic resources available to users, and now guides of suggested apps and mobile websites are starting to appear. New questions emerge: Do the users use the Android platform on their smartphones or tablets? Do they have an iPhone or an iPad? What about Windows phones or Blackberry devices? How do you determine what platform/operating system your users have on their mobile devices? Does it matter? In suggesting mobile apps to library users, it does matter. The DynaMed app that you can download to your iDevice, for example, is not the same app that you download to an Android smartphone or tablet. The health science library itself might have a mobile app or website. A bit of investigation is necessary to determine what platforms are predominantly used by users.

MOBILE PLATFORM DETERMINATION

Viewing electronic resources such as e-books and e-journals on a standard computer screen is usually not a problem for most users. It does not matter if you are using a Windows-based PC or a Mac. However, if you have users who are viewing certain resources via a smartphone or tablet device, it can become an issue. For example, Unbound Medicine is a health care knowledge company that creates mobile products in multiple platforms. One of their products, Taber's Medical Dictionary for Mobile and Web, can be used on a full-screen browser and can also be viewed on a smartphone like the iPhone.

It is not only determining platforms that are being used by the patrons that is important, but also what will be supported by the institution's Information Technology (IT) department. Knowing which platform is most widely used will help determine what is created and possibly supported. Apps for the various platforms are made in different computer languages. Developing an app is usually more complicated than creating a mobile website.

A questionnaire went out to MEDLIB-L,[5] an email list for medical librarians, in November 2011 asking health sciences librarians how they determine the platforms that are being used at their institutions, as well as how they select and promote appropriate resources for use with mobile devices. Here are some of the responses in regard to platform determination.

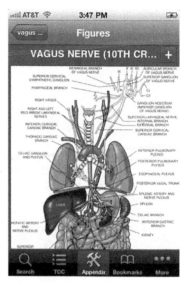

Figure 12.1

Taber's Medical Dictionary for iPhone.

- Christina Seeger, University of the Incarnate Word, Feik School of Pharmacy, replied, "IT is forthcoming with that information; however we have had to push the envelope in the library in explaining why we needed to explore the non-supported platforms as well." Regarding policies for mobile resources, Seeger said, "We do not have a separate policy for mobile resources, they must fall into our collection development philosophy to be considered."
- Marie Ascher of the New York Medical College replied, "Officially supported by our institution? We reached out to our CIO at the time and were told the only officially supported platform was Blackberry, and the only web browser supported is IE. We went out on our own and developed a site based on the iPhone that works on all three major mobile platforms. We surveyed our users to see what they are currently using. More than half of mobile users use some sort of Apple mobile device (iPhone, iPad, iPod Touch)."
- Emily Vardell from the University of Miami, Calder Memorial Library, replied, "One year ago I went through our list of databases and individually explored each one to determine which mobile platforms were supported. I often found the information on the databases' About Us section, but when not, I used my Android device or borrowed an iPhone to see if the database worked on those databases."
- Peg Burnette from the University of Illinois at Chicago replied, "My institution does not officially support a specific platform. As a librarian I tried to identify the resources that were available for all platforms."
- Chris Bishop from Community Health Network in Indiana said, "If I have question about what our organization supports I ask some people I know in IT. I personally have focused solely on Apple and Android. I think Blackberry is too far behind."
- Sarah Jewell from Memorial Sloan Kettering replied, "We contacted the IT department to obtain purchasing statistics. We also took a survey of what devices employees were using."
- Jill Boruff from McGill University said, "McGill IT does not provide any official support for mobile devices. The support is ad hoc—for example, our IT knowledgebase has an entry on Blackberrys [*sic*] only because someone in IT has one and decided to write an entry."

In some cases, there is not a clearly supported platform at each institution, and in others the librarian has managed to be a part of the conversation with IT in determining support. From casual conversations with health science librarians, the author has found that in some instances it is just a matter of observing what the patrons are using. Some hospital librarians have described just going into the doctor's lounge to see what devices they were using, which helped them determine what to promote or create.

Another method for viewing mobile resources is straight from a mobile-enabled website. The benefit of this is there is no platform with which to be concerned. It is simply a website that has been converted to be viewed on a mobile device. Sometimes it is a matter of creating a cascading style sheet that can do the converting for the viewfinder; other times it requires creating a mirror website—like Mobile MedlinePlus,[6] which can be viewed easily on a smaller screen.

Figure 12.2
MobileMedlinePlus.

ELECTRONIC RESOURCE SELECTION CRITERIA

The selection process for electronic resources involves an imperative need to understand the library's user community. The goals and mission of the institution should be considered as well as policies regarding the types and kinds of resources that will be offered to users. "The selection decisions a library must make therefore necessarily involve a form of intellectual triage" (Gregory and Hanson 2006). Conducting a needs assessment for mobile resources asks similar questions to the following:

- Who are the users?
- What resources have the patrons requested?
- *What resources are available in mobile format? Websites? Apps?*
- *What are the trends in which mobile platforms are being used?*
- *What apps are available for the various platforms?*

The last three points include new questions to be considered when investigating mobile resources. The book by Gregory and Hanson listed in the resources section gives some helpful information on selecting electronic resources. While this is not specifically for mobile resources, the information gleaned about selection can be customized for the mobile environment. Selecting apps to promote to users depends on the platforms used. For vendor-supplied resources it depends on what the vendors can make available as well. With mobile websites, on the other hand, it is less important to know what platforms are used than it is to know how likely a mobile website will look similar on different platforms. Access to subscription-based resources is another question. There are many free health-related mobile websites available to promote to users. Some examples include CDC Mobile,[7] Mobile MedlinePlus,[8] and PubMed for Handhelds.[9]

Other free or low-cost apps include WISER,[10] Epocrates,[11] and Diagnosaurus.[12] Paid apps such as those that come from Unbound Medicine[13] are definitely worth investigating, and, because there is a cost involved, a review of the apps' applicability to your institution is suggested.

Another popular platform that is evolving is downloadable e-books. As of mid-2011, the Library of the Health Sciences at the University of Illinois at Chicago (UIC-LHS) had thousands of e-books in the health sciences with more being added regularly. The library has purchased e-books from Springer, Wiley, Ebrary, and others. Oxford University Press is another e-book supplier, and the collection from this publisher at the library focuses on public health, epidemiology, and neuroscience.

Some providers of e-books for academic libraries are starting to include options that allow for download to e-readers that have built-in expiration dates. Some of the chapters or sections in various platforms can be loaded onto mobile devices.

"Selection criteria for mobile resources" was a question asked of health science librarians in November 2011 on the MEDLIB-L email discussion list. Here are some of the responses:

- Christina Seeger replied in regards to selection criteria at her institution for mobile apps, "Again, we use our collection development philosophy. I maintain an 'app blog' (on our

Blackboard site) in the discipline that I serve to share apps of interest—not just healthcare-specific, but organizational tools, leisure, health and wellness, etc."

- Marie Ascher said in regards to selection criteria, "We do not have official collection criteria for mobile resources. We are primarily linking to and listing on our mobile site those products we currently have that have mobile functionality. I'd be very happy to see others' criteria and collection policies related to mobile resources." And on the subject of updating mobile resource pages, she said, "We are also talking about adding mobile app/site recommendations to the academic department pages maintained by our librarian liaisons."

- Emily Vardell replied, "We simply supply information about mobile resources that are available for our normal databases." In regards to selection criteria for mobile apps, "Right now we only support mobile apps for the databases we already provide. We have not explored selecting additional apps for our patrons."

- Susan Fowler from Washington University in St. Louis: "As far as e-books and e-journals go, we have a collections committee that has a set of criteria they use but I don't know what the specifics are outside of what is posted to the public which is . . .

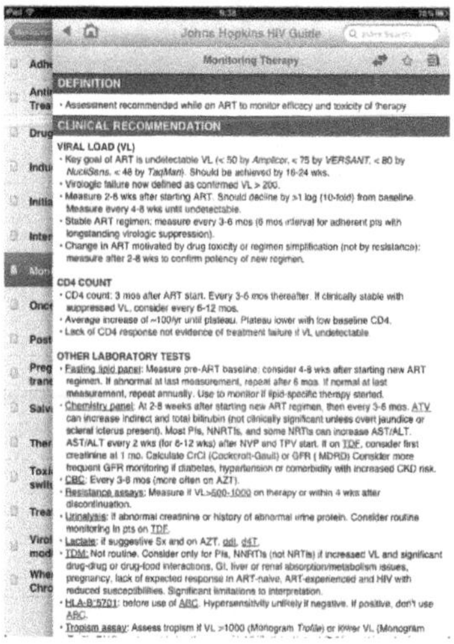

Figure 12.3
Johns Hopkins HIV Guide App for the iPad.

'The Library welcomes recommendations for additions to its collection. A member of the Collection Management staff will evaluate your request.

The criteria for purchasing items is based on:

- the subject scope of the recommended item
- budgetary considerations
- the topic's demand
- potential users
- electronic license terms
- availability (whether or not the item is in print)

Required and suggested textbooks and monographs for student class work are purchased for course reserves upon receipt of requests from faculty.

Duplicate copies of monographs are purchased only if the title is very heavily used and funds are available. Second copies of journals are not purchased.

Missing/lost/damaged books are not automatically replaced, even when the library is reimbursed for these items. The decision to replace an item is based on use, subject matter and relevance to the needs of faculty and students, date, cost, and availability.'

On selection criteria for mobile apps, Fowler said, "Mobile applications do not fit into out [sic] current collection development policy or work flow. I have built our collection based on what comes as part of our licenses and subscriptions, what is recommended by patrons, online reviews, and what I discover myself."

- Bille Anne Gebbs from Frontier Nursing University said, "[We] don't really have selection criteria, basically just keep in mind what is available with our existing electronic resources." And about mobile apps, she said, "Preferably downloadable (i.e. doesn't require an Internet connection to use) and available on Apple platform."

Figure 12.4
Guide to icons used in the mobile resource guide.

- Jill Boruff: "We do not select specifically for mobile electronic resources. Currently, we decide which mobile resources (from the electronic resources that we already have access to) we are going to promote depending on how well they work and how well they serve our population. We have created a mobile subject guide to promote the mobile-optimized sites and mobile applications for resources requiring McGill authentication. Most of these have been chosen for their usefulness as point-of-care tools."
- Peg Burnette said, "The mobile applications that we promote are generally available as part of an institutional subscription to an electronic, web-based resource. The selection criteria for content would be the same as for any medical resource: scope and quality, authorship, up to date, etc. For mobile apps it is also important that the product is easy to get onto the device and easy to use; readability & navigation are also important." Selection criteria for apps include "Scope & quality, evidence-based, current with frequent updates, easy to procure and easy to use, and comfortable to read on a small device."
- Xan Goodman replied, "The following mobile apps we use are a part of our electronic resource offerings, Micromedex, Clinical Pharmacology, MD Consult, Facts & Comparisons and such. Selection criteria is not based on the mobile function instead if a resource meets our goals and fits within our collection development guidelines we purchase the resource— and if a mobile app is available we then market that app to our student and faculty population."
- Chris Bishop stated, "I have not selected any mobile e-resources specifically. I have only provided instruction and links for the mobile resources that free—case in point the NEJM mobile app or items that come in combination like say Micromedix."
- Sarah Jewell said, "We limited our list to mobile apps for Android, Blackberry, iPhone, and iPad devices. We also included selected mobile websites, which can include journals and databases." Memorial Sloan-Kettering Cancer Center Library has a Mobile Resources Collection Development Policy.[14]

Besides looking at what resources other libraries include in their collections, you can review the contents of the Apple iTunes Store, which has a "medical" apps category.[15] Some of the apps may be questionable as to their appropriateness for your institution, so librarians should do a proper review of the resource, just as they have done for years for Internet resources. Another resource example is Skyscape.[16] While the app itself is free, the hundreds of resources available through Skyscape are not.

PROMOTING ELECTRONIC RESOURCES TO USERS

Librarians are known for making information guides for patrons and sometimes even for their fellow librarians. A visit to most any library website will bring you to webpages with database and subject guides. Hospital library websites are usually behind strict firewalls, so it was difficult for the author to gain access to see how they promote electronic resources. As an academic health science library example, the UIC-LHS staff has created a "Mobile Medicine @ UIC" guide using LibGuide software. In fact, they have created two guides. One is formatted for a desktop computer, and another one is formatted for mobile devices. Along the sidebar of the desktop formatted guide, they have included a list with icons showing the various devices they refer to for each resource.

In UIC-LHS's mobile resource guide, they include tabs of lists popular tools, an A–Z list of resources, UIC Mobile services, UIC licensed services, an FYI, and a "Need Help?" tab. In particular, under the tab for licensed resources, a description is given as to how to access a particular resource: "Some UIC licensed resources require registration. This is sometimes simply a matter of knowing your netid and password at UIC, but other times it is more complicated with special codes, keys, etc. The following links will take you to the registration page, download page, or to a page with details about the registration process. Please do not hesitate to contact us if you need any assistance."[17] UIC has promoted its subscriptions to electronic resources as well as mobile apps and websites to users via word of mouth, flyers, table tents, and its Facebook page.[18] Other promotional methods include Twitter, blogs, and widgets on webpages. Refer to Appendix A to see examples of mobile resource guides created by libraries, including the one for UIC.

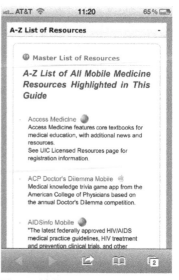

Figure 12.5

UIC-LHS A–Z List of Resources as it appears on an iPhone.

Conferences are a venue for librarians to talk about their mobile electronic resources as a poster session or as a presentation. Medical librarian Bohyun Kim has a presentation[19] on SlideShare about mobile access to licensed databases as yet another example of innovative ways to promote mobile electronic resources. And finally, participants at a Mobile Technologies for Medical Librarians roundtable[20] at the Medical Library Association 2011 meeting suggested the importance of discussing medical apps during orientation for new students. Some medical librarians reported having a "clinical skills" day where mobile resources were integrated into the curriculum. Consider creating either formal or ad hoc training sessions to assist users with accessing mobile resources, and promote these sessions as much as possible, using some of the methods described here.

GAUGING USAGE OF ELECTRONIC RESOURCES

Determining how resources have been used in a library used to be fairly easy. Since library systems have been automated, it is simple to pull up counts of checkouts for print resources in the library. With electronic resources, whether they be journals, books, or even the library's own mobile app, determining usage is a lot more difficult. A question related to this was asked in the same questionnaire discussed earlier, and here are some of the responses for gauging usage of mobile resources.

Figure 12.6

Facebook page for UIC-LHS promoting mobile electronic resources.

- Christina Seeger: "Vendor stats, google [sic] analytics on the pages with download links."
- Marie Ascher: "Varies. Can't get download stats for Dynamed from EBSCO. Boo. But for most mobile sites, yes, I believe stats are available."
- Emily Vardell: "We have not yet explored this. I will say that the blog posts I write on our mobile databases are the ones that receive the largest number of views."

Figure 12.7
University of Utah, Spencer S. Eccles
Health Sciences Library blog posting
about a mobile app.

- Susan Fowler: "We do not currently do anything to gauge the use of mobile apps. Our only indicator of use is how often our mobile guide is accessed. We do measure use of our online e-books, e-journals, and desktop online platforms like UpToDate using stats we get from our vendors."
- Peg Burnette: "We can only get hits from the libguide [*sic*] for mobile apps."
- Xan Goodman: "That is an excellent question. One way we gauge use is by the request of special codes for some of the apps, specifically Clinical Pharmacology, with the others I am unsure if stats are available."
- Chris Bishop: "Have not yet gone as to get usage stats from vendor."
- Sarah Jewell: "LibGuides gives us some statistics on who clicked to go to a particular app or website we have listed, but it can't really tell us whether or not the app was actually downloaded, and whether or not the app was used or liked. To our knowledge, none of our vendors are offering usage stats on mobile apps and websites yet."

LibGuides do give statistics on usage for each guide that is created. Looking at the statistics for 2011 for the "MobileMed@UIC" guide (the guide that is formatted for smartphones), it is clear that there was more usage in June and July of 2011, and usage actually decreased from there. The usage statistics for the guide "Mobile Medicine @ UIC," which is formatted for desktop computers, shows a steady increase in usage. A possible explanation of the decreasing usage of the mobile guide formatted for smartphones might be one of increased awareness with increased use of smartphones.

It is unlikely you will really know which mobile apps that are being promoted by your institution are actually being used. Those statistics are proprietary, and the company might be unwilling to release such information. If you are creating your own mobile app or website, usage statistics can be obtained, though it is easier to get them for mobile websites than for mobile apps. There are companies that claim to be able to report real-time app statistics. It is important to do your homework on the platform for which you plan to develop to see what types of statistics are available.

CONCLUSION

The lab coat hasn't changed much, but what goes into the pockets has changed (Burnette 2010). The pockets used to be overloaded with formularies and medical dictionaries. Now you might see iPhones and Android-based phones or even iPads. At a medical library conference in the fall of 2011, the author spoke with some medical librarians from Emory University who described how residents had started sewing larger pockets on the inside of their lab coats. One reason was because in traditional lab coats iPads do not fit in the pockets, and a second reason was so the device would be harder to steal. As Burnette points out in her article, opportunities remain for libraries to provide the appropriate resources and services to their mobile users. She ruminates that "a mobile-friendly Web site will soon be a given."

Look at how other libraries have enabled access to mobile resources. Attend sessions at conferences or take advantage of other educational opportunities on creating access to mobile content or the content itself, if possible. Survey your users to find out what they need and how they access mobile resources. Keeping up with the fast-paced nature of changes in mobile technology is important for medical librarians if they want to remain relevant. As an example, in mid-2011 the South Central Chapter of the Medical Library Association held an online free introduction to mobile resources[21] in health science libraries. Some of the topics included mobile trends and issues in academic and hospital library environments and promoting mobile resources. As another example, a wiki of best practices on a variety of topics called "Library Success"[22] includes a set of pages about "M-Libraries."[23] This section is not specific to medical libraries or electronic resources but does include a section on vendors and publishers.

Mobile technology is evolving at an amazing pace and is here to stay for the foreseeable future (until the next new shiny technology is introduced). By the time this book is published, it is likely some of the information will be outdated. However, as Burnette points out in her article, "it falls to librarians to do what we have always done: provide our users not only with information but with the tools they need to find and evaluate information in support of education, research, clinical practice, and life-long learning." The author of this chapter interprets this to mean staying on top of the technological changes and applying them as best as possible to your environment.

APPENDIX A: EXAMPLES OF MOBILE RESOURCE GUIDES AND WEBPAGES

This is a short list of what guides and webpages have been created and is not meant to be comprehensive.

- Duke University Medical Center: http://guides.mclibrary.duke.edu/mobile
- Florida International University Medical Library (mobile site): http://medlib.fiu.edu/m/
- Johns Hopkins Welch Medical Library: http://www.welch.jhu.edu/internet/mobile.html
- McGill University (mobile site): http://m.library.mcgill.ca/touch/healthsciguide/
- Medical College of Wisconsin, http://www.mcw.edu/mcwlibraries/mobileresources.htm
- Memorial Sloan-Kettering Cancer Center Library: http://libguides.mskcc.org/mobile
- New York Medical College: http://library.nymc.edu/informatics/pda.cfm
- New York Medical College (mobile site): http://library.nymc.edu/m/
- Oregon Health & Science University: http://www.ohsu.edu/xd/education/library/research-assistance/handheld-pda-resources.cfm
- Roseman University of Health Sciences: http://usn.libguides.com/content.php?pid=123788
- University of Illinois at Chicago, Library of the Health Sciences: http://researchguides.uic.edu/MobileMed
- University of Miami, Louis Calder Memorial Library: http://calder.med.miami.edu/electronic_databases.html (includes handy icons for supported devices)
- University of Nebraska Medical Center (mobile site): http://www.unmc.edu/library/m/index.html
- University of Virginia Claude Moore Health Sciences Library: http://mobile.hsl.virginia.edu/
- Washington University School of Medicine in St. Louis: http://beckerguides.wustl.edu/mobileresources
- Yale Cushing/Whitney Medical Library (mobile site): http://doc.med.yale.edu/m/

Most hospital library websites are behind strict firewalls so including URLs of their resources was not permitted.

NOTES

1. Association of Research Libraries DRM Policies, http://colldev.mlanet.org/resources/professional_resources.htm

2. Medical Library Association Collection Development Section—Professional Resources for Librarians, http://colldev.mlanet.org/resources/professional_resources.htm

3. EZProxy, http://www.oclc.org/ezproxy

4. DynaMed, http://dynamed.ebscohost.com/access/mobile

5. MEDLIB-L, http://www.mlanet.org/discussion/medlibl.html

6. Mobile MedlinePlus, http://m.medlineplus.gov/

7. CDC Mobile, http://m.cdc.gov/

8. Mobile MedlinePlus, http://m.medlineplus.gov/

9. PubMed for Handhelds, http://pubmedhh.nlm.nih.gov/

10. WISER, http://itunes.apple.com/us/app/wiser-for-iphone-ipod-touch/id375185381?mt=8

11. Epocrates, http://www.epocrates.com/products/android/

12. Diagnosaurus, http://books.mcgraw-hill.com/medical/diagnosaurus/

13. Unbound Medicine, http://www.unboundmedicine.com/

14. Memorial Sloan-Kettering Cancer Center Library, Mobile Resources Collection Development Policy, http://libguides.mskcc.org/content.php?pid=220316&sid=1829269

15. Apple iTunes Medical Apps, http://itunes.apple.com/us/genre/ios-medical/id6020?mt=8

16. Skyscape, http://www.skyscape.com/intro/iPhoneIntro.aspx

17. UIC Licensed Resources—Mobile Medicine @ UIC, http://researchguides.uic.edu/content.php?pid=195898&sid=1667236

18. Library of the Health Sciences—UIC, https://www.facebook.com/LHSChicago

19. SlideShare—Mobile Access to Licensed Database in Medicine & Other Subject Areas, http://www.slideshare.net/bohyunkim/mobile-access-to-licensed-databases-in-medicine-and-other-subject-areas

20. Chapter Council Report, http://www.chaptercouncil.mlanet.org/roundtables/2011/19_Mobile_Technologies.pdf

21. Get Mobilized, http://sites.google.com/site/getmobilizedmla/

22. Library Success Wiki, http://www.libsuccess.org/index.php?title=Main_Page

23. M-Libraries, http://www.libsuccess.org/index.php?title=Main_Page

REFERENCES

Burnette, Peg. 2010. "Mobile Technology and Medical Libraries: Worlds Collide." *Reference Librarian* 52(1/2): 98–105.

Gregory, Vicki L., and Ardis Hanson. 2006. *Selecting and Managing Electronic Resources*. New York: Neal-Schuman.

Hallerberg, Gretchen, et al. 2011. "Collection Technical Management," in *The Medical Library Association Guide to Managing Health Care Libraries*, edited by Margaret Moylan Bandy and Rosalind Farnam Dudden, 157–184. Chicago: Neal-Schuman.

Havelka, Stefanie. 2011. "Mobile Resources for Nursing Students and Nursing Faculty." *Journal of Electronic Resources in Medical Libraries* 8(2): 194–199.

Klatt, Carolyn. 2011. "Going Mobile: Free and Easy." *Medical Reference Services Quarterly* 30(1): 56–73.

Shearer, Barbara S., Carolyn Klatt, and Suzanne P. Nagy. 2009. "Development of a New Academic Digital Library: A Study of Usage Data of a Core Medical Electronic Journal Collection." *Journal of the Medical Library Association* 97(2): 93–101.

Ugaz, Ana G., and Taryn Resnick. 2008. "Assessing Print and Electronic Use of Reference/Core Medical Textbooks." *Journal of the Medical Library Association* 96(2): 145–147.

FURTHER READING

Blecic, Deborah. 2011. "E-books in the Health Sciences." *E-ppendix: Online Newsletter of the UIC-Library of the Health Sciences* 2(2). http://ojphi.org/htbin/cgiwrap/bin/ojs/index.php/eppendix/article/viewFile/3784/3063.

Ennis, Lisa A., and Nicole Mitchell. 2010. *The Accidental Health Sciences Librarian*. Medford, NJ: Information Today.

Kim, Bohyun, and Marissa Ball. 2011. "Mobile Use in Medicine: Taking a Cue from Specialized Resources and Devices." *Reference Librarian* 52(1/2): 57–67.

13

Smartphones, QR Codes, and Augmented Reality in the Library

Harry E. Pence

Key Points

- Augmented reality (AR) applications, which combine digital information with the real world, offer several constructive ways for libraries to respond to the shift toward mobile information services and the virtual information commons.
- AR applications, which are already being used by several museums and libraries, include the two-dimensional barcodes, situated narratives, and location-based services.
- These developments not only provide patrons with expanded information access but make libraries more visible to the young technology users who will represent the library patrons of the future.

INTRODUCTION

We are rapidly reaching a tipping point in terms of the number of people in this country who have web-enabled cell phones, often called smartphones.[1] A study from December 2009 reported that 42 percent of U.S. consumers had a smartphone, and this percentage has been increasing rapidly for some time ("Android Surges among Handset Purchasers" 2010). A study by Pew reports a somewhat lower percentage of smartphone users but also finds that 25 percent of those with smartphones prefer to access the Internet using their phones (Leggatt 2011). This tendency to access the Internet with smartphones is even higher among college students. A recent article in the *Chronicle of Higher Education* reports that 40 percent of college students use the Internet on mobile devices every day, and students increasingly expect that all their college services will be available from their phones (Keller 2011).

AR is not a new idea, but the widespread adoption of mobile devices is reviving interest in this technology. The 2010 Horizon Report predicts that "augmented reality has become simple, and is now poised to enter the mainstream in the consumer sector" (Johnson, Levine, Smith, and Stone 2010). Mobile devices, such as smartphones and tablet computers, are creating a *mobile ecosystem*, which is becoming the preferred portal to the Internet. The mobile ecosystem can be defined as the combination of mobile devices, apps, operating systems, physical objects, and networks that integrates information retrieval and communications.

If information access is no longer limited to a specific location and time, how will this affect libraries? Some time ago, libraries began to move towards the idea of an information commons (Lippincott 2006). To serve the mobile ecosystem, libraries will have to move into virtual space, creating a virtual information commons. There is already considerable progress in this direction, with most libraries offering access to online journals and databases, support for campus learning-management systems, and 24-hour reference service by cell phone text messaging. AR provides another way to create the virtual information commons.

SMARTPHONES AND AR

Augmented (or virtual) reality has been discussed since the late 1960s, but access was too expensive and cumbersome to be useful (Pausch, Proffitt, and Williams 1997). The combination of the power of AR with the convenience of the smartphone is now creating important applications for communications, research, industry, and the arts. Although there may not be a widely accepted definition of AR, for the purposes of this chapter it will be defined as the combination of digital information with the real world (Bimber and Raskar 2005). AR differs from true virtual reality in that a computer-generated component is added to the real environment, whereas in virtual reality the entire experience is computer generated.

There are basically two main types of AR currently in use on cell phones. *Marker-based AR* requires a specific label, such as a QR bar code, to access information. *Marker-less AR* combines position data from a phone's global positioning system (GPS) and compass with an internal accelerometer or gyroscope, which determines the orientation of the phone, to determine what information is to be overlaid on the image provided by the cell phone camera. There are several free online sites available that allow an individual to create two-dimensional (2D) bar codes for website addresses (IDAutomation.com, Inc. 2009) and various apps, which work with all the major types of smartphones, that can open a web link from the universal resource locator (URL) in a bar code. Microsoft has created its own tagging system (which is in color) that creates tags and a free smartphone app to read the tags (Microsoft 2010). Tolliver-Nigro (2009) gives more suggestions about using QR codes, including phone compatibilities for a number of free sites that create these codes.

Markered AR puts a label on an object that is read by the smartphone, which then accesses a website that contains more information. This is often more convenient than trying to type in a URL. The 2D bar code (shown in Figure 13.1) represents more information because it is a more complicated pattern of squares, dots, hexagons, or other geometric patterns than the familiar one-dimensional (1D) code (sometimes called a "zebra code"). Figure 13.1 also shows a 1D barcode for comparison. Currently the most common 2D coding pattern is called quick response (QR) code. The QR code was first used in Japan in 1994 and is now becoming popular in the United States. A 2D bar code can represent several thousand characters, much more than a 1D barcode and more than enough to stand for the URL of a website. A QR code can direct a phone to access a website, dial a number, or send a text message.

Figure 13.1

1D barcode (left) and 2D barcode (right).

There are several advantages to using a 2D barcode to refer to a web page. It is quicker than typing in a long URL, especially on a cell phone, and when the web page is changed the modification is available immediately to the users. Markered applications are the easiest way to develop AR, although some would argue that a code or tab that simply redirects a device to a traditional website is not true AR.

An advantage of traditional web pages is that it is easy to power browse from site to site using hyperlinks embedded in the web page. An ordinary piece of paper that includes a 2D bar code is called a smart or intelligent object because it can connect to digital information on the web (Pence 2011). Thus, 2D barcodes make objects in the real world clickable, somewhat like a web page. Finally, some companies have created proprietary apps that respond to the label on a record album or even a coffee cup to present a digital advertisement.

Several companies have created markerless phone apps that combine camera views with digital data, including Layar, Tagwhat, and Junaio. This allows location-related content, such as the location of nearby schools, museums, restaurants, transportation, and health care, to be layered on top of the live camera feed. Some smartphone programs, like Google Goggles, do an image search to identify an object or landmark and then add information to the camera image (Leckart 2011).

GEOLOCATION APPLICATIONS

Another approach to markerless AR is geolocation smartphone applications, such as Foursquare, Yelp, Loopt, and Checkin, which uses the GPS from a smartphone to search the local area for services; check in at clubs, bars, and restaurants; recommend locations; share photos; or locate friends who are nearby (Miller 2010). Those who frequently check in at a site may be named as the "mayor" of the location (until someone else checks in more often) or have access to special offers. Other location-based cell phone applications, like Wikitude, allow individual users to customize the viewer experience by adding URLs, phone numbers, or addresses to each point of interest, a process called geotagging (Wikitude 2010).

Thus far, geolocation applications are used by relatively few people. Only about 6 percent of the adults in the United States use geolocation apps, and this is up from 4 percent in 2010. Only 2 percent of U.S. adults use this type of application more than once a week (Heussner 2011). Despite this, these early adopters are relatively young and technologically sophisticated, making them more influential. Initially, male users predominated, but this is shifting, with the most recent figures showing that female users have increased from 22 percent in 2010 to 37 percent in 2011.

SITUATED NARRATIVE

Situated (or locative) narrative ties digital storytelling to some specific physical or geographic location. AR offers one way to accomplish this. For example, a location, such as the steps of the Lincoln Memorial in Washington, DC, can trigger a cell phone to access a video of Martin Luther King's famous "I Have a Dream" speech. The surroundings then act to enhance the experience of listening to the speech. The physical world around us becomes a platform for narratives delivered by AR applications based on the cell phone. Several institutions are already experimenting with situated narrative in combination with AR.

In a blog entitled "The End of Museums as We Know Them," Ori Inbar asks, "Where do kids prefer to be on a summer day, at a museum, a theme park, or staying home and playing video games?" (Inbar 2008). Then he suggests that all three of these experiences can be combined and gives seven examples of museums that are having considerable success doing this. His examples range from bringing the ancient city of Pompeii to life to providing historical background for a cemetery in Atlanta, Georgia. Inbar argues that learning can be more enjoyable when it is combined with a good story, regardless of whether the experience is indoors or outdoors.

More and more museums are exploring this educational tool. For example, The Museum of London has cooperated with The History Channel to create StreetMuseum, Londinium, an AR app for iPads and iPhones based on historical art and photographs that show the evolution of London since the Roman period (Lucas 2010). The apps even allow the user to "virtually excavate" sites to reveal coins or other artifacts as images on the screen. More recently, the Museum of London has created iPhone and iPad graphic-novel apps that use the writings of Charles Dickens for a narrated tour of the 19th century London slums.

It would be a mistake to assume that situated narratives are limited to institutions with extensive resources that are in locations rich in historical events, like London or Pompeii. The basic idea is broadly applicable. Every location has its own history, which can be shared with both local citizens and visitors. The beauty of AR is that it is accessible to institutions with relatively modest investments of time and resources.

HOW LIBRARIES CAN USE AR

Almost all libraries are currently facing financial exigencies, and most library staffs are already stretched to the limit. Any new initiative must be justified by comparing how much work and expense is required to the extra service the project will provide for the patrons. Each library will also have to consider how technologically aware their patrons are. Will there be enough usage to justify the investment? The need to reach new populations is also relevant. The young people who will hopefully become tomorrow's patrons are most likely to be users of the latest technology, so it is necessary to keep in mind the actions that will make them more aware of library services.

Probably the technology that promises the greatest benefit for the least effort is QR codes. The software needed to create and read QR codes is free, and QR codes can be used to enrich material that most libraries are already producing, like room schedules, supplemental materials, library guides, or book reviews. The blog Bibliothekia suggests that it will be possible to set up QR codes for different sections of a collection so that patrons could be informed any time a new book is added to that section. The same blog quotes Nate Hill, from the Brooklyn Public Library, who proposes that every book should have its own web page ("QR Codes and Libraries" 2008). Phillips Memorial Library at Providence College uses QR codes to provide directions, play tutorial videos, and access contact information (Pulliam and Landry 2010). In an article in *Library Journal*, Contra Costa County Library, California, reports that it is placing QR symbols in high-traffic areas to connect patrons with library services (Hadro 2010). The Read-WriteWeb blog suggests some other ways to use QR codes (Perez 2008).

The combination of situated narrative and true AR to create an information overlay for programs like Layar requires somewhat more time and effort, but the results can be valuable. This is an opportunity to make a library's archival material more accessible to the public. It can create a visual local history, whether it be of a campus, a city, or the local region. This not only enriches the experience of visitors and local patrons but also brings the library to the attention of potential patrons who might not otherwise be engaged.

The WolfWalk application created by the library at North Carolina State University (NCSU) is an excellent example of this approach. This smartphone app overlays historical images from the NCSU library archives at over 50 major sites of interest on the NCSU campus (Sierra 2011). According to the college website, both iPad and iPhone versions of WolfWalk are currently available. The Oregon State University Libraries have created a similar smartphone tour called BeaverTracks (Oregon State University Libraries 2010).

Geolocation software seems to be the least important application for most libraries, but there is still a need to be aware of this activity. Users who write reviews for sites like Foursquare are creating an online database that will be read by many potential patrons. It is important at least to be aware of these comments to understand how they may affect the patrons' attitudes.

NEAR-TERM CONSTRAINTS ON QR CODES AND AR

Expanded implementation of AR is constrained by the fact that many patrons do not yet have smartphones, which, in turn, is related to the high cost of data plans that service these devices and the lack of dependable connectivity in some areas. In addition, many websites are not yet optimized for mobile devices, and the many different types of phones and screen sizes in use make can optimization difficult. In the long run, this situation will correct itself as more people purchase these devices and use them to access the World Wide Web. It is important to note that AR is most often a supplement to existing services, so adding AR may not even be noticed by those who lack access to these new services. Because young people are most likely to own cell phones, this group is most likely to have access. Many libraries are eager to attract this next generation of library users.

Another limitation is that thus far many people who own smartphones do not know how QR codes work. Although many advertisements include QR codes, much of the public is not yet aware that a special app is required to read them. For example, a marketing company recently showed a picture of a QR code to over 500 students on 24 college campuses across the country and found that even though 81 percent of the students owned a smartphone, only 21 percent of this presumably tech-savvy group were able to scan a QR code (Aguirre 2011).

The solution to this problem would be to include a scanner with the smartphone purchase, but this is currently limited by the wide variety of codes and readers in use. There are several competing tag formats that require different readers. This lack of standardization also makes it more difficult to protect phones from viruses and other malware embedded in the tag or code. It is important to access only QR codes from reliable sources because hackers can use AR applications to attack your device just as they can use normal URLs, and security efforts are just beginning to respond to this new threat.

The other main problem is content. Few people desire to see more advertisements than they already encounter, and until the codes lead to more interesting content, it will be difficult to attract the public. When Benedict and Pence did a project using QR codes to access directions for using instruments in a chemistry lab and for adding videos to complement work sheets, they found the students to be extremely enthusiastic (Benedict and Pence 2012). An anonymous survey of the students involved showed that 77 percent of the students agreed or strongly agreed with the statement that "Having a video that could be accessed on a worksheet makes it easier to visualize problems in class," and 48 percent of the students strongly agreed or agreed with the statement, "I enjoyed using 2D barcodes to access online material for this class." This response was despite the fact that only a little over half of the students had smartphones, and the class was given a mere five minutes of training on creating and using barcodes. The difference here was that the content was more relevant to the users.

Brian Wassom (2011a) points out that most of the legal ramifications of AR have not yet been explored in the courts of this country. Wassom raises a number of potential legal problems, ranging from how the fair-use concept will apply when AR messages are superimposed on brand advertisements to the probably inevitable law suits that will result from those who claim that their injury resulted from their being distracted by the AR image on their cell phone. In a more recent post, Wassom (2011b) reports that four consumer advocacy groups have filed suit against an AR advertising campaign by Doritos claiming that it deceptively blurred the line between advertising and entertainment. Some commentators, such as Jamie Cascio in an article in *The Atlantic* (Cascio 2009), argue that in the long run AR applications will cause problems ranging from spam to loss of civil liberties.

THE FUTURE OF AR

Smartphones are increasingly being used for text, web browsing, games, and even watching television, but the relatively small size of most current smartphone screens is a disincentive to long-term viewing (Wortham 2010). Despite this, a 2010 survey indicates that there are over 20 million people who watch mobile video, and they spend an average of 3 hours and 37 minutes per month doing this ("What Consumers Watch" 2010). David Murray argues that the small screen is still very usable for routine reference library work (Murray 2008).

This suggests several possible future directions for AR. Tablet computers, such as the iPad, are becoming increasingly popular, and because most of the modern tablet computers include a camera and a GPS, they can be used for either markered or markerless AR. In the future, phones may be replaced with a pair of glasses that overlay an AR image onto any surface. There are already military applications of this technology, called heads-up displays (HUDs), being used for modern aircraft flight controls and even for combat soldiers (Jean 2010). Patti Maies from Massachusetts Institute of

Technology has demonstrated what she calls a Sixth Sense, which combines a personal projector, camera, and a phone and uses colored finger tabs to control the devices (Maies and Mistry 2009). The Sixth Sense devices cost about $350 with off-the-shelf components, so with economies of scale units like this should be affordable.

If HUDs or magic glasses become widely used, this will create a number of interesting possibilities. Soryn Voicu, an architecture student, has visualized this possibility in a video that he created as his thesis project at the Valle Giulia Faculty of Architecture in Italy (Voicu 2008). As Voicu imagines it, when a book is viewed through these special glasses, virtual tabs appear that allow the reader to manipulate the illustrations, run a movie, or even convert a floor plan into a 3D image. Beyond these "magic glasses," the next possible step is contact lenses that will provide the same functionality with optoelectronics that will display a data field overlaid upon the real-world images. This may not be as futuristic as one might expect. Parviz (2009) states that "a contact lens with simple built-in electronics is already within reach."

There are a number of interesting developments that are either already in use or else are close to commercial availability. Recently, a program called Aursma has become available that doesn't require the creation of a QR code in order to connect physical objects with web pages (Marks 2011). QR Voice is a program that converts a text message of 100 characters or less into a QR code that can be read aloud by a voice synthesizer program when the code is scanned (Dennis 2011). This will probably be even more useful when combined with a color 2D coding system, called Mobile Multi-Colour Composite, which is currently under development. It can store much more information than current 2D bar codes (Wilson 2009).

One potential competitor to AR is near-field communications (NFC). This technology creates two-way information sharing between smartphones and other devices when they are brought close to each other. For example, Google Wallet stores one's credit card information and allows payment at some stores by simply tapping your phone (Google 2011). According to a recent report, Microsoft has expanded its own tag technology to include both QR codes and NFC tags (Clark 2011).

As noted above, widespread public acceptance of AR will ultimately depend on access to content that the public finds to be useful or interesting. Situated narratives certainly represent one possible direction that may find public favor, but the most likely candidate is probably going to be an online AR game (Steen 2011).

In the longer term, AR is a first step towards the Internet of Things. More and more of the physical objects around us include sensors, which provide a continuing stream of data about the world, and smartphones will increasingly be able to tap into this data stream. This information could be supplied to people by way of AR overlays. Thus, a bus stop sign could indicate when the next bus is actually going to arrive based on a GPS on the bus; facial recognition software could offer informative reminders about people we meet; and a car could offer suggestions about the best way to avoid traffic problems on the way to a destination.

CONCLUSION

AR offers many advantages for libraries. QR applications can be developed for minimal investment of time and money, and they integrate mobile access into normal library operations. Location-based programs may require a somewhat greater commitment but can make the special collections and archives more visible for public access.

AR offers many new opportunities for innovation and meshes well with the current public interest in social networks. Geolocation is becoming a routine component of social network sites like Facebook. Perhaps the best way to summarize the potential impact of AR on libraries is through one librarian's comment: "When I shift my thinking about AR to the physical library space I see our whole collection opening up before our eyeballs. Imagine the ability to walk down an aisle and see the reviews and popularity of an entire shelf of title just by pointing the camera lens on your phone at the spines (or the outfacing covers)" (Schnell 2009).

NOTE

1. The distinction between feature phones and smartphones is not always clear, but, generally, a smartphone can run applications (apps) but a feature phone cannot.

REFERENCES

Aguirre, Don, Bart Johnston, and Libby Kohn. 2011. "QR Codes Go to College." Archrival: Youth Marketing. http://www.archrival.com/ideas/13/qr-codes-go-to-college.

"Android Surges among Handset Purchasers." 2010. *eMarketer: Digital Intelligence*, January 13. http://www.emarketer.com/Article.aspx?R=1007462.

Benedict, Lucille, and Harry E. Pence. 2012. "Teaching Chemistry Using Student-Created Videos and Photo Blogs Accessed with Smartphones and Two-Dimensional Barcodes." *Journal of Chemical Education* 89(4): 492–496.

Bimber, Oliver, and Ramesh Raskar. 2005. *Spatial Augmented Reality: Merging Real and Virtual Worlds*. Natick, MA: A. K. Peters.

Cascio, Jamais. 2009. "Filtering Reality." *The Atlantic Monthly*, November. http://www.theatlantic.com/magazine/archive/2009/11/filtering-reality/7713/.

Clark, Sarah. 2011. "Microsoft Adds NFC to Tag Platform." *Near Field Communications World*, December 13. http://www.nfcworld.com/2011/12/13/311911/microsoft-adds-nfc-to-tag-platform/.

Dennis, Tony. 2011. "QRvoice Converts Speech into QR Codes for Listening To." *GoMo News*. http://www.gomonews.com/qrvoice-converts-speech-into-qr-codes-for-listening-to/.

Google. 2011. "What Is Google Wallet?" http://www.google.com/wallet/what-is-google-wallet.html.

Hadro, Josh. 2010. "QR Codes to Extend Library's Reach in Contra Costa, CA." *Library Journal*, January 14. http://www.libraryjournal.com/lj/technologylibrary20/853479-295/qr_codes_to_extend_libraryaposs.html.csp.

Heussner, Ki Mae. 2011. "Why Geolocation App Users Matter to Marketers." *AdWeek*, December 6. http://www.adweek.com/news/advertising-branding/why-geolocation-app-users-matter-marketers-136950.

IDAutomation.com, Inc. 2009. "Free Data Matrix ECC200 Barcode Image Creator." http://www.bcgen.com/datamatrix-barcode-creator.html.

Inbar, Ori. 2008. "The End of Museums as We Know It." *Games Alfresco*, August 22. http://gamesalfresco.com/2008/08/22/the-end-of-museums-as-we-know-it/.

Jean, Grace V. 2010. "Taking 'Heads-Up' Displays to the Next Level." *National Defense*, March. http://www.nationaldefensemagazine.org/archive/2010/March/Pages/HeadsUpDisplays.aspx.

Johnson, Larry, A. Levine, R. Smith, and S. Stone. 2010. *The 2010 Horizon Report*. Austin, TX: The New Media Consortium. http://www.nmc.org/pdf/2010-Horizon-Report.pdf.

Keller, Josh. 2011. "As the Web Goes Mobile, Colleges Fail to Keep Up." *The Chronicle of Higher Education*, February 23, A1. http://chronicle.com/article/Colleges-Search-for -Their/126016/.

Leckart, Steven. 2011. "What Is That? Let Your Smartphone Have a Look." *New York Times*, August 31, B6.

Leggatt, Helen. 2011. "Pew: 25% Prefer Internet Access via Smartphone." *BizReport*, July 12. http://www.bizreport.com/2011/07/pew-25-prefer-internet-access-via-smartphone.html.

Lippincott, Joan K. 2006. "Linking the Information Commons to Learning." In *Learning Spaces*, edited by Diana G. Oblinger, Chapter 7. Boulder, CO: EduCause.

Lucas, Gavin. 2010. "StreetMuseum iPhone App." *Creative Review Blog*, May 24. http://www .creativereview.co.uk/cr-blog/2010/may/streetmuseum-app.

Maes, Pattie, and Pranav Mistry. 2009. "Pattie Maes and Pranav Mistry Demo SixthSense." *TED Talk*, February. http://www.ted.com/talks/pattie_maes_demos_the_sixth_sense.html.

Marks, Paul. 2011. "Aurasma App Is Augmented Reality, Augmented." *NewScientist*, May 20. http://www.newscientist.com/blogs/onepercent/2011/05/how-the-reverend-bayes-will-fi .html.

Microsoft. 2010. "Microsoft Tag Homepage." http://tag.microsoft.com/consumer/index.aspx.

Miller, Claire Cain. 2010. "Cell Phone in a New Role: Loyalty Card." *New York Times*, May 31, B1.

Murray, David C. 2008. "iReference: Using Apple's iPhone as a Reference Tool." *The Reference Librarian* 49(2): 167–170.

Oregon State University Libraries. 2010. "OSU History Goes Mobile." http://osulibrary .oregonstate.edu/beavertracks.

Parviz, Babak A. 2009. "Augmented Reality in a Contact Lens." *IEEE Spectrum: Inside Technology*, September. http://spectrum.ieee.org/biomedical/bionics/augmented-reality-in-a -contact-lens/0.

Pausch, Randy, Dennis Proffitt, and George Williams. 1997. "Quantifying Immersion in Virtual Reality." http://www.cs.cmu.edu/~stage3/publications/97/conferences/siggraph/ immersion/.

Pence, Harry E. 2011. "Smartphones, Smart Objects, and Augmented Reality." *The Reference Librarian* 52(1–2): 136–145.

Perez, Sarah. 2008. "The Scannable World, Part 3: Barcode Scanning in the Real World." *ReadWriteWeb*, September 25. http://www.readwriteweb.com/archives/the_scannable_world _barcodes_scanning_in_the_real_world.php.

Pulliam, Beatrice, and Chris Landry. 2010. "QR in the Library." [LibGuide] Phillips Memorial Library, Providence College. http://providence.libguides.com/content.php? pid=76255&sid=565728.

"QR Codes and Libraries." 2008. *Bibliothekia Blog*, September 28. http://bibliothekia.blogspot .com/2008/09/qr-codes-and-libraries.html.

Schnell, Eric. 2009. "TechTips: Augmented Reality." *The Ohio State University Libraries Blog*, September 21. http://library.osu.edu/blogs/techtips/2009/09/21/techtips-augmented -reality/.

Sierra, Tito. 2011. "WolfWalk." NCSU Libraries. http://www.lib.ncsu.edu/dli/projects/wolfwalk.

Steen, Greg. 2011. "Why Location-Based Gaming Is the Next Killer App." *Mashable*, July 24. http://mashable.com/2011/07/24/location-based-gaming/.

Tolliver-Nigro, Heidi. 2009. "Making the Most of Quick Response Codes." *Seybold Report: Analyzing Publishing Technologies* 9(21): 2–8.

Voicu, Soryn. 2008. "Augmented Reality—The Future of Education." http://vimeo.com/2341387.

Wassom, Brian D. 2011a. "The Coming Conundra: Real Laws in an Augmented Reality." *The Wassom.com Blog*, March 22. http://www.wassom.com/the-coming-conundra-real-laws -in-an-augmented-reality.html.

Wassom, Brian D. 2011b. "Beyond Doritos: How Else Might AR Be Called 'Deceptive'?" *The Wassom.com Blog*, November 15. http://www.wassom.com/beyond-doritos-how-else -might-ar-be-called-deceptive.html.

"What Consumers Watch: Nielsen's Q1 2010 Three Screen Report." 2010. *NielsenWire*, June 11. http://blog.nielsen.com/nielsenwire/online_mobile/what-consumers-watch-nielsens-q1-2010 -three-screen-report/.

Wikitude. 2010. "Home Page." http://wikitude.me/.

Wilson, March. 2009. "Barcodes Can Now Hold Entire Videos and Games." *Gizmodo*, March 16. http://gizmodo.com/5170695/barcodes-can-now-hold-entire-videos-and-games.

Wortham, Jenna. 2010. "Everyone's Using Cellphones, But Not So Many Are Talking." *New York Times*, May 14, B1.

14

Mobile Technologies and Archives: Using the New to Preserve the Old

April Karlene Anderson

Key Points

- Initially, many library services incorporating mobile technologies were developed reactively.
- Librarians are now in a position to be proactive about their use of mobile technologies to advance services and streamline professional work.
- Most early studies of mobile technology use in libraries have focused on users.
- This article describes how archives faculty and staff used iPads to improve and accelerate the process of taking inventory.
- Using the iPad in the stacks to take inventory reduced the time needed almost by half, compared to using pencil and paper and then transcribing the inventory into a computer.
- This pilot project utilized the mobility and usability of the iPad with great success to complete the inventory project in a timely manner.
- The potential applications of mobile technologies in archives are many.

Whether you have a smartphone, flip phone, or no phone, there's no getting around it—mobile technologies are here to stay. Laptops at one time may have seemed like the ultimate leap forward in mobile computer technology. These days, computer users demand on-the-go information that does not require booting up a computer or looking for an Ethernet port. Smartphones, iPads, Nooks, and Kindles are sci-fi visions, dreamed up by writers and watched on TV by our younger selves, one day wondering if we were ever going to own a flying car. While the flying car isn't yet on the market, mobile technologies are, and they are changing the way we live both personally and professionally. This chapter briefly looks at the use of mobile technologies in libraries at an administrative level and how they can be effective tools for information management. I will also look at the use of mobile technologies in my own archival setting to see if traditional methods of information management stand up to the newcomer, the mobile device.

MOBILE TECHNOLOGIES IN THE LIBRARIES:
PATRONS VERSUS STAFF

Library services supporting mobile technologies have developed reactively rather than proactively. And that's not to say that libraries weren't prepared—mobile technology has grown and morphed at such a rapid pace that librarians were experiencing new devices just like any other consumer. It's when the librarian goes to use the device as a consumer in her or his professional life that the idea for creating or improving upon a particular type of mobile technology service is hit upon. Now that librarians have been exposed to this fast-paced movement for a few years, they can be more proactive rather than reactive in preparing services for the next generation of mobile technology devices. However, the librarian is still a consumer of these technologies and is looking for ways to not only improve the patron experience but his or her own professional experiences in the workplace.

In his chapter from *Museum Informatics: People, Information and Technology in Museums*, Paul F. Marty explains that as technologies improve and become more accessible, institutions are looking at every option for utilizing these services:

While museums have for centuries employed paper-based information systems for managing their collections data, the recent availability of stand-alone and networked computer systems has encouraged even the smallest and poorest museums to purchase computerized collections management systems. Even museum professionals who do not wish or cannot afford to purchase "off-the-shelf" systems (which can range from a few hundred to tens of thousands of dollars) can develop "home-grown" collections management systems fairly easily using spreadsheet applications like Microsoft Excel or database applications like Microsoft Access or Filemaker Pro. (Marty 2008, 79)

In his book *Managing Archival and Manuscript Repositories*, Michael J. Kurtz echoes Marty's statement: "Most archives are not on the cutting edge of the technology continuum. Rather, most have to use existing technologies and applications" (Kurtz 2004, 109). Kurtz takes the idea of using technology a step further by explaining the need of technology in an archival setting:

Managers need access to data for day-to-day operations to be able to schedule work, track hours worked, and quantify units of work completed. Whether in the public or private sector, archival managers must justify the effectiveness and efficiency of their programs, and automated management systems have increasingly become a requirement of doing business (Kurtz 2004, 102).

However, Kurtz's statement on immediate access to materials is the most telling of a modern-day archives problem: "customers expect to have immediate or nearly immediate access to the archives services and holding by means of Web technology" (Kurtz 2004, 102). Kurtz explains that it is archival managers' job to merge their archival skills with their collection records and information technology in order to provide better service.

As mobile technology has advanced, so have the types of services libraries offer to meet patron needs. And with these new mobile services have come surveys, analyses, and reports on how these services are working. Most published papers and reports focus primarily on users—do they use the services offered? Do they demand variations of the service or different services altogether? For example, the California Digital Library (CDL) completed a study in the summer of 2010 that suggested that while the libraries in their study were proactive in providing mobile services, only a small number of library patrons were using them. The CDL discovered that patrons preferred laptops and desktops over other mobile devices. Users commented that the services offered were hard to use on small smartphone screens (Hu and Meier 2011). Because this study was conducted in 2010, tablet devices had only started moving into consumer circles, so the "small screen" observations make a bit of sense. Now that tablets are in heavier use, it would be interesting to see what patrons at those CDL libraries say about the provided mobile technologies.

Little has been written about the use of mobile technologies by library staff for administrative duties, perhaps due to the furious rate at which mobile technologies evolve in a small period of time. Some library directors may be apprehensive about or economically unable to adopt the use of mobile technologies in their buildings. Debra A. Riley-Huff and Julia M. Rholes (2011) conducted a survey of librarians with technological skills and demonstrated that library school programs still lack advanced technology classes to meet current demands. Even with the rise of the iSchool movement, Riley-Huff and Rholes assert that library programs have stuck to teaching core courses, offer a limited number of technology-based classes, and do not require enough technology courses for graduation. While the type and number of technology courses vary from program to program, Riley-Huff and Rholes show that there is a lack of technological education in new librarians, and they rely on the workshops, classes, and courses offered or paid for by the library for which they work. Riley-Huff and Rholes's survey showed that 89 percent of libraries in their survey set aside money in their budgets for educational endeavors they know they need in order to have correctly trained personnel (Riley-Huff and Rholes 2011).

Kurtz (2004) takes a different perspective and suggests that implementation of new technological systems is made difficult by staff resistance:

In many ways, the most difficult challenge for the archival manager comes with the introduction of a product or service involving information technology. Issues involving resistance to change and training needs come to the fore during the implementation phase. Resistance occurs for a variety of reasons. Some staff can feel unfamiliar or threatened by the introduction of a new system. For others, particularly in management, information technology can be perceived as a threat to status or power (Kurtz 2004, 111).

What does this mean for mobile technology use in a library in an administrative capacity? If librarians aren't being trained and patrons aren't utilizing services, what is the point of supporting mobile technologies for administrative work? As with all studies, it helps to have a real-world scenario. In our case, we were using technology to build something out of nothing.

THE ARCHIVES DILEMMA

I came to Illinois State University (ISU) in April 2011 as the new university archivist. At the time, the materials I was charged to organize and make accessible had little intellectual control and no online presence. My number-one priority was to get the materials inventoried as quickly and efficiently as possible. Once I could identify the number of collections we had and the amount of linear feet they occupied, I could establish a workflow that would allow for efficient processing of materials and the creation of encoded finding aids for online use. I emphasize "efficient" because I knew that no matter how ambitious I planned to be, my library and campus duties were going to keep me away from steadily working at an inventory. Three months later I was able to bring in an archives assistant who I trained to process collections and write encoded archival description (EAD) finding aids. We also acquired several interns for the start of the fall 2011 semester who processed collections for school projects. My prediction of being too busy to steadily work at an inventory had come true—our plates were extremely full. I needed to come up with a way to perform the inventory in an efficient manner so that the time we could devote to the inventory would be as productive as possible.

At the beginning of the inventory process, I estimated we had between 8,000 and 10,000 linear feet of material. This was split up among eight shelving units with 68 ranges each, several map drawers, an art rack, and a cold room. The inventory we were creating was not from scratch. We did have a previous inventory that represented most of these storage areas, but it was extremely limited in the information it provided. It was created in Excel, and it indicated where various collections were located on certain ranges, but the accuracy was in question. The materials were given a type of overview listing where only the title of the collection (or the record group it belonged to) should be. For an example, see Figure 14.1.

Not only was I new to the university, I was new to the region and the state. As a new employee of the university, as well as the state of Illinois, I knew little about most of the collections, and I had to do some initial research to understand what may be contained in them. Following this preliminary inventory, I had no idea how many boxes each collection contained, the linear feet they encompassed, and so on.

Adding to the difficulty, many of the boxes on the shelves were not labeled. The Archives stacks area is situated on one side of a larger warehouse that is shared with Central Receiving. The shelving units in which the materials sit are old bookshelves from a local library. The shelves are narrow and not very deep. Many of the boxes are old, half-foot Hollinger-style boxes or old office storage boxes turned on their sides. Shifting and sorting through the boxes, trying to figure out what was in the unlabeled containers, was challenging.

Clearly our new inventory needed more information than what was originally gathered. I decided that we needed to make the following adjustments:

- Changes to the locations labels. Instead of "R" for Range, I renamed this to "Unit." The label "Sec" became "Range," and "Sh" remained "Shelf." Office information was removed and now indicated in the acquisition spreadsheet.
- Titles of collections were fleshed out where needed. Acronyms and personal names were spelled out, official titles were given where appropriate (President, Provost, etc.), and collections with multiple titles were split up.
- A column was added after "Dates" labeled "Linear Feet" where the approximate linear feet of each collection was calculated. Another column called "Boxes" was added to indicate what kind of boxes were used (size 0.5 boxes, 1 linear foot boxes, newspaper boxes, etc.) and how many of each.
- Any and all pertinent information not included in the line item was added to the "Notes" column. We found that we often needed an extra space to record additional information.

R	Sec	Sh	Office	Title	Dates	Size
	10	1		Accreditation AATC	1942	
				Accreditation North Central	1972, 1977, 1982	
		2		Accreditation North Central	1977, 1983, 1985	
		3		Accreditation North Central	1995	
		4		Accreditation North Central	1995	
		5		Accreditation North Central	2004	
		6		Accreditation North Central	2004	
	11	1				
		2				
		3				
		4				
		5		Hovey		
		6		Hewitt		
	12	1				
		2		Edwards		
		3		Edwards		
		4		Edwards		
		5		Edwards		
		6		Edwards		

Figure 14.1

Example of the original inventory fields.

I wanted to expand the original inventory not only to provide a map to the location of materials but also to make it keyword searchable. I was still learning about the university and needed to be sure I could find materials in every way possible, even if I didn't know what those materials were about. I also have found that patrons can reference one item in a variety of ways. Having as much information listed as possible makes it easier for us to search the inventory to find what the patron is looking for.

Some might ask why we did not immediately go to an archives database system, particularly one of the open-source systems on the Internet. I felt at the time that we needed to quickly get a handle on our information and to use every person possible to complete this task. As with all systems, training is involved. Most of my outside help would be coming from students, and I was confident they would be able to use Excel without needing extensive training. I also needed time to investigate the various databases available to see which one would be the best match for our materials and our needs. Creating an Excel spreadsheet would be the most time- and cost-effective option. Once the information had been gathered, I could manipulate that spreadsheet in a variety of ways to injectit into a database at a later date.

Inventory issues aside, the Archives also had some physical and technological limitations. For starters, we are not located on campus. Several years ago, the university took advantage of an opportunity to buy a warehouse that had been used by a local printing company. The warehouse was converted into a one-stop delivery location for all university mail and packages. Part of the warehouse was also given to the university library, which was in need of space for its fast-growing collections. The area that housed the Archives on campus was in terrible shape; the staff had problems with a buckling floor and leaks in the ceiling. Given that the building they occupied would not be repaired anytime soon, the library decided to move the Archives out to the warehouse.

Though we share space with Central Receiving, our stacks are securely locked in their own section of the warehouse. Because our offices are located at the front of the building, we have to walk through Central Receiving to get to the stacks at the back of the building. The stacks area is completely cut off from the rest of the building and does not have a phone line or Internet terminal. In short, our stacks area is like a dead zone with little to no communication capabilities except for a set of walkie-talkies we use. The building itself was built in the early 1980s and is completely made of metal. This causes a number of problems for cell phone users who not only can't place calls but also have difficulty connecting to a 3G or 4G network. The warehouse also is not equipped with any wireless routers. Patrons wanting to connect to the Internet must bring their own hotspot or use the one hardwired computer in our Reading Room. Though we need to be mobile because of the physical locations of our offices and stacks area, our actual mobility is extremely limited. We are technologically tied to the desktop and can't move about our space as freely as our staff counterparts in the main library building. This would hinder us in finding mobile solutions to our inventory problem.

For the first few months of my new job, it was just me. I spent my afternoons with the inventory, writing notes and entering them into my computer. I made it through only 500 linear feet by the end of June. My plans to have the inventory completed during the fall term quickly vanished. It wasn't until the library offered to check out iPads to faculty and staff did I have an idea: Why not try the iPad to take the inventory? The iPad would give me the ability to stay mobile while I picked through cumbersome boxes. Though we would not have wireless access with the iPad in the warehouse, I could still take the iPad to the stacks, record the inventory, bring it back to my desktop, and upload the information. Laptops were also an option we tested, but they proved to be clunky and hard to maneuver while I was sorting boxes and taking notes. During that trial run, I set my laptop on top of a book cart while I sorted through boxes. There were several occasions that my new library-issued laptop almost met its fate with the concrete floor. The iPad was light, small, and easy to place on the shelf—no book cart required.

There is some agreement in the computer world about the physical superiority of the iPad over laptops in these types of situations. In his winter 2011 article, Jamal Cromity points out that "Unlike stationary touchscreens, such as the HP TouchSmart, the iPad can lie flat. This makes it less awkward when typing more than two words" (Cromity 2011, 27). Cromity also comments on how iPads do not produce heat and they far outlast the physical wear a laptop usually gets when being moved around.

Because the iPads did not come with any Microsoft Office products, I installed a $10 spreadsheet program from the Apple App Store called Numbers. The program had similar characteristics to Excel and offered an export function. By this time, my new archives assistant had started, so I traded her paper and pencil for the iPad and sent her to the stacks. I asked her to keep track of her average inventory time for each method. With a handwritten inventory, the user must duplicate her or his work by reentering the handwritten information into a computer. It had not occurred to me that using

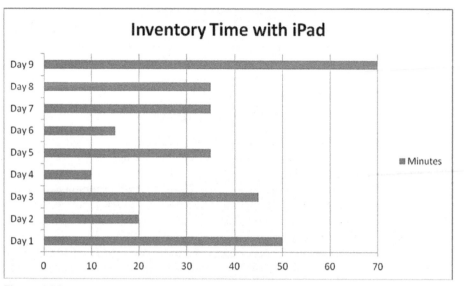

Figure 14.2
714 linear feet; total: 5 hours and 25 minutes.

the iPad would eliminate this step, and thus we found our time spent recording an inventory cut in half:

To take the inventory with pencil and paper took almost 10 hours versus the 5-1/2 she spent using the iPad. She was able to enter her information directly into the spreadsheet rather than transcribing her information later. Our time spent on inventory was sharply reduced during the fall term, and two-thirds of the inventory was completed by December.

I did run into some technical glitches with using the iPad in the inventory process. The simplest yet most frustrating of problems was that I was only allowed to check out one iPad, which meant we had to share. When we both had time or when we had in a volunteer, only one person could use the iPad. That meant the other person had to revert to using pencil and paper, resulting in more time spent reentering information from the written notes. Given our time commitments on other projects that term, this was not a common problem. The software proved to be a trickier issue.

As I mentioned earlier, the iPads were not loaded with any Microsoft Office products and thus no Excel software. I had to find software through the Apple App Store that would allow me to convert from an Apple app to Excel. I explored several different options until I settled on Numbers. Due to time constraints, I relied on an occasional volunteer during the fall term to work on the inventory. The volunteer, an undergraduate education major, found the program to be difficult at first. I believe that it was her inexperience with using a tablet device that gave her trouble. Though she was extremely familiar with Excel, the concept of using finger swipes in place of a mouse caused her some problems. But once she became comfortable with using the iPad and the Numbers app, she settled into the project nicely.

For me, it was getting the information converted into Excel that proved difficult. Even though the information was being entered into one Numbers spreadsheet, the app converted the information into several Excel spreadsheets within one workbook during the export process. Rather than fighting the file Numbers created and forcing Excel to read it, I copied the information from Numbers into a new Excel spreadsheet and formatted from there. Formatting the first couple of completed unit inventories was tricky and took more time than I had anticipated. Once I established a workflow, the transfer process became quick and routine.

AFTER THE INVENTORY—WHAT NEXT?

Our situation shows that with some ingenuity and available resources we could make mobile technologies work in a less-than-perfect situation. And now that we've used this technology, we want to expand upon its capabilities and apply it to other administrative situations. However, we weren't the only ones to come up with a solution to a library inventory problem using a mobile device. At the Bergen County Cooperative Library System (BCCLS) in New Jersey, Guy Dobson created a web-based weeding system using the BCCLS's database. Dobson used the system application program interface (API) to create a web-based program called Paperless Online Weeding (POW) that would pull little-used items from the library's database into an inventory list. The API enabled staff members using a tablet or a smartphone to access POW on the web and begin the weeding task. They could see the checkout history of an item and make an on-the-spot decision. The downside to this solution is that the BCCLS will be moving to another system in 2012, and should they want to continue using POW, new code will need to be written (Rapp 2011).

From a public services perspective, Cromity (2011) suggests another use:

In academic settings, be aware that mobility can potentially equate visibility. In times where academic libraries are reporting fewer reference interactions, tools such as tablet computers can easily be carried around to engage users and help increase the library's visibility, sparking usage while illustrating the librarians' valuable services. (Cromity 2011, 26)

Certainly we had some software and hardware problems in using the iPad for our inventory process. But, with some creative solutions, we made it work for our needs. Cromity (2011) points out that while mobile devices are great tools, they are limited by their Internet accessibility—something we experienced. Though we couldn't use the iPad for its wireless potential, we utilized its mobility with great success. The ease of data entry and comfort of use on the iPad was better for us as users versus pencil and paper or even a laptop. There is so much potential for this technology in the archives field, and showing its capabilities with the simple task of taking inventory is only the start. I already have other uses planned for the iPad in the Archives, including the following:

- Instant updating: Use the iPad to update collection storage locations, collection processing, and other accession-related information by accessing a web-based archives database. Once we are able to put a wireless router in the Archives, we will be able to edit an archives database via the iPad's web browser and have information update in real time for the patron. This will give us the ability to walk through our stacks and instantly update our holdings.
- Tracking materials: The iPad2's camera could be used in a scanning capacity for QR codes or some similar barcode method. In a traditional barcoding system, one would use a wand to scan boxes and books to track their use and movement. Scanning a barcode would be a one-button

solution for updating an inventory or archives database rather than taking the time to manually enter each book or box.

- Patron use: As Cromity (2011) suggests above, we could be mobile within our offices and the Reading Room and assist patrons in finding relevant collections with the iPad rather than with a traditional wired desktop machine. This would allow us to interact and engage with our patrons rather than sitting them down and leaving them to search a database on their own. Also, instead of a laptop, patrons could use the iPad for research use. This option saves space in the Reading Room. When the iPad was not in use, staff could use it for other projects.
- Processing: We currently use Notetab to create our EADs in-house on dedicated computers. Our desks are not big enough to allow processing near a computer. An archivist could easily move the iPad where needed (even to the stacks when a collection is too large to take all the boxes at once) to both do research and create a finding aid. So, rather than moving the boxes to the archivist, the archivist can move with the boxes.

I agree with Cromity (2011) when he writes that even though the pros outweigh the cons in utilizing an iPad for administrative use, the iPad will not replace the laptop or desktop computer. The iPad is a fantastic mobile tool that should be integrated into the workflow of any library or library department. Its ease of use, physical capabilities, and ability to save time have been huge benefits for the ISU Archives. Though slightly skeptical at first, I am amazed at how mobile technology has helped me in preserving its paper-based predecessors. Hopefully, library school programs will offer additional technology classes and give greater focus to the expanding world of mobile technologies.

REFERENCES

Cromity, Jamal. 2011. "Tablet Computers: Enterprise Solutions for Information Professionals." *Online* 35(1): 25–28.

Hu, Rachel, and Alison Meier. 2011. "Planning for a Mobile Future: A User Research Case Study from the California Digital Library." *Serials: The Journal for the Serials Community* 24(3): S17–S25. http://uksg.metapress.com/content/41w6145986193813/.

Kurtz, Michael J. 2004. *Managing Archival and Manuscript Repositories*. Chicago: Society of American Archivists.

Marty, Paul F. 2008. "Information Organization and Access." In *Museum Informatics: People, Information and Technology in Museums*, edited by Paul F. Marty and Katherine Burton Jones, 79–83. New York: Taylor and Francis.

Rapp, David. 2011. "Innovation Goes POW." *Library Journal* 136(12): 19–20. http://www.libraryjournal.com/lj/communityacademiclibraries/890914-265/innovation_goes_pow.html.csp.

Riley-Huff, Debra A., and Julia M. Rholes. 2011. "Librarians and Technology Skill Acquisition: Issues and Perspectives." *Information Technology and Libraries* 30(3): 129–140.

Part 4

Mobile Reference

15

SMS-Based Reference

Rene J. Erlandson

Key Points

- Is SMS reference right for your library?
- How do you implement SMS reference in the library?
- Who is your audience and what are your goals?
- Who should be involved?
- What service models exist?
- What are software and service options?
- What are best practices?
- How do you market and promote the service?
- How do you assess the service?

Between 2009 and mid-2011, the number of mobile subscribers globally increased from 4.6 billion to 5.9 billion (ITU 2009, 2011). As the number of mobile-device users continues to increase at an unprecedented rate, the number of libraries offering reference assistance via short-message service (SMS) is also growing. With 6.1 trillion text messages sent in 2010 (ITU 2010), even librarians and administrators who may not send many text messages themselves understand the potential SMS has to reimagine reference service at their institutions. SMS allows cell phones and other mobile devices to send and receive text messages of up to 160 characters per message. The technology also allows transmission of 160-character messages between cellular devices and email accounts. Until now, telephone reference was the most portable form of reference assistance, with email and IM (instant message or chat) requiring a computer and associated connectivity limitations. However, SMS reference assistance moves beyond the limitations of telephone, email, and IM reference to connect users with information and resources through the same device from which the queries originate, wherever a user happens to be at a given moment.

For example, SMS reference makes it possible for someone receiving a diagnosis from a doctor to text a librarian for contact information of local support groups and schedule a consultation with a counselor or advocate before leaving the doctor's office. A student can text a librarian from the book stacks to ask about other materials on a specific topic and download articles and e-books directly onto his or her device.

As early as 2001, libraries experimented with SMS for delivery of services. Helsinki University Library in Finland devised an SMS mechanism by which users sent general queries to librarians and the library sent SMS circulation reminders, renewal notices, and tables of contents to users (Pasanen and Muhonen 2002). By 2004, librarians at Curtin University Library in Australia piloted SMS reference assistance to the university community (Giles and Grey-Smith 2005). In the United States, Southeastern Louisiana University offered SMS reference service in early 2005 (Stahr 2010, 9). These pioneers, along with other early adopters like the College of Charleston (2007), New York University (2008), East Carolina University (2008), and Cornell University (2009), laid the groundwork for local SMS reference and collaborative initiatives throughout the United States.

This chapter outlines how to implement SMS reference locally. Questions such as whether SMS is right for your library, who should be involved in the implementation process, what the library's local service goals are, what service models might be used, and what software and service options are available are addressed. In addition, best practices and tips for promoting and marketing the service are highlighted as well as a definition of success as a method of assessment.

IS SMS RIGHT FOR YOUR LIBRARY?

Much like the early days of email and IM reference (which are now core methods of delivery for reference assistance), the value, necessity, viability, and sustainability of SMS reference is frequently questioned when libraries begin to explore implementing such an initiative. There is no one-size-fits-all answer. Libraries must assess community support and sustainability of SMS reference service locally. The proliferation of unlimited-text-message plans and their adoption within U.S. communities are indicators people are comfortable using SMS messaging. However, whether or not people are interested in communicating with librarians through text messaging is a question that must be answered locally before an SMS reference program is initiated. Survey users and community members to find out if they are open to communicating with librarians via text message, informally observe texting habits in your community, and analyze reference service data to identify trends in telephone, email, and IM reference use over time. Each of these tools will assist in determining whether SMS reference is a good investment of library resources.

While this may seem obvious, it is important to remember SMS reference should benefit users and the community. Developing an SMS reference service simply because other libraries are doing it should not be the driving force behind the undertaking. Like any other initiative, implementing SMS reference assistance takes planning, resources, and commitment to be successful. There are no benchmarks for how long it will take SMS reference service to catch on within a community. However, if the service fills a need it is much more likely to be successful for the simple reason that people who use it will like it and talk about it. Often the best form of publicity for any service is word of mouth. Therefore it is important to identify a need for, or support of, the service before implementing such a program.

IMPLEMENTATION

If local interest in SMS reference supports implementation, it is important to plan for success. No one can predict how quickly a new initiative will be embraced. However, sure ways to fail are lack of planning and low expectations. Therefore, plan and antici-pate success.

Audience and Goals

Begin by considering audience and goals. Identify user groups who may utilize the service. In an academic community, user groups may be categorized as students, fac-ulty, staff, and alumni or be refined further by rank, major, discipline, department, and college within the broader categories. In public libraries user groups may be defined by demographics or some other local scale, such as teenagers, reader-advisory partici-pants, multilingual community members, child-reading-hour attendees, and so forth. It is also important to be aware of mobile-use and text-messaging habits of specific sub-sets of the population. Nationally, African Americans and English-speaking Latinos are more likely to own a cell phone and to send and receive text messages regularly than their white counterparts. While nine in ten 18- to 29-year-olds own a cell phone, 95 percent of those young cell phone owners regularly send and receive text messages (Smith 2010, 4–5). Identifying potential users early in the process will assist in devel-oping and promoting the service over time.

Next, define goals for the program. What does the library hope to achieve with SMS reference? How will the service benefit users? What are the benefits to the library? What types of questions will the service respond to? While one might assume the types of questions sent via SMS will be ready reference and/or directional, librarians who staff SMS reference services report a wide degree of variation in the types of questions received. During 2008 and 2009, New York University (NYU) reported 60 percent of the questions received via SMS were directional with very few ready reference ques-tions, which left a little less than 40 percent of incoming questions being standard refer-ence questions (Pearce, Collard, and Whatley 2010, 259–260). Southeastern Louisiana University (SLU) reported 86 percent of SMS questions received between 2006 and 2010 were reference questions (Stahr 2010, 14). Meanwhile, Bruce Jensen, a member of the service team of the My Info Quest (MIQ) SMS collaborative reference service, noted that most questions received through MIQ focused on a single fact or issue and were much less complex than queries submitted through non-SMS reference venues (Jensen 2011, 269). The variation in these reports may be due in part to differences in user base between academic communities like NYU and SLU and the predominately public-library-focused MIQ. Therefore, it is important to consider targeted user groups and the types of questions received through other local reference methods, like IM, to anticipate the depth and complexity of questions that may be submitted to SMS refer-ence staff.

Defining user groups and goals for the service early on provides the foundation to focus development and keep the project on track over time. However, remember that flexibility is vital to sustaining any technology-based initiative. As the makeup and needs of the community change, user groups and goals may change. For example, as children who have used mobile technology since preschool join student bodies on college campuses, there may be a need to devote more library resources to mobile technologies, including SMS reference. Do not create goals and identify user groups at the beginning of the process and file them in a drawer (or on a server). Revisit and adjust stated goals and defined user groups as experience dictates or circumstances change—this is critical to the long-term success of the initiative.

WHO SHOULD BE INVOLVED?

When launching any new initiative, the more support garnered early on, the more likely the service will be successful. It is important to have administration involved in the project from the beginning. Even in the pilot phases, SMS reference should be viewed as a long-term commitment, which means budget allocations for equipment, software, staffing, training, and marketing for the service must be projected on an annual basis.

Everyone on the reference staff and the information technology staff should be included in, or kept up to date on, the development, implementation, and assessment of the service. These individuals will be instrumental when testing, evaluating, implementing, and sustaining the service. In addition, because access services staff members are often the front line for fielding questions about facilities and services in the library, it is important they are kept in the loop when developing a SMS reference service. Once implementation begins, individuals staffing all library service points will need to understand how SMS reference works, who may use it, who staffs it, and who administers it in order to answer questions that may arise.

Because e-resources are heavily used in any virtual reference service, it is important to ensure that SMS reference staff members know about newly purchased works. In addition, when electronic resources are under review for purchase, the availability of a mobile interface for the resource should be considered when purchase decisions are made, as this feature is especially critical for SMS reference users. Therefore, if SMS reference staff are not part of the purchase process and administration of e-resources, communication avenues need to be established between technical services and SMS staff to facilitate exchange of information.

Other individuals to include in the SMS reference-service planning process include members of library friends groups, advisory boards, and the library foundation team. While these individuals do not need to be included on the actual planning and implementation team, they may be useful in finding monetary support for the initiative, and they definitely will be useful in promoting the launch of the new service. Including as many people as possible in the early stages of development helps build support for the service and obtain diverse perspectives on service models and platform options.

SERVICE MODELS

There are two common service models for SMS reference: dedicated smartphone and SMS-to-email. SMS reference via a dedicated smartphone provides users with a specific local phone number for the service, which they can store in their mobile devices for easy access. The dedicated-smartphone model allows librarians to take the phone with them wherever they go and respond to queries as they come in, making the service synchronous. Some drawbacks to this service model are problems transferring the phone from librarian to librarian when shifts change, lack of easy access to supporting tools like URL shorteners, cheat-sheets and similar resources, and nonintegration of SMS reference into email, IM, and walk-up reference service workflows. The dedicated-cell-phone service model was popular in the early days of SMS reference, but many libraries found the need to keep separate reference schedules for SMS reference, the dependence on ever-changing mobile-carrier pricing structures, and the lack of integration into established workflows problematic.

The SMS-to-email service model is used widely among libraries that currently offer SMS reference. In this model, users submit text messages to either a dedicated local phone number or short code, after which the message is routed to a web-based email service, where librarians craft and send responses from a computer or web-enabled mobile device via email that is translated into a SMS response sent to users. The ability to respond to SMS queries along with incoming email and IM queries in one platform or location allows SMS reference to be easily incorporated into other virtual reference service workflows.

SMS Reference Service Models
- Dedicated cell/smartphone
- SMS-to-email

Software and Service Options

Platform options vary depending on the service model selected. If the desired service model is a dedicated cell phone, the service can be accomplished using any web-enabled smartphone from a number of mobile carriers in the United States. Contact local carriers for packages and costs. In addition, one of the SMS-to-email platform options outlined below, Altarama, also offers cell/smartphone response.

Altarama, an Australian company, was the first vendor to offer an SMS platform to libraries for reference service, SMSReference. Users send text messages to a local dedicated phone number set up by Altarama. Librarians reply using email, a webapp, smartphone, or cell phone. This is the only company that provides libraries the option of answering reference queries via cell phone or email. Regardless of the method librarians use to respond to the query, responses are sent via SMS to users. One of the advantages of this service is the dedicated phone number users can store in their mobile devices for easy access to the service. Altarama provides a number of standard and custom reports for assessment. Libraries also have the option of hosting SMSReference locally or subscribing to a hosted version of the service that includes the features noted here. Contact Altarama for pricing: http://www.altarama.com/Products/SMSreference.

Mosio created Text-A-Librarian specifically for libraries. The hosted platform combines email, IM, and SMS into one dashboard where librarians see incoming messages and respond to queries from every medium. A user send texts to Mosio's short code—66746—and then enters the library's keyword and the question. Inquiries are routed to the web dashboard where library staff craft responses sent to users via SMS. The dashboard is browser-based and can be logged into at any time to view new messages, or the system can send message alerts to librarians via email or IM. Pricing starts at $65/month for 350 outbound texts per month or billed annually beginning at $780/year for 350 outbound texts per month. Consortia and collaborative projects may obtain discounted pricing for annual access to Text-A-Librarian. In addition, subscribers of both Text-A-Librarian and OCLC QuestionPoint are now able to incorporate incoming SMS reference questions into the collaborative QuestionPoint email and IM queues and obtain 24/7 SMS reference along with email and IM reference; see http://www.textalibrarian.com/.

Springshare, vendor of the widely used LibGuides content-management system, added an SMS module to the LibAnswers platform in 2010. LibAnswers incorporates questions from email, IM, Twitter, and SMS into one platform and allows librarians to collaborate on answering incoming queries in a web environment. The hosted platform assigns a local phone number for each library and provides access to a number of standard and custom reports. The SMS module is part of the broader LibAnswers platform, with subscription prices varying based on type and size of library. After subscribing to LibAnswers there is a one-time setup fee of $149 for the SMS module and additional charges starting at $30/month for up to 600 messages per month; visit http://springshare.com/libanswers/.

Canada-based Upside Wireless also offers U.S. libraries a local phone number where users may send SMS reference inquiries. Questions are routed to an existing library email account librarians use to send responses back to users' mobile devices via SMS. Prices vary and begin at $15/month: http://www.upsidewireless.com/library _text_messaging.htm.

LibraryH3lp allows libraries to integrate IM and SMS reference. Via a library-created Google Voice phone number or a library-purchased phone number from Twilio, users send text messages to the library that are then rerouted to the LibraryH3lp interface and picked up by librarians. Responses to SMS inquiries are sent via chat or SMS. There is a charge for LibraryH3lp based on library size and type, as well as $12/year for a Twilio-created phone number and $.03 per incoming or outgoing SMS message. See http://libraryh3lp .com/ and http://twilio.com/.

A low-cost alternative to independently sustaining SMS reference is the collaborative MIQ project. Currently, individuals from 26 libraries and a few independent librarians from around the United States staff the service. MIQ uses Mosio's Text-A-Librarian platform where users text to the 66746 short code, then type in the identifying code of the local participating library; librarians pick up the questions and respond via SMS through the web-based dashboard. The cost of the service is divided between participating libraries. More information is available at http://myinfoquest.info/.

Google Voice is a no-cost alternative some libraries are using to offer SMS reference service. A library establishes a new phone number through Google Voice, and then incoming text messages can be picked up from the browser-based Google Voice interface or rerouted to other phones or a Gmail account (which in turn can be set up to reroute to an established reference-desk email). If you are logged in to Google Voice in your web browser, you can respond directly to a text message via SMS from the browser. However, if the service is set up to reroute to an email account, replies will be sent via email, not SMS. There is no charge for the service. See http://voice.google.com.

Service Platforms

- Altarama SMSReference: http://www.altarama.com/Products/SMSreference
- Text-A-Librarian: http://www.textalibrarian.com/
- LibAnswers: http://springshare.com/libanswers/
- Upside Wireless: http://www.upsidewireless.com/library_text_messaging.htm
- LibraryH3lp and Twilio: http://libraryh3lp.com/, http://twilio.com/
- My Info Quest: http://myinfoquest.info/
- Google Voice: http://voice.google.com

BEST PRACTICES

Once a service model and platform have been decided on, it is time to develop the governing policies for the SMS service. The Reference and User Services Association (RUSA)'s *Guidelines for Implementing and Maintaining Virtual Reference Services* (http://www.ala.org/ala/mgrps/divs/rusa/resources/guidelines/virtrefguidelines.cfm) are the guiding principles for remote forms of reference service. While instances are noted in the literature that SMS reference inquiries are sometimes made by users sitting inside the library and in close physical proximity to librarians, SMS reference is conducted electronically, not face to face, and therefore falls under the RUSA definition of virtual reference.

As SMS reference service is developed and implemented, it is important to provide users and library staff with access to adequate documentation for the service. Many documents should be produced prior to launching the initiative. However, it is also important to update documentation as the service evolves. Some fundamentals that should be included in SMS reference documentation are hours, policies, and maximum response time.

What hours will the service be available? Will service hours vary depending on time of the semester or year? What holidays will be observed by the service, and how will holidays affect response times? Clearly post hours the service is available within advertising and promotional materials as well as on the library website. If the service is unavailable at given times, also note exceptions within the documentation (i.e., "M–F 7 a.m.–12 a.m. except when classes are not in session").

Be sure to document all governing policies for the service. Is the service open to anyone? If not, clearly define who may submit inquiries to the service and how someone may become eligible to use the service. Will the service answer any question received, or is the service meant to handle specific types of reference inquiries only (like short answer/ready reference)? Guidelines should be developed to determine if an incoming question falls within service parameters and what a staff member should do if faced with a question outside service boundaries. If the service will not answer certain types of questions, such as inquiries for personal or confidential information or inappropriate questions, define "personal information," "confidential information," or "inappropriate questions." Defining question parameters assists staff to categorize inquiries and alerts users to the types of questions that will not be answered if submitted. Craft specific wording to be used by staff when replying to inquiries that fall outside of service parameters in order to ensure consistent responses and take the burden off individuals staffing the service to come up with a polite response to such queries.

There may be times when librarians answering SMS reference questions determine the user needs to actually speak with a reference librarian or schedule a consultation with a subject specialist librarian. Therefore, it is a best practice to develop guidelines for determining when a reference query should be referred to another mode of communication or alternative reference service. In addition, crafting standard wording for messages to be used by staff to refer users to alternative services is useful in expediting communication.

Response time to inquiries should also be defined for users and staff. At some institutions where SMS reference has been implemented, staff noted the service is more asynchronous than synchronous. If SMS reference is being incorporated into activities at a busy reference desk where walk-up users and telephone users have priority, it is possible SMS queries may not be responded to for many minutes or hours. Therefore, it is important to note anticipated SMS-inquiry response turn-around time in documentation, on promotional materials, and on web pages so patrons know what to expect. Some services like Mosio's Text-A-Librarian allow subscribers to create automated responses that are sent out when the service is not available or a response is not made by library staff within a specified timeframe, such as, "Text-a-Librarian is available M–F 7am–12am, we will respond within 2 hours on the next business day" or "Your question is important to us and has been added to the queue, we will respond within the next hour." These automated responses let users know their question has been logged and the timeframe for a response, and they take the burden off reference staff to acknowledge all incoming queries immediately.

Charges associated with the service also need to be included in the documentation. While the reference service is free, standard SMS usage charges will apply to all messages. Although many people subscribe to unlimited texting plans, some users may not. Therefore, be sure to include a statement about standard SMS charges applying to all queries and subsequent responses within the written documentation of the service and on all promotion materials. Also consider adding a brief statement about incurring standard charges to outgoing responses. If using one of the services that provide response templates, this could be added to the beginning or end of every initial response message.

Although librarians may feel hampered by the 160-character constraints of the text-message medium, it is important to provide SMS reference service users with high-quality responses while being mindful of the number of messages sent to the user. In order to maximize efficient use of the available 160 characters, incorporate basic SMS language or texting shorthand, emoticons, and use of short URLs into responses. For staff who may not regularly send text messages themselves, create a cheat-sheet of texting shorthand and emoticons (b4 = before; ty = thank you; ? = I have a question; :S or %-) = I'm confused) and keep it on hand wherever the service is staffed. It may also be useful to bookmark or load a SMS translator site or tool on the device used to respond to queries so staff unfamiliar with texting shorthand can look up abbreviations as needed. Because URLs are often included in responses as links to further information or to document the source of a provided answer, make sure a URL shortener is readily available on the device used to craft responses. Any URL shortener such as bit.ly, tinyurl.com, or goo.gl reduces the number of characters needed to refer a user to a specific URL, thus using fewer characters to transmit the information.

In addition to good written documentation and SMS language and emoticon cheat-sheets, it is critical to train staff to provide SMS reference service. Even if only certain individuals will regularly staff the service, every reference librarian and reference staff person should be trained to respond to SMS queries. Training of all reference staff is important so everyone is comfortable and confident when required to cover SMS shifts due to illness, vacations, and so forth. Training all reference staff also ensures everyone understands the service and they are able to answer questions about the service when asked.

It is also important to give the service a human touch whenever possible. Even though it may seem difficult to be perceived as approachable and interested in a virtual environment, it is not impossible. Users will feel SMS reference is approachable if they know about the service and the service is available during posted hours. Acknowledgement when a query is received may also be perceived as approachability by users, whether done immediately by staff or a system-supplied automated response. In addition, when completing a transaction, end it with personal initials or an agreed-upon acronym and encourage the patron to use the service again, if characters allow. In a texting environment, these simple acts are perceived as personal touches.

While all SMS reference-service communication between librarians and users is confidential, it is useful to strip off identifiers, such as incoming cell-phone number, and collate incoming queries and assess the types of questions, number of texts used during transactions, length of response time, date and time questions were received, and other information. Taking the time to analyze when the service is used, the types of questions received, how long it is taking staff to respond to queries, and so forth can be used to adjust service focus and staffing as needed.

Best Practices
- Clearly display hours service is available.
- Provide access to written governing service policies.
- Develop guidelines for service parameters.
- Craft responses to be used in specific instances.
- Plainly identify anticipated response time.
- Create SMS language/emoticon cheat-sheet for staff use.
- Use a URL shortener when crafting responses.
- Train all reference librarians to staff the service.
- Make the users experience personal by being approachable and interested.
- Assess/analyze service data.

MARKETING AND PROMOTION

A new service no one knows about is doomed to failure. Develop a marketing and promotion strategy during the planning process. Create a custom logo for the service, and brand all marketing and promotion materials with the service logo. Make sure the logo is appealing and clearly discernable on a small screen. As with any logo, simple is better. Keep in mind that text embedded in a logo may not be readable when viewed on a mobile screen. If possible, create a variety of logos that incorporate institution colors and ask people outside the library to vote on the designs. The whole point of marketing and promotion is to appeal to users, and an ugly logo that is unidentifiable will not sell the service.

It is fine to do an initial low-profile, soft launch in order to have time to address any unforeseen issues that may arise. However, it is imperative to set a date for a full-out, high-profile launch of the service. Craft a press release and send it to local newspapers, radio, and TV stations. Make sure the press release going to print media is informative, succinct, and well written. The easier it is for editors to turn the press release into a story, the more likely it will be printed. Press releases going to broadcast media should highlight what's in it for the community and users of the service. If there is a catchy tagline for the service, be sure to include it in all press releases.

Use the marketing and promotion budget allocated to the project by the administration to purchase ads and promotional materials to announce the service. Consider buying ads in local newspapers and magazines. If your community is active on Facebook, create a targeted ad that will appear to everyone within the targeted demographic from your geographic area when they log on to Facebook. This is a good way to connect with local community members who may not use the library but are ardent users of online social media. Also regularly post notices about the service to the library Facebook fan page, Twitter account, library blogs, and any other social media outlet where the library has a presence.

Posters and flyers are tried-and-true methods of getting the word out about a new service. Depending on the service platform, create a quick-response (QR) code that direct-dials the SMS reference-service phone number, and include the code on all advertising and promotion materials. Plaster public meeting spots with posters and flyers. Some libraries report promoting their new services by flyers adhered to surfaces in restrooms—whatever works. For college campuses, consider creating table tents with the phone number or short code and hours of operation for placement on dorm cafeteria tables or on tables in the student union, bowling alley, and other public areas.

Other useful promotion tools are business cards printed with pertinent details, which can be handed out from all library service desks and stuck in out-going circulating books. Purchasing custom scratch paper and sticky note pads and placing them around the library in public spaces is also a good tactic. Remember to include service information on all bibliographic instruction handouts and on online research guides. Promoting the service to individuals who already use the library is as important as garnering new users.

Placing announcements on the library website and on digital signs located on campus, around town, or in the library will also alert community members to the new service. Ask library friend and library foundation groups to promote the service and provide them with promotion materials. If your library serves a learning community, such as a school, college, or university, ask established student groups, like student government, honors programs, sororities, and fraternities, to get the word out.

If the budget allows, have promotion items like travel mugs, flash drives, ear buds, and MP3 speakers made up with the service logo and QR code or phone number/short code. In the beginning, saturating the market with the service information is the goal. After the service is established it is important to continue to market the service, but word-of-mouth buzz about the service may ultimately be as effective as promotion materials later on.

ASSESSMENT

As with any new or existing library service, SMS reference should be assessed regularly to find out if the service is used, who is using it, how it meets user needs, what aspects work, what facets to adjust, and potential growth areas. Therefore, be sure to build assessment dates and goals into your SMS reference-service implementation plan.

Initially, evaluate use, incoming questions, workflows, and policies frequently to ensure the service is on track and library staff understand service parameters, policies, and so forth. Beyond early assessment, formal evaluation is generally undertaken at 6- to 12-month intervals. At this point, there are no national benchmarks for assessing text-message reference services. Therefore, libraries need to define success locally and share their measures of success globally.

As noted in the *Guidelines for Implementing and Maintaining Virtual Reference Services* (http://www.ala.org/ala/mgrps/divs/rusa/resources/guidelines/virtrefguidelines.cfm), implementing any virtual reference service should be a long-term commitment. Therefore, it is important to give the service time to succeed. Mobile use by community members, question response time, user satisfaction, marketing, and promotion of the service are just a few of the factors that affect use. It is important to use focus groups, advisory boards, and user surveys to go beyond usage data to discover if marketing and promotion strategies are working and if users are satisfied with the service.

CONCLUSION

SMS is another way to connect users to the library. Although SMS reference may never supplant other forms of reference service, it can be a useful tool in serving segments of the population who regularly use text messaging. It will be interesting to see if, like telephone, email, and IM, SMS reference becomes a core component of ask-a-librarian programs over the next few years. We live in interesting times!

REFERENCES

Giles, Nicola, and Sue Grey-Smith. 2005. "TXTing Librarians @ Curtin." Paper presented at the Australian Library and Information Association Information Online Conference and Exhibition, Sydney, Australia, February 1–3. http://conferences.alia.org.au/online2005/papers/a12.pdf.

International Telecommunication Union (ITU). 2009. *The World in 2009: ITC Facts and Figures.* Geneva: ITU. http://www.itu.int/ITU-D/ict/material/Telecom09_flyer.pdf.

International Telecommunication Union (ITU). 2010. *The World in 2010: ITC Facts and Figures.* Geneva: ITU. http://www.itu.int/ITU-D/ict/material/FactsFigures2010.pdf.

International Telecommunication Union (ITU). 2011. *The World in 2011: ITC Facts and Figures.* Geneva: ITU. http://www.itu.int/ITU-D/ict/facts/2011/material/ICTFactsFigures2011.pdf.

Jensen, Bruce. 2011. "SMS Text Reference Comes of Age: The My Info Quest Collaborative." *The Reference Librarian* 51(4): 264–275.

Pasanen, Irma, and Ari Muhonen. 2002. "Library in Your Pocket." Paper presented at the International Association of Scientific and Technological University Libraries Conference, Kansas City, Missouri, June 2–6. http://www.iatul.org/doclibrary/public/Conf_Proceedings/2002/Muhonen.pdf.

Pearce, Alexa, Scott Collard, and Kara Whatley. 2010. "SMS Reference: Myths, Markers, and Modalities." *Reference Service Review* 38(2): 250–263.

Smith, Aaron. 2010. *Mobile Access 2010.* Washington: Pew Research Center. http://pewinternet.org/~/media//Files/Reports/2010/PIP_Mobile_Access_2010.pdf.

Stahr, Beth. 2010. "Text Message Reference Service: Five Years Later." *The Reference Librarian* 52(1–2): 9–19.

16

Using Mobile-to-Mobile Messaging to Deliver Health Information at the Point of Need

Tammy A. Magid

Key Points

- Libraries' role in public health information programs is explored.
- Designing health information systems that use SMS messaging effectively is outlined.
- Mobile health information services meet three distinct needs: treatment adherence, appointment notifications, and health literacy messages.
- The Mobile 4 Women SMS-based health information service for HIV+ African American women is proposed.

WHAT IS MHEALTH?

The k4Health website defines mobile health (mHealth) as "the use of mobile technology to support health outcomes. The varied definitions and opportunities of mHealth are evolving rapidly, but they all provide a tool to support your goals—improving health outcomes in developing countries." Low-resource-setting countries have successfully connected a variety of populations to health information and treatment adherence using these programs. SMS technology is a cost-effective and scalable solution that can deliver short, text-based health information messages to critically ill populations. Text messaging is a nonintrusive mode of communication that can reach these populations at the point of need. This chapter investigates the relationship between librarians and health information technology to supply the public health domain and health care providers with a tool to engage vulnerable populations in their individualized health outcomes.

LIBRARIANS AND MHEALTH PROGRAMS

Librarians have a long history of providing traditional and emerging health information services to public health agencies, community-based organizations, and patients in a variety of settings. This chapter seeks to define the librarian's role in collaborating with health care providers and other agents to develop mHealth programs in the United States. In the fall of 2011, a research project was conducted that evaluated the potential efficacy of using SMS technologies to improve health literacy and treatment adherence among high-need populations. This research project was named Mobile 4 Women. Mobile 4 Women examined how SMS technologies could potentially improve the lives of HIV+ African American females.

Mobile 4 Women is the culmination of a two-year research project investigating the librarian's role in community-based SMS health programs in the United States and Africa. The aftermath of Hurricane Katrina prompted my interest to first investigate how text-message services could potentially locate people, save lives, and reunite families during natural disasters. Over the next year my interest in women and mobile-based health information services formed. Medical librarians, health science librarians, and clinicians in academia, nongovernmental organizations, and leading biomedical research libraries in the United States and Africa were contacted to discuss their roles in designing health information systems using SMS technology. My research took me to Kenya to study how mHealth programs are shaping the lives of remote populations that have limited access to information, communication, and technology (ICT) resources. In contrast to owning a laptop, iPad, or both in the first world, people in developing regions may either own or have access to a cell phone in the near future. Africa has seen an explosion in cell-phone ownership in the last several years, and ownership rates continue to grow. The International Telecommunications Union estimates that in late 2011 there were 5.9 billion active mobile/cellular phone subscriptions worldwide, with diffusion rates of 79 percent in the developing world (ITU 2011).

While in Kenya I met with the programme manager of library and information services at Family Health Options Kenya (FHOK). FHOK is the Africa Regional Office of the International Planned Parenthood Federation, a leading provider in sexual and reproductive health services in Kenya for over 50 years. During our conversation, the programme manager spoke about FHI 360's program Mobile 4 Reproductive Health (M4RH), which connects Kenyans to general family planning and reproductive health information using SMS text messages. M4RH was created through U.S. Agency for International Development (USAID) funding and FHI 360's commitment to marrying research and public health programming to deliver a ubiquitous service that reaches all Kenyan citizens. In addition, she advocates for the integration of health-related information to improve the knowledge of health care workers and Kenyan citizens across the country. She also works on multimedia initiatives that disseminate health information for different populations in a variety of settings. She provides outreach and training on programs like M4RH. She plans to expand the scope of mHealth programming into the areas of mental health and gender violence. These future services seek to increase access to health information for mental health patients and gender violence victims in Kenya who require discreet and confidential communication about their conditions (http://www.fhi360.org/en/Research/Projects/Progress/GTL/mobile _tech.htm).

DESIGNING MOBILE 4 WOMEN PILOT PROJECT

The impetus to design the Mobile 4 Women project was a culmination of these research activities. A grant has been written for this project and will be submitted to a select group of funders. At present, Mobile 4 Women seeks a sponsor that will headquarter the project during the development and implementation phases pending full funding. The project would explore how SMS technology can potentially reduce health care disparities among HIV+ African American females in the United States. Recent studies conducted in Africa show positive results that SMS interventions can improve treatment adherence among HIV+ populations. A study by Pop-Eleches et al. (2011) found that an intervention group that received weekly reminders adhered better to their antiretroviral treatment protocol when compared to the control group. Their randomized controlled trial shows evidence that librarians and medical researchers should collaborate to pursue conducting trials on the efficacy of similar programs for HIV+ populations in the United States. Successful studies could lead to funded public-health-based SMS programs that mobilize information resources to address the unmet needs of high-risk populations at the point of need. Although there is more prevalent cell phone usage in the United States, there has been less adoption of this technology in the public health domain. Libraries are uniquely positioned to address the health information management challenges faced with the adoption of this specialized service in the United States.

At present, African American females have the fastest-growing rate of new HIV infections in the United States. The Centers for Disease Control and Prevention (2011b) published 2009 infection rates in their report titled "HIV among Women." In 2009, an estimated 11,200 new HIV infections were reported among women in the United States. African American females reported the highest rate of occurrence at 57 percent. Whites reported at 21 percent, and 16 percent of cases were among Hispanics/Latinas. The December 2010 California AIDS Surveillance Quarterly Report cited females living with HIV/AIDS made up 13 percent of all cumulative cases (California Department of Public Health 2010). In 2010, San Francisco's Department of Public Health published its HIV/AIDS Epidemiology Annual Report citing that African American women make up only 8 percent of the total female population and account for 42 percent of all HIV/AIDS cases in the city and county of San Francisco.

Traditionally, women living with HIV/AIDS have not been targeted for outreach and intervention programs and lack an extensive support network. In contrast to this population, gay men have a long history of HIV/AIDS outreach and intervention programs that support treatment adherence and promote health. African American females living with HIV/AIDS have limited access to personalized health support and specialized health information. Furthermore, the CDC's webpage on HIV/AIDS and African Americans reports that barriers such as social constraints and community stigma, high-risk behavior, access to medical treatment and services, limited financial resources, and government funding impact positive health outcomes for this infected population. Women in the African American community find it especially hard to manage their medical needs while retaining privacy and independence.

Social media provide powerful tools for developing mHealth programs that directly connect women to health-related information services at the point of need. This population needs access to confidential modes of health information. This project would engage members of the population to make behavior changes to improve their own personalized health outcomes. Using social media is potentially a gateway to building health literacy and autonomy for this disadvantaged population.

NEEDS ASSESSMENT

The Mobile 4 Women project conducted a needs assessment, collecting data and information about HIV/AIDS intervention programs for high-risk female populations in San Francisco, California. Medical professionals were interviewed on current patient-engagement programs and health communication strategies for HIV+ African American females. Our findings show a lack in public health interventions for HIV/AIDS using social media to connect women to health- and disease-related information services. For example, Planned Parenthood uses pamphlets to supply information to infected patients. At present, San Francisco community-based health providers have not collaborated with librarians to design a health information system that engages women in taking a more active role in their health care.

Mobile 4 Women would support these unmet health information needs to empower patients to take ownership of their treatment. Librarians trained in developing health information systems should seize this opportunity to disseminate health information using social media as the cornerstone of mobile services. A health sciences library is perfectly positioned to administer mobile health information services for patient engagement programs because of the expert librarians, the history of successful community collaboration, and the commitment to quality of public service to both providers and patients.

LITERATURE REVIEW

Mobile 4 Women intends to use the evidence from its research and literature review to design an mHealth intervention that addresses the needs of disadvantaged populations. Mobile 4 Women's research builds upon a growing body of studies investigating SMS treatment interventions for high-risk populations. The researcher considered the following relevant studies in designing the pilot program.

Franklin et al. (2006) examined the efficacy of sending SMS messages to juveniles for treatment adherence. Participants taking intensive insulin therapy (IIT) and receiving text messages showed the most improvement in treatment adherence. The experiment found that SMS text messaging engaged a hard-to-reach population. Similarly, Menon-Johansson et al. (2006) assessed the effectiveness of text messaging in reducing the time between diagnosis and treatment. Patients who received their diagnosis via text message returned to the clinic for treatment in less time compared to the recall group. Menon-Johansson et al. found that more patients selected text-message notification to receive their diagnosis than telephone follow up.

More relevant to the Mobile 4 Women initiative is Ybarra and Bull's (2007) study, which reviewed current advances in technology-based HIV prevention and intervention programming. Ybarra and Bull's meta-analysis suggested that using technology-based interventions had a positive effect on behavior change. SMS messaging is an efficient way to reach adolescent and adult populations seeking information and needing adherence support. Their review of available adolescent and elderly studies indicated the potential feasibility of SMS text messaging for women infected with HIV. This study was particularly useful in designing our own.

Additionally, Krishna and Boren (2008) evaluated SMS messaging interventions across a broad population. Krishna and Boren conducted a meta-analysis review of the literature about diabetic/obese patients concerning improved health status using cell phone messaging interventions. Diabetic patients require a daily plan of care to maintain their health and need to track their daily sugar levels and respond with prescribed medical treatments. Krishna and Boren's research shows that SMS messaging is an effective tool for aiding patients who require frequent reminders to regulate their disease. SMS messaging provides diabetics with a powerful coping tool for managing their condition.

Finding additional relevant studies encountered literature suggesting that this technology would be useful to a broad range of populations, diseases, and settings. Krishna, Boren, and Balas (2009) evaluated studies on the use of voice and text-messaging intervention programs for improving health outcomes. The researchers evaluated 25 studies in their systematic review. They found that standard care coupled with SMS messaging services improved both compliance for patients and processes for providers. This meta-analysis demonstrated to us the global potential of cell phone voice and text-messaging interventions. More recently, Cole-Lewis and Kershaw (2010) conducted a meta-analytic study of mobile phone text-messaging tools for behavior change and disease management in a variety of applications. The study included only preventions that used text messaging as a primary mode of communication. Cole-Lewis and Kershaw found that 8 of 25 studies showed evidence that supported text messaging as a tool for behavior change. Because SMS texting is a new technology, the authors had no choice but to analyze studies that used this intervention in a variety of settings with diverse populations for different diseases. The authors found the behavior change to be similar in all environments. This meta-analysis synthesizes the literature and demonstrated to us the potential efficacy of mobile technologies to deliver health-related information services.

The research conducted by Hardy et al. (2011) is especially relevant to this proposed program. Hardy et al. compared a cell phone reminder system versus a beeper notification system for enhancing adherence to antiretroviral therapy (ART). Twenty-three HIV-infected subjects participated over the course of two phases. Phase-one participants received an SMS text-message reminder to take their ARTs over a two-week period. Phase two used beepers to remind patients to take their drugs. Phase-one participants self-reported taking their ARTs. The beeper group was tracked through MEMS (micro-electromechanical-systems (MEMS). This study is significant because it discovered that cell phones had better short-term improvement in adherence to ART over the beeper reminder system. Even though the study shows that cell phones improved adherence, it could have had a larger sample size. Also, Hardy et al. (2011) do not elaborate on their findings to make potential recommendations that suggest using SMS messaging in practice.

RESEARCH PROBLEM

An SMS-based intervention will address the research problem: how best to improve the health outcomes of high-needs populations that have not been targeted for technology-based interventions? Specifically, this program will consider how message content and type of message (information/inspiration) contribute to treatment outcome and health literacy. Health information and treatment at the point of need has significant potential to improve health outcomes for chronically ill populations. This mobile opt-in

SMS text-messaging service seeks to connect participants to three distinct areas of health-related information services: treatment adherence, appointment reminders, and health-literacy-based activities. The Mobile 4 Women project will develop a comprehensive set of messages along with its coalition of partners to send to program participants. Participants will receive daily treatment reminders, notifications of upcoming medical appointments, health literacy materials relating to HIV/AIDS, and supportive messages.

U.S. MHEALTH PROGRAMS

Mobile 4 Women is closely studying the success of Text 4 Baby (http://www .text4baby.org/), the largest private-public partnership mHealth program in the United States targeting expecting and new mothers. Text 4 Baby is an education-based SMS program that delivers messages to expecting and new mothers who opt in to the service. Text 4 Baby created 250 messages to address a variety of prenatal, health, and consumer topics for women in both English and Spanish. Johnson & Johnson funded the Text 4 Baby program. Healthy Mothers, Healthy Babies operates the program with over 600 public health and health care providers and community-based organization partners. The program has enrolled over 250,000 participants in two years. In November 2011, Text 4 Baby published its first study data. A small study in San Diego County found that expecting and new mothers improved their heath literacy skills from Text 4 Baby messages. Women were more likely to ask their health care providers questions about messages they received. Most women surveyed found the service to be helpful and rated it highly.

Real Talk DC (http://www.facebook.com/realtalkdc/) is an opt-in SMS program that targets teens seeking information on HIV/AIDS and reproductive health. Washington, DC, has a very high prevalence of HIV/AIDS among its African American population. Teens are prone to infection without proper information and knowledge about how HIV is contracted. Teens can text Real Talk DC for free HIV testing centers in their local area. Real Talk DC connects teens to health-related information through quizzes on sexually transmitted infections (STIs), contraceptives, and HIV/AIDS. This program has enjoyed great success in the Washington, DC, area. Other cities have designed similar programs that address teen needs for health information.

Text 4 Baby and Real Talk DC are examples of how mHealth programs can reach populations at the point of need to engage in their individualized health outcomes. Librarians have the opportunity to capitalize on our skills to play a key role in designing these programs. Libraries have the information assets and expertise to develop sustainable programs. Community-engagement models bring together key players from a variety of agencies to address issues affecting their local populations. This model has the potential to grow relationships among the librarians, public health agents, health care providers, and community activists who seek to reduce health disparities among their community.

METHODOLOGY

Three resources—PubMed, Web of Science, and Google Scholar—were searched to find studies on SMS or cell-phone-based interventions that improved participant behavior. Behavior-change studies examined the efficacy of sending text-message reminders to an intervention group to show improved treatment adherence over those participants who did not receive messages. The main search terms "cellular OR mobile phone," "AIDS," "HIV," and "health education" were combined with "treatment outcome," "disease management," "program evaluation," and "medication adherence" to amass articles for review. Health care professionals, librarians, and technologists were also consulted. The search yielded several studies that supported designing a program for the public heath domain. Mobile 4 Women designed a project based on the literature review and the needs-assessment findings.

If funded, Mobile 4 Women's goal is to enroll 100 participants recruited from a variety of programs focused on women's health from the public and nonprofit sectors. The pilot's targeted population is HIV+ African American women age 21 to 49 living in San Francisco County. This patient-engagement program increases the provider's role in supporting a patient's access to care at the point of need.

The program will provide cell phones with unlimited text plans to participants who do not have them. A 12-month, double-blind, randomized control trial will split the participants into three groups. Group one will receive treatment and appointment reminders only. Group two will receive treatment, appointment reminders, and short health-education-based messages. A third group will receive treatment, appointment reminders, and a long health-education-based message with an inspirational quote. A group of medical librarians, health care providers, and public health experts will form a coalition to develop a set of culturally competent messages for the intervention. The comprehensive messages will address HIV/AIDS health care maintenance, exercise, family planning, mental health, personal communication, nutrition, and substance abuse. Inspirational quotes will be added to health-education messages to supply additional support to encourage participants to engage in managing their personal health care. By contrast, the short messages will provide only scant information on the long-message topics and will be limited to 160 characters. Both long, short, and no health literacy message groups will receive their daily treatment and appointment reminders with equal frequency. The long and short text message reminders can be sent out at the same time with the same frequency. Mobile 4 Women will employ an open-source framework similar to those of Real Talk DC or Text 4 Baby to send messages to and receive them from the participants.

DATA-COLLECTION STRATEGIES

Data will be collected from participating health care providers that survey enrollees during routine appointments. Sample survey questions may include the following:

1. Did you receive a daily reminder to take your ART drug? Yes or No
2. Did you take your daily dose? Yes or No
3. Did you receive an SMS appointment reminder 24 hours before your scheduled office visit? Yes or No
4. Did you keep your appointment? Yes or No
5. If no, did you immediately contact your health care provider to reschedule your appointment? Yes or No
6. Did sending and receiving text messages to and from your health care provider between visits improve your HIV/AIDS status? Yes or No
7. Would you rate your overall health and well-being as good, fair, or poor today? If poor, why?
8. Overall, would you rate Mobile 4 Women's service as good, fair, or poor? If poor, why?

Participants will also be surveyed on health-information topics for attitude towards their health and increased literacy from long and short messages. The control group (which receives no text messages) will be surveyed using the same questions as well. Additionally, the long- and short-message groups will receive periodic text messages on HIV/AIDS and health topics to test their knowledge. The text-message quizzes promote interactive communication between the provider and patient. Answers from the text quizzes can be downloaded for analysis by health care providers and reported to the Mobile 4 Women project team.

RISKS AND LIMITATIONS

Mobile 4 Women has identified some risks and limitations of their proposed program. The program leadership will seek guidance from mHealth experts, medical practitioners, and health care providers to address these critical issues. Compliance with the Health Insurance Portability and Accountability Act (HIPAA) of 1996, is one challenge. Personal information such as telephone numbers under HIPAA regulations are considered patient health information (PHI) and therefore confidential. PHI guidelines limit message content that participants can receive. To adhere to HIPAA guidelines, participants enrolled in the Mobile 4 Women pilot program would consent to receiving messages related to the diagnosis and treatment of their disease. All participants would sign a consent form allowing the provider to send messages that explicitly reference their diagnosis. Participants who decline consent would be eliminated from the pilot program. Mobile 4 Women would consult with HIPAA experts on how to ensure privacy for participants who consented to the pilot program.

Lack of patient access to mobile phone devices is another challenge. The program would provide a limited number of cell phones for participants who don't own phones. Mobile 4 Health would develop a tracking system to inventory phones for distribution through our community health providers. The project leadership would set up a patient tracking schedule to monitor handsets for loss or theft. These data would be collected directly from the health care provider that manages the patient's care. Participants who use program phones need a tracking system to ensure messages are delivered to the prepaid handsets. Mobile 4 Women would develop a message that requests participants to text their number of minutes during different intervals, which could be downloaded in a report for the project team.

Collecting data will be a challenge, too. Health care providers would be asked to survey participants during in-person appointments about treatment adherence, health literacy, and program satisfaction. The providers would agree to upload or transmit data about compliance over the course of the pilot program. Data collection on compliance would be used to evaluate the efficacy of the intervention at the end of the program. Compliance includes receiving messages for treatment adherence, appointment notification, and the participant's attitude towards supportive messaging and changes in health literacy.

Message content also needs to be carefully crafted. Literacy rates among participants are unknown. The intervention targets African American women ages 21 to 49. The enrolled participants are expected to have varying levels of literacy. The messages will be designed to have a low barrier to literacy. The text messages will be developed based on average literacy rates and educational statistics known about this population. Mobile 4 Women sees this as potential limitation and plans to ensure that most participants will understand the messages they receive.

Tracking of Mobile 4 Women outcomes and challenges will begin during year two of the project. Monthly tracking will monitor the program for participant adherence to the trial and provider communication. Monitoring will be a combination of in-person meetings, virtual meetings, and online surveys for both patients and providers. Mobile 4 Women seeks to present the most accurate outcome possible from data collected during the trial. The main challenge will be to engage busy medical professionals to meet and respond to surveys. The project team will work closely with providers to ensure timely data are collected.

CONCLUSION

The potential success of our project aims to serve as a model for the institutionalization of SMS technology in the public health domain. Mobile 4 Women strives to expand its capacity to reach other African American women living in cities that have a high prevalence of HIV/AIDS and suffer from its stigma. The program can be adapted to meet the needs of other populations that live with chronic diseases. Mobile 4 Women promotes improving public health using a community-engagement model. Community-based organizations and social services can benefit from the integration of an SMS intervention that links to a participant's electronic health record, thus making health care services more portable and accessible to high-needs populations that suffer from chronic illnesses requiring complex health monitoring.

It is the library's intention to advocate for universal adoption of SMS-based interventions with these populations in the public health domain. Furthermore, medical librarians and medical professionals believe that this intervention has the potential to bolster health literacy among these populations with other, unintended positive consequences, such as increased self-care and preventive lifestyles. This pilot study aims to show that SMS-based interventions are an excellent medium for transmitting health literacy and improving treatment outcomes, and that this protocol will have a significant impact in transforming care delivery to people with chronic illness.

REFERENCES

California Department of Public Health, Center for Infectious Diseases, Office of AIDS. 2010. "HIV/AIDS Surveillance in California." Accessed January 2, 2012. http://www.cdph.ca .gov/programs/aids/Documents/SSQtr4Dec2010.pdf.

Centers for Disease Control and Prevention. 2011a. "HIV among Women." Atlanta, GA: Centers for Disease Control and Prevention. Accessed January 2, 2012. http://www.cdc.gov/hiv/ topics/women/pdf/women.pdf.

Centers for Disease Control and Prevention. 2011b. "HIV/AIDS and African Americans." Atlanta, GA: Centers for Disease Control and Prevention. Accessed January 2, 2012. http://www.cdc.gov/hiv/topics/aa/index.htm.

Cole-Lewis, Heather, and Trace Kershaw. 2010. "Text Messaging as a Tool for Behavior Change in Disease Prevention and Management." *Epidemiological Review* 32(1): 56–69.

Franklin, Victoria L., A. Waller, C. Pagliari, and S. A. Greene. 2006. "A Randomized Controlled Trial of Sweet Talk, a Text-Messaging System to Support Young People with Diabetes." *Diabetic Medicine* 23(12): 1332–1338.

Hardy, Helene, Vikram Kumar, Gheorghe Doros, Eric Farmer, Mari-Lynn Drainoni, Denis Rybin, Dan Myung, Jonathan Jackson, Elke Backman, Anela Stanic, and Paul R. Skolnik. 2011.

"Randomized Controlled Trial of a Personalized Cellular Phone Reminder System to Enhance Adherence to Antiretroviral Therapy." *AIDS Patient Care and STDs* 25(3): 153–161.

International Telecommunication Union (ITU). 2011. "The World in 2011: ICT Facts and Figures." Geneva, Switzerland: International Telecommunication Union. http://www.itu.int/ITU-D/ict/facts/2011/material/ICTFactsFigures2011.pdf.

Krishna, Santosh, and Susan Austin Boren. 2008. "Diabetes Self-Management Care via Cell Phone: A Systematic Review" *Journal of Diabetes Science and Technology* 2(3): 509–517.

Krishna, Santosh, Susan Austin Boren, and E. Andrew Balas. 2009. "Healthcare via Cell Phones: A Systematic Review." *Telemedicine and e-Health* 15(3): 231–240.

Menon-Johansson, A. S., F. McNaught, S. Mandalia, and A. K. Sullivan. 2006. "Texting Decreases the Time to Treatment for Genital Chlamydia Trachomatis Infection." *Sexually Transmitted Infections* 82(1): 49–51.

Pop-Eleches, Cristian, Harsha Thirumurthy, James P. Habyarimana, Joshua G. Zivin, Markus P. Goldstein, Damien de Walque, Leslie MacKeen, Jessica Haberer, Sylvester Kimaiyo, John Sidle, Duncan Ngare, and David R. Bangsberg. 2011. "Mobile Phone Technologies Improve Adherence to Antiretroviral Treatment in a Resources-Limited Setting: A Randomized Controlled Trial of Text Message Reminders." *AIDS* 25(6): 825–834.

San Francisco Department of Public Health. 2010. "The HIV/AIDS Epidemiology Annual Report." http://www.sfdph.org/dph/comupg/oprograms/hivepisec/default.asp.

Ybarra, Michele L., and Sheana B. Bull. 2007. "Current Trends in Internet and Cell Phone-Based HIV Prevention and Intervention Programs." *Current HIV/AIDS Reports* 4(4): 201–207.

_____

17

_____

Text a Librarian: Ideas for Best Practices

Lili Luo

Key Points

- The affordances of text messaging as a medium for reference service are examined.
- Research into My Info Quest, the first national text reference collaborative, is discussed.
- Several start-up issues and decision points are reviewed.
- Strategies are shared for promoting the service.
- The core competencies of text reference service providers are reviewed.
- The special service aspects of a collaborative, multitype service are explored.

INTRODUCTION

Text messaging, or texting, has become an increasingly popular communication venue. A new form of reference service, based on texting, has been added to libraries' digital reference suite. Such a service enables library users to send in reference questions and receive answers via texting and is usually referred to as text reference service. As more and more libraries embrace this new service conduit, it is important to establish a solid professional understanding of the affordances of texting as a reference medium and develop best practices and guidelines. In this chapter, the author draws upon the empirical research conducted on My Info Quest (http://myinfoquest.info/), the first national text reference collaborative, and discusses ideas to effectively establish and deliver text reference service.

There are two different ways for libraries to deliver text reference service: adopting a dedicated mobile device (usually a smartphone) or utilizing computer applications like email, instant messenger (IM), or a vendor-developed system to process users' texts. The latter is a more frequently employed method among libraries as it allows text messages to be integrated into existing virtual reference services and because librarians can answer text reference questions from a computer, an environment they are already familiar with, and it offers more power in finding an answer to a user's question quickly and easily than via a smartphone. The learning curve is as flat as possible in terms of technology and requires usually minimal training. At My Info Quest, the training session for new service providers, covering a step-by-step technical demonstration of how to provide service and an introduction of service policies and procedures, only lasts about one hour. Given this, the new form of service is likely to be welcomed with a more positive attitude among librarians.

Some free email and IM applications like AIM or Gmail support the sending and receiving of text messages. Libraries can instruct users to text their questions to an email address or an IM screen name. While these free services offer a great opportunity to explore text reference service, especially for libraries with budget constraints, there are a few concerns. First, user privacy is not ensured. For example, Google archives all of its data, meaning users' phone numbers and their text messages stored in a Gmail account can also be accessed by Google. Second, general-purpose applications like AIM or Gmail do not necessarily have features that serve the specific purpose of providing text reference service. For example, Gmail, like other public email services, does not have an effective system to announce new message arrival and may lead to delayed responses. Reference transactions cannot be easily organized and retrieved by users' phone number when librarians need context to help answer a follow-up question. Furthermore, when a question is being answered, there is no indication in Gmail that the question is "claimed," and this could be problematic when the service is provided by multiple libraries collaboratively. Third, librarians may still have to learn how to use an application such as AIM or Gmail if it is not already used by the library for chat and email reference service. Finally, libraries have no control over these free service providers and are subject to whatever changes they make, and thus sustainability issues may arise.

To alleviate the above concerns, libraries often opt for software specifically designed for text reference service. Currently, such commercial software used by most American libraries includes Altarama SMS Reference,[1] Mosio Text a Librarian,[2] and LibraryH3lp.[3] Detailed features and pricing models vary for these different services.

My Info Quest (MIQ) is a nationwide collaborative text reference service with 30 members (as of November 2011) including not only academic and public libraries but also volunteer practitioners whose libraries or institutions are not associated with MIQ. Launched in July 2009, MIQ chose the route of vendor-developed software for service delivery. It piloted with Altarama SMS Reference for about a year and a half, and switched to Mosio Text a Librarian in January 2011. On average, MIQ answers over 700 questions per month. Detailed information about MIQ such as participating libraries, service hours, and service policies can be found online.[4] To better understand the practice of text reference service, an in-depth research study supported by the Institute of Museum and Library Services was conducted to examine MIQ with regards to the types of information needs fulfilled by the service, user perceptions and expectations, collaborative service management, and competencies requisite for the provision of the service. Research methods used in the study included content analysis of text reference transactions and a survey and interviews among library users and MIQ librarians. Findings from the empirical research form a solid foundation to develop best-practices guidelines and help interested libraries make informed decisions about their text reference services.

SETTING UP THE SERVICE

Choosing the service software is the first step in implementing a text reference service. Given the different options discussed previously, libraries have a lot to consider before making this important decision. Lippincott (2010) listed some broad questions to consider when planning text reference service:

- What is the current state of mobile device deployment at your institution or for your population?
- What are your goals for providing service, and what are your strategies?
- Who should you work with in your institution or service area?
- How will you know if you are successful?
- What is your strategy for the next two to three years?

These questions, according to Lippincott, are "fundamental questions that can assist libraries in framing and planning process" for text reference service (Lippincott 2010, 2). They can help libraries determine service needs and establish service goals and policies accordingly. In addition to these broad questions, it is also necessary to consider a few specific ones related to libraries' budget, staffing, and usability concerns. Such questions include, but are not limited to, the following:

- How costly are the different service delivery models?
- What is financially feasible both in the short term and in the long run?
- Should text reference service be integrated into existing virtual reference services (e.g., email, IM/chat) for question processing or run as a separate service point?
- Is it preferable to maintain the current staffing schedule or to use a different schedule for text reference service?
- How much extra work is reasonable for librarians to adapt to the new service venue?
- What is the acceptable amount of instruction for users?
- When considering features of the service software (e.g., message organization and display, character limit per response, capability to accommodate collaboration among libraries, capability to send and receive graphics), what is important?
- What built-in tools of the service software are necessary—character counter, URL shortener, new-message alert sound, mechanism to claim questions, texting glossary or translation software, or others?

Once these questions are answered, libraries should be able to paint a clear picture of what they hope to achieve via text reference service and therefore choose the software that is able to meet their needs.

PROMOTE THE SERVICE

Effective promotion is critical to successfully creating awareness of the service among users and attracting them to use it. Methods of outreach and promotion documented in the current text reference literature had a focus on academic library users (Giles and Grey-Smith 2005; Hill et al. 2007; Kohl and Keating 2009; Pearce 2010; Weimer 2010) and usually applied to the entire suite of the Ask A Librarian digital reference service. Here is a list of examples:

- Announce the service on the library website, library digital signs, library blog, and library pages on social networking sites like Facebook and Twitter.
- Set up an information kiosk outside of student gathering places (e.g., student union) to distribute information about the service.
- Promote the service when interacting with students during reference transactions, information literacy instruction sessions, and library orientations.
- Promote the service via campus media.
- Hold a contest with prizes to encourage students to use the service.
- Distribute promotional material such as flyers, small business cards, scrap note paper, and posters across campus.

According to a survey conducted among MIQ users, they found out about the service in different ways—from the library website (21.1%), from a librarian (21.1%), from a personal acquaintance (10.4%), and from promotional materials created and distributed by the library (47.4%). This finding suggests that print and digital promotional materials are most effective, and word-of-mouth advertisement is also helpful to making the service known to users. While it is important to promote the service to the entire user community, a particular user demographic might warrant special attention as they are the largest population of texters and could be the greatest benefactors of text reference service—teens. The Pew Internet & American Life Project (Lenhart 2010) found that 75 percent of 12- to 17-year-olds now own cell phones, rising from 45 percent in 2004. Cell phones have become indispensable devices in teen communications, and texting is considered the preferred channel of basic communication between teens and their friends. Nowadays 72 percent of all teens, or 88 percent of teen cell phone users, are texters, up from 51 percent in 2006. More than half of teens (54%) are daily texters, and one in three sends more than 100 text messages on a daily basis (Lenhart 2010). However, teens seem to lack awareness of the text reference service offered by their libraries. Among the 40 teen users of MIQ member libraries who participated in focus group interviews about their use and perceptions of text reference, only one was aware of the service, and none had used it. In order to better reach this user population, libraries need to be more active in promoting the service to them. Consider the following approaches: holding a contest (a scavenger hunt) with prizes, promoting the service at teen events like gaming and teen advisory board meetings, setting up promotional displays in teen areas, having teen librarians introduce the service to teens in reference encounters or informal conversations, and encouraging teens to spread the word about the service.

When texting a librarian, library users may be concerned about sharing their mobile phone numbers with a third party that might lead to unsolicited advertisements and texting spam. Thus, it is important to ensure them that their phone numbers will be well protected and libraries take privacy issues seriously. Privacy protection should be highlighted in all promotional activities. Some text reference software automatically masks

Figure 17.1
Info Quest buttons.

users' phone numbers, displaying only an identification code to responding librarians. Libraries may consider adopting such software to buttress the privacy-protection guarantee.

DELIVER THE SERVICE

Making the service easy to use is an important component of text reference service delivery. Clear instructions should be provided that detail how to use the service, especially when patrons need to enter a library code in their initial message or text to an IM name/email address rather than a 10-digit phone number. It is also helpful to display a mobile barcode that stores the service phone number, enabling smartphone users to scan and save the number easily and quickly.

In addition to the technical instructions, it is necessary to make sure users understand the nature of the service and how to benefit most from it. In the aforementioned focus group interviews with teen library users, some reported hesitation toward using the service because they were uncertain about the types of questions they can ask and proper etiquette such as how to address librarians in a text message. Teens tend to associate texting with informal communications between family and friends, and when they are offered the opportunity to use this venue for formal information needs, they might feel confused or even a little uncomfortable. Thus, libraries need to help users better understand what they can gain from the service and use it comfortably. For example, it is helpful to provide information on questions that are most appropriate for the service medium. Luo and Weak (2011) found that the majority of text reference questions (69.8%) were ready reference questions that required simply a brief and straightforward answer. Thus, letting users know what kinds of questions the service is best suited to answer will encourage users to use it effectively and hence maximize the value of the service for them.

In the meantime, information on service policies such as service hours, response time, and what is considered inappropriate use of the service should be provided as well so that users understand what to expect from the service. Enforcing these policies is equally important. During the hours when the service is closed, it is important to set up an autoresponder alerting users about the service hours and letting them know when they can expect an answer. Users should be properly acknowledged when their questions cannot be handled immediately, and scripted messages can be employed to notify users that it might take more than the promised response time to answer their questions or encourage them to use other means of reference services like email for more in-depth assistance.

Given the informal nature of texting, adding a personal touch to the service may soften the façade of seriousness that is often associated with libraries. For instance, libraries may consider creating a universal screen name for the service or encourage individual librarians to conclude their responses with a signature, welcome users to continue their regular texting style such as using abbreviations when they text a librarian, or use "word contact" such as using emoticons or common abbreviations in their greetings and closings. The key is to make it clear that, while maintaining professionalism, librarians who provide a text reference service can be friendly, personal, and informal, reflecting the common perceptions of texting as a communication venue. Meola and Stormont's (2002) advice for chat reference librarians can also be applicable in texting: don't sweat a few typos; drop the formality, but don't get too cute; be concise, but don't be rude; and use scripted messages, but don't become librario-bot.

As mentioned earlier, the majority of text reference questions are ready reference questions that can be answered with a brief and definitive answer. This indicates that users are aware of the affordances of texting as a communication venue (e.g., each text message only allows 160 characters) and intuitively choose to text simple and straightforward questions to librarians. Accordingly, librarians providing the service consider skills that could help them effectively locate/interpret/convey information via texting to be most important. In a study identifying competencies requisite for text reference, the top five were as follows:

1. Ability to compose answers to patrons' questions concisely, quickly, and accurately.
2. Ability to construct effective search strategies and skillfully search online information sources.
3. Ability to quickly evaluate information and determine the validity, credibility, and authoritativeness of sources.
4. Knowledge of information resources, especially online information resources.
5. Ability to interpret patrons' information needs with the limited context provided in brief text messages.

These competencies reflect the need for a concise, speedy response to questions without much contextual information. Occasionally there are questions that represent more complex information needs and may require a comprehensive interview, and librarians can let the user decide whether they want to continue the transaction, or if they would rather be referred to other reference services. Sometimes even when answers are straightforward, they are not necessarily brief (e.g., lyrics and recipes) and need to spread across multiple messages. Librarians may offer users the option to receive the answer in multiple messages or to receive a URL that contains the information. Users with immediate information needs and no web access may prefer the former, and users who are cost conscious (each text message costs about 25 cents) may select the latter.

When there is not a definitive answer to a question and users have to be referred to a source, it is helpful to provide an informational summary along with the source because not all users have access to the mobile web. If they need the information immediately, the summary will give them a quick preliminary overview, and they can examine the details at a later time. By the same token, when referring users to a third party (e.g., an organization, a merchant, etc.), it is necessary to include a phone number rather than simply providing a URL or an email address.

Among the top five competencies requisite for text reference service, three are about online information sources knowledge and search skills, suggesting that text reference questions are primarily answered with online information sources. Subsequently, in text reference service training, online information searching should be emphasized. To help librarians effectively and efficiently compose their answers, an easily accessible cheat sheet containing useful sources on the web, tools like URL shorteners, word counters, common abbreviations, and information on how to consult colleagues will be helpful.

When text reference service is provided by a consortium of libraries, local library questions are often answered by nonlocal librarians. Thus it is important to ensure consistency across the responses. For example, when facing questions about library collections, it is likely that some librarians search the local library's catalog and provide a specific answer, while others simply ask users to go to their library catalog for information. To avoid such inconsistency and its negative impact on user satisfaction, clear service policies and procedures are necessary to any collaborative text reference service. In general, it seems that text reference users prefer direct answers, not URLs, citations to sources, or referrals to other agencies, unless that is absolutely necessary.

CONCLUSION

As more and more libraries start offering text reference service to their users, it is essential to develop a solid professional understanding of how to best use this service medium to fulfill users' information needs. Based on research findings from studying MIQ, ideas for best practices of establishing, promoting, and delivering text reference service have been discussed in this chapter. The goal is to help interested libraries understand the affordances of texting as a reference service venue, how text messaging impacts reference transactions, and therefore how to effectively and efficiently provide reference service via this medium. Libraries may draw upon ideas suggested in this chapter to help them plan and implement their own text reference services.

NOTES

1. http://www.altarama.com
2. http://www.textalibrarian.com/
3. http://libraryh3lp.com/
4. http://www.myinfoquest.info

REFERENCES

Giles, Nicola, and Sue Grey-Smith. 2005. "Txting Librarians@ Curtin." Paper presented at the Information Online Conference, Sydney, Australia, February 1–3. http://conferences.alia .org.au/online2005/papers/a12.pdf.

Hill, J. B., Cherie Madarash Hill, and Dayne Sherman. 2007. "Text Messaging in an Academic Library: Integrating SMS into Digital Reference." *The Reference Librarian* 47(1): 17–29. doi:10.1300/J120v47n97_04.

Kohl, Laura, and Maura Keating. 2009. "A Phone of One's Own." *College & Research Libraries News* 70(2): 104–106, 118.

Lenhart, Amanda. 2010. "Cell Phones and American Adults." Pew Internet & American Life Project, September 2. http://www.pewinternet.org/~/media//Files/Reports/2010/PIP _Adults_Cellphones_Report_2010.pdf.

Lippincott, Joan K. 2010. "Mobile Reference: What Are the Questions?" *The Reference Librarian* 51(1) (December 21): 1–11. doi:10.1080/02763870903373016.

Luo, Lili, and Emily Weak. 2011. "Texting 4 Answers: What Questions Do People Ask?" *Reference and User Services Quarterly* 51(2) (Winter): 43–52.

Meola, Marc, and Sam Stormont. 2002. *Starting and Operating Live Virtual Reference Services: A How-to-Do-It Manual for Librarians*, 1st ed. New York: Neal-Schuman.

Pearce, Alexa. 2010. "Text Message Reference at NYU Libraries." *The Reference Librarian* 51 (4): 256–263. doi:10.1080/02763877.2010.503314.

Weimer, Keith. 2010. "Text Messaging the Reference Desk: Using Upside Wireless' SMS-to-Email to Extend Reference Service." *The Reference Librarian* 51(2): 108–123. doi:10.1080/ 02763870903579729.

Part 5

Mobile Professional Development and New Opportunities

18

Expanding a Community College Library's Mobile Presence on a Shoestring Budget

Cate Kaufman and Brittany Osika

Key Points

- Readers will learn tips to increase visibility and services for mobile patrons.
- A cost-effective mobile presence will be discussed.
- The authors will discuss implementing and sustaining a mobile presence at a community college with three sites and a relatively small staff

---

OVERVIEW

Change is the one thing you can always count on, especially in the library field. The library of Illinois Central College (ICC), a mid-sized community college located in East Peoria, Illinois, has not been immune to change. In fact, we have seen significant shifts in priorities and staff in the last few years. Much of this change can be seen by examining our annual program plan. This plan outlines goals for the coming year as well as project progress updates from the previous year's plan. Although the goals were laudable in the past, they did not always push the boundaries of what staff could accomplish.

Beginning in 2009, the ICC Library began making mobile services more of a priority. Increased emphasis was placed on developing tools for patrons who would be viewing our resources on a smartphone or other mobile device. Given the economic climate, however, it was essential that the services were cost-effective or free. It was also crucial that staff could continue providing outstanding service to our in-person patrons while our mobile services were being developed.

A unique opportunity presented itself when we had an opening for an electronic resources librarian in 2011. We decided to focus on finding a candidate with a specific set of interests and the ability to learn new skills. While it was important for the candidate

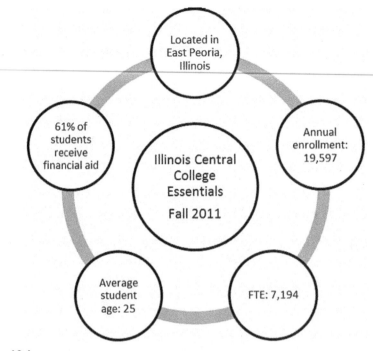

Figure 18.1
Essential information about Illinois Central College.

to have experience with database maintenance and vendor contracts, his or her ability and interest in growing the library's mobile presence was even more important. A self-motivated and technologically savvy candidate was sought and found, allowing the library to refine its goals.

Since then, the ICC Library has taken on a number of low-cost mobile initiatives that bring our services and resources to our mobile patrons. Each project was chosen for its ability to increase our mobile presence while minimizing the impact on the budget and staff time needed for development.

MOBILE WEBSITE

Cost: $
Staff Time: 16–20 hours

The ICC Library website was specifically designed to display acceptably on a mobile screen. However, later a decision was made that a dedicated mobile website was needed. While many low-cost options exist, the Mobile Site Builder add-on to Lib-Guides was chosen. Allowing for complete content control, the Mobile Site Builder offered us the opportunity to feature the areas that we felt were most likely to be used by a mobile visitor: library account and catalog access, directional and hours information, and access to mobile-optimized resources. Rather than developing content from scratch, much of the information for the mobile website was sourced from existing ICC Library websites and electronic resource vendors who had developed mobile optimized products.

In addition to our mobile library website, the ICC Library also was able to customize a mobile version of our library catalog. As a benefit of membership in the Consortium of Academic Research Libraries in Illinois, we were provided with the option to provide a mobile online public-access catalog (OPAC). All features of the traditional OPAC are available on the mobile OPAC, including account information, searching, and item renewal, as well as some branding with ICC colors. While there is not currently automatic redirect to the mobile catalog for our patrons, a direct mobile URL is available and has been featured on our mobile website.

Making our mobile website available for our patrons is a priority for the ICC Library. Posters and signage have been developed with QR code links and short URLS that allow easy access. Additionally, mobile patrons who visit our website from their device are automatically redirected to our mobile website.

QR CODES

Cost: Free
Staff Time: Less than 10 hours

Integrating QR codes into the library was a quick, easy, and inexpensive way to interact with and disseminate information to its mobile users. The primary QR code initiative allowed us to foster the link between our electronic resources and print collection. New signs were created that had the subject, call number range, and two links to a LibGuide, online research guides created and maintained by librarians. A text link was placed on each sign to encourage all patrons to visit our LibGuides, and i-nigma was used to generate a free QR code that linked patrons directly to the LibGuide. Each LibGuide featured electronic resources, websites, journals, and other materials students may find useful in their research.

Signs were printed and placed on the end caps of stacks at our East Peoria Campus, and smaller signs were placed among the books at our two smaller campuses, where stack space is limited. Because LibGuides are automatically optimized for mobile browsers, only QR codes and signage needed to be created.

Additionally, QR codes have been featured as a part of the library's marketing campaign. Every poster featuring ICC Library events such as the Edible Book Festival, Summer Reading Program, and Book Club corresponded with a LibGuide that contained additional information. A QR code and a text link to each LibGuide were added to the posters to ensure that mobile and traditional patrons had access to all information.

E-BOOK DOWNLOAD STATIONS

Cost: Free
Staff Time: Less than 10 hours

ICC Library migrated from a generic large academic collection in July 2011 to a patron-driven acquisition model of e-book purchasing. This allowed the Collection Development Committee to select specific titles that were

Figure 18.2

Signs with QR codes placed on the end caps of stacks.

tailored to curriculum and assignment needs. This shift gives patrons a focused collection for their research requirements.

When the option to download titles became available, the library decided to develop an easy way for patrons to participate. As the ICC Library already provided laptops for student checkout, only the addition of free software, Adobe Digital Editions, and staff training was necessary. Each laptop is checked out for in-house use and has a login profile that allows downloading to take place, a permission that is not available on our student desktop computers. After the laptop is checked out, students use it to locate, download, and transfer e-books to their phones or e-readers. ICC Library student workers and circulation staff are responsible for deauthorizing Adobe Digital Editions after each patron use.

LIBRARYH3LP

Cost: $
Staff Time: 16–20 hours

In order to offer a streamlined virtual reference package to patrons, ICC Library subscribed to Libraryh3lp in summer 2012. This innovative service allowed the library to develop personalized chat widgets that allowed for precise statistic keeping, as well as a way to determine where our patrons were accessing our service points. An add-on subscription to Twilio's text-message service seamlessly integrated incoming text messages into the library's chat client.

Chat widgets were placed on the ICC Library's website, LibGuides, and Facebook. Because the widgets are also optimized for a mobile screen, a separate widget was created and placed on the mobile website. These services were featured on the poster marketing campaign as well as during instruction sessions and on the library Facebook page and websites. To encourage use, we ran a contest that entered each chat or text patron into a weekly drawing to remove library fines from a patron's account. As part of their entry, patrons were required to ask a question or offer feedback on a library service or resource. This was a free way for us to receive student feedback and encourage use of our new service.

Figure 18.3
Poster marketing campaign encourages use and feedback.

ELECTRONIC RESOURCE APPLICATIONS

Cost: Free
Staff Time: Less than 10 hours

Many electronic resource vendors offer mobile adaptations free of charge, only requiring institutions to opt in. Some vendors provide a mobile website, like Encyclopedia Britannica and ProQuest, while many others offer applications for mobile phones. EBSCO, for example, provides free applications for EBSCOhost and the Nursing Reference Center, and Gale has created a series of free Access My Library applications for academic, public, K–12, and special libraries. All of these mobile interfaces allow patron access to subscription-only content with many features available.

These mobile adaptations were featured on the library mobile website, as they were often the easiest to use on a mobile device. Also, marketing materials such as posters and table tents to the larger resource were provided free of charge, and information about mobile access was added. A LibGuide featuring mobile resources was created and featured in the library marketing campaign.

OBSTACLES

Integrating mobile technologies into library services and resources has its difficulties. It is imperative to avoid discrimination against those who do not have mobile technologies. ICC Library has combated this by including a text link wherever a QR code is located. An additional obstacle for patrons is the affordability of the data and text-messaging plans to access these services. While we do not charge the patrons to access any mobile service, we do not subsidize the additional cost a patron may incur by utilizing these services.

ICC Library implemented these mobile technologies while trying to minimize the strain on staff and budgetary resources. The budget was of the utmost concern to all involved in the mobile initiatives, but projects were chosen that would allow for a maximum return on investment of time and money. Inexpensive resources and the use of free tools gave the opportunity to provide a variety of mobile access points to our patrons.

With a staff of five full-time and seven part-time librarians spread over three campuses, ensuring that staff members were able to take on mobile initiatives while completing normal duties was necessary. This was accomplished by using resources that were already created and marketing them to a different audience. For example, librarians had already created LibGuides featuring electronic and online resources for the majority of subjects, so providing direct access to those looking for print materials was our next step. Many of the initiatives were able to be completed by staff members who possessed the basic skills needed as well as the interest to learn additional skills as required.

However, ensuring librarians and support staff were properly trained to assist mobile patrons' access to our new services posed a unique challenge. With seven points of service, it remains critical that all staff remain familiar with our offerings and are able to work with mobile patrons to access services and materials. Instructional materials were provided, and verbal directions and reminders are given as required. Additionally, one-on-one staff training sessions were completed when necessary.

LOOKING AHEAD

As with any project, implementing new services and technologies does not mean the work is complete. Maintenance of the mobile website, development of QR codes and LibGuides for each Library of Congress classification, and offering of Libraryh3lp and e-book downloading stations will continue until the technologies are no longer relevant. Beyond the upkeep of current services, we will be looking to expand our mobile offerings. One way this may occur is by adding QR codes to individual items, such as books and journals. The codes would then link the physical material to the same electronic resource. For example, an issue of *Scientific American* would have a QR code on it that would direct patrons to the same issue of the electronic journal. Books that are also held in our e-book collection would be connected via QR codes as well.

In addition, we will be investigating tools that will link an item's location in the catalog to a map of the library stacks. Our hope is to implement a service that will allow patrons to look up an item through the mobile catalog, click on a link, and have the location of the item within the physical library displayed on their mobile device. Both proprietary and open-source options are available for this type of service.

Library applications of mobile technologies will continue to expand with time. Although it is hard to predict what the next advance may be, the ICC Library plans to carefully review and adopt the technologies that make the most sense based on budget and staff resources.

RESOURCES

All price estimates are based on enrollment numbers and negotiated contracts.

- *Springshare* (LibGuides, Mobile Site Builder)
  www.springshare.com
  sales@springshare.com
  Springshare, LLC, 801 Brickell Ave, Suite 900 Miami, FL 33131
- *Library H3lp/Twilio Add-on*
  libraryh3lp.com
  support@libraryh3lp.com
  Nub Games, Inc., P.O. Box 354, Carrboro, NC 27510
- *i-nigma* (QR code creator)
  http://www.i-nigma.com/

19

Mobile Empowerment: Lifelong Learning at Your Fingertips

Rebecca K. Miller

Key Points

- The author will discuss the significance of continuing education and professional development for all types of library practitioners.
- Three major ways mobile technologies revolutionize professional development will be introduced.
- Readers will learn about transformation of existing opportunities for professional development and continuing education through mobile technologies.
- Readers will be able to identify of apps, tools, and other key resources for using mobile technologies in professional development opportunities.
- The author makes recommendations for keeping current on the topic of mobile technologies and libraries.

INTRODUCTION AND OVERVIEW

ALA's Core Competences for Librarianship recognizes "the necessity of continuing professional development" for the successful practice of librarianship in any and all types of library settings (ALA 2009, 4). For many librarians and other information professionals, continuing professional development signifies a multifaceted approach to keeping up with trends, technology, skills, and strategies, all with the ultimate goal of fostering a certain level of engagement and understanding within the profession. An individual librarian's approach to current awareness, professional development, and continuing education may include structured courses or webinars, blogs, social networks, books, journals, conferences, and even other people. For the purposes of this chapter, the terms "professional development" and "continuing education" are used interchangeably, both generally referring to opportunities and activities related to supporting librarians and library staff in developing skill sets and expertise in order to stay relevant and informed. Overall, this chapter focuses on how all types of librarians and library staff can leverage the power of mobile devices—smartphones, tablets, e-readers, and laptops—to participate in and enhance professional development and other opportunities for continuing education and lifelong learning.

CONTINUING EDUCATION IN THE LIBRARY PROFESSION

Librarians and other information professionals have long been concerned with continuing education and professional development as an important part of maintaining the vitality and relevance of the library and those who operate it. Even before libraries faced the sort of radical transformation that they do today, library professionals recognized the need for and benefits of continuing education. "We are under a duty to *inquire*," pronounced one librarian from 1938 (Waldron 1938, 442). Throughout the history of librarianship, librarians have directed their inquiries toward building specific skills sets and participating in subject-specific scholarship. More recently, the direction of this inquiry and the opportunities related to continuing education for librarians and library staff point toward developing critical workforce competencies specific to the evolving role of libraries in an increasingly digital and networked world. A recent issue of *Library Trends* devoted to workforce issues in library and information science identifies competencies that librarians and library staff may need at present: instructional design, business administration, management, social work, urban planning, popular culture, disciplinary expertise, and, of course, knowledge of topics related to technology and Web 2.0 (Marshall et al. 2010, 2).

Regardless of the popular issues or trends that influence the particular directions of inquiry for librarians, it remains the love and pursuit of lifelong learning that drives library and information professionals to continue to inquire and to discover in all areas of life. As librarian Alice Waldron wrote in the early twentieth century, "the average librarian (if there is one) is consumed with the desire to know everything . . . we want to possess it completely" (Waldron 1938, 442). In fact, this may be one of the few areas of librarianship that has not changed over the past century of professional growth and evolution. While *ALA's Core Competences for Librarianship* may emphasize the "necessity of continuing professional development," and while institutions may require a certain amount of continuing education for promotions or salary increases, librarians ultimately seek knowledge because we embrace the value of lifelong learning—not only for our users but also for ourselves (ALA 2009, 4).

Because you made the choice to pick up this book and are, right now, taking the time to read it to advance your understanding of mobile technologies, this section of the book may be preaching to the proverbial choir. However, take a moment to think: You may be reading this book on a Kindle, an iPad, or even an iPhone. You may be on a bus, in a class, or in bed. How are mobile technologies changing your experience of inquiry and discovery, and what exciting potential do they contain for the future of professional development, continuing education, and lifelong learning? The rest of this chapter offers a few answers to these questions but mainly endeavors to inspire you to harness the power of mobile technology and consider how you can—and perhaps already do—engage with the library profession on new, more convenient, and more meaningful levels.

THE MOBILE REVOLUTION

The rise of ubiquitous computing through mobile devices absolutely has revolutionized the way that librarians and library staff can engage with professional communities for development and learning opportunities. Specifically, related literature, surveys, and reports converge on three chief reasons why mobile technologies empower library and information professionals to manage individual continuing education as we have never been able to in the past. Mobile technologies help develop formal and informal learning communities, incorporate new possibilities for interactivity and engagement, and offer easy and pervasive access to inexpensive or free professional development options. With these three intersecting changes, mobile technologies completely transform the professional development landscape. The next section of this chapter explores specific examples and ways that library practitioners can capitalize on these three changes; this section focuses on the background and principles driving the mobile revolution in continuing education for library practitioners.

Identity and Community

With the emergence of portable personal digital assistants (PDAs) in the early 1990s, the divide between personal and professional time began to diminish. The explosion of cell phones, smartphones, and tablets over the past decade now ensures that the personal/professional distinction has all but disappeared. Many professionals have begun to express concerns over the idea of the "continuous workday," a circumstance that occurs because of the eminent accessibility of work-related material through technology and an accompanying expectation that individuals be available through their mobile devices even when at home. Courts are even investigating labor issues related to mobile technologies and the ways that they are changing the concept of the workday and expectations for employees (Sands and Cho 2011). While these issues remain genuine concerns for everyone trying to negotiate a work-life balance, the widespread adoption of personal portable computers and other devices also has brought with it new opportunities for professional engagement and learning.

The quick and easy access to social networks that mobile technologies provide further compounds this blending of the personal and professional worlds. Like the continuous-workday issue, the fusion of professional and personal identities in a digital environment generates anxiety for nearly all types of professionals. A recent study from the Pew Research Center found that 66 percent of online adults use social media platforms like Facebook, LinkedIn, or Twitter, and that adults mainly used these platforms for staying in touch with acquaintances and connecting with others about a personal interest or hobby (Smith 2011). Clearly, this blending of personal and professional life can have repercussions that may not be positive. Although shared networks and communication spaces create a new type of learning environment and are able to foster new exchanges and interactions, these spaces can also foster negative exchanges. Professionals communicating personal opinions, political thoughts, or controversial ideas can alienate colleagues and endanger reputation and opportunities. Similarly, sharing certain types of personal information in public spaces can place a user, his or her information, and even his or her family at risk. In this environment, experts acknowledge the impossibility of maintaining two different identities for professional and personal purposes and suggest that professionals need to employ common sense in the type of information shared and maintain a certain level of professionalism while remaining open to new kinds of interactions with personal friends, current colleagues, and future employers, all in the same space (Markgren 2011, 32). This constant and pervasive communication essentially changes the way that library professionals interact with, collaborate with, and view each other. A light example of this phenomenon can be seen in the way professional librarians now are able to organize events and meet-ups surrounding hobbies, in addition to those focused on professional interests, at major library conferences. During the ALA Midwinter 2012 conference in Dallas, Texas, professional librarians used social media outlets to organize CraftCon, an event celebrating crafting that was held in the ALA Networking Uncommons in the Dallas Convention Center. The impact of social media and mobile devices on professionalism in librarianship represents a topic ripe for future study; for now, we will continue to look at the ways that these technologies affect and enhance professional development and learning.

Mobile technologies give users instant and constant access to these shared communication spaces within social networks, and one major concept arises out of this union of technology and networks: informal learning communities. Learning communities, professional learning networks, personal learning networks, and personal learning environments are all concepts that, on some level, can be used to discuss pervasive learning environments that originate out of individuals coming together and capitalizing on available technology to facilitate collaborative learning experiences and discussions. While learning communities can be formal groups devoted to the study of a particular topic, many library practitioners are starting to view their social networks as learning communities. In their 2011 article on learning communities in libraries, Paul Signorelli and Lori Reed discuss the "Twittersphere" and how Princeton (NJ) Public Library assistant director Peter Bromberg cites this space as "one of the best learning communities he has joined" (Signorelli and Reed 2011, 58). Other library professionals talk about creating a network of resources through social tools like Facebook, Twitter, and LinkedIn, following and keeping up with specific blogs, library leaders, professional associations, and journals in their networks (Kell 2009).

George Siemens, a social media strategies and learning technologist, explores this new type of learning aided by mobile devices and social networks in his research revolving around a new theory of learning: connectivism. Connectivism, unlike learning theories that precede it, addresses concepts such as informal contacts through social networking, how the tools learners use can define their learning experiences, and how learning and work-related activities are no longer distinct (Siemens 2004). While many researchers in the field of education and instructional technology view Siemens's theory with some skepticism, his work nonetheless emphasizes the way that learning has shifted in the digital age and how mobile devices fit into this new schema.

Increased Engagement

New research and practices coming out of the field of instructional technology underscore the interactive learning capabilities that mobile devices deliver. Indeed, professionals from many different fields—including health care, finance, and education—are starting to leverage mobile devices in their instruction and even marketing plans in order to engage their intended audiences. Examples of increased engagement through mobile devices include interactive tablet and smartphone games designed to teach elementary-aged students math principles, audience response systems used to enhance radiology residents' long-term retention, and tablet-based interactive workshops and investment tools offered to investment-plan participants to encourage participants to take a more active role in retirement planning (Liao et al. 2010; Collins 2008; Steyer 2011). Indeed, emerging educational research validates these examples by describing the advantages of using mobile technologies to enhance learner participation and invent new ways of helping individuals gain knowledge and skills (Ng 2010). The 2011 Horizon Report underscores the benefits of using mobile technologies to increase student participation in class, assess student learning, and actively involve participants in research, science, and the arts (Johnson et al. 2011).

All of these examples from education and instructional technology research can be applied to continuing education for library practitioners. Conference presentations, asynchronous online web courses, and even professional reading no longer need to be, and should not be, static experiences. Rather, mobile technologies make it possible for librarians and library staff to take part in dynamic conversations and learning experiences both online and in person. During conferences, for example, attendees can use tablets or phones to communicate with presenters and other attendees through Twitter and real-time polling software. Similarly, various apps and e-readers can help library practitioners manage, annotate, and participate in discussions occurring through professional blogs and journals. Learners' ability to participate in learning experiences on this more profound level, while definitely aiding in the retention of new knowledge and skills, also plays a large role in the development and growth of formal and informal learning communities.

Convenience and Access to a Variety of Opportunities

Recent economic issues have encouraged many library administrators and staff to consider free or inexpensive ways to gain new skills or stay on top of trends and hot issues. The networked personal computer has played a significant role in facilitating new opportunities for professional development and continuing education through online workshops, virtual conferences, websites, electronic journals, and blogs. Essentially, the same rapidly changing world of technology that creates the need for librarians to maintain current awareness also ensures that library practitioners are able to do so in many innovative and fairly inexpensive ways. These new education opportunities are discussed in more detail in the next section; before reading about these, consider three main ways that mobile technologies change the way that library practitioners can experience these learning opportunities: location, time, and area (Hanewald and Ng 2011). In other words, in addition to ensuring that participants no longer remain tethered to a certain location in order to participate in learning interactions, mobile learning can happen on the participants' own schedule, and participants mix and match areas of interest (e.g., personal hobbies and professional interests) all in one place. While virtual conferences, online courses, and electronic journals and books have been around for some time now, mobile technologies empower library practitioners easily to fit these various types of continued education into their busy lives.

The inherent flexibility of mobile technologies also lends to the convenience they offer their users. Tablets, smartphones, and even e-readers now come equipped with many different functionalities, including annotators, accelerometers, global positioning, digital capture and editing, video, audio, and imaging (Johnson et al. 2011). The combination of portability and flexible functionality contributes to the way that these mobile technologies can easily open up new realms of professional engagement for many library practitioners.

RESOURCES AND TOOLS FOR ENGAGING IN PROFESSIONAL DEVELOPMENT OPPORTUNITIES

Library literature contains no scarcity of articles discussing the various ways that librarians and library staff can engage in continuing professional development. Some articles defend the enduring value of the in-person professional conference (Harrison 2010; Tomaszewski and McDonald 2009). Other articles argue that while the professional conference remains relevant, other professional development opportunities must supplement the interactions that these conferences afford (Bell 2009; Blakiston 2011; Pan and Hovde 2010; Partridge, Lee, and Munro 2010; Pierce 2010). Again, the current economic environment also encourages librarians and library staff to seek cost-effective methods of professional development whenever possible, and most of the recent literature published on continuing education for library practitioners focuses on this cost-saving aspect.

Overall, library literature emphasizes several distinct classifications of professional development and continuing education in which library practitioners most often engage. These categories include professional reading, interpersonal networking, research and scholarship, virtual workshops, structured courses, and in-person conferences. Because of the ways that mobile technologies have transformed continuing education and development, library practitioners are now able to engage in these different types of professional development activities in new ways that may be both more meaningful and more convenient. This section focuses on specific apps, tools, and other resources that library practitioners can use with their mobile device(s) in order to participate in each of these categories of professional development and continuing education. For specific suggestions about relevant blogs to follow, learning communities to join, or virtual workshops to attend, see Rebecca Blakiston's article on this topic (2011).

Professional Reading

Aside from conference attendance, professional reading remains the most popular professional development activity among librarians and library staff. According to a recent *Chronicle of Higher Education* article, academic librarians spend an average of 22 minutes a day reading print publications related to their jobs and 10 minutes a day reading library-related blogs (Laster 2010). Smartphones, tablets, and of course e-readers are optimized to help librarians and library staff manage large amounts of professional reading in order to stay on top of trends, issues, and research in the library field.

E-books can be managed a number of ways, and across multiple devices. Library practitioners interested in exploring e-books in a new way can download free Kindle or Nook apps for their smartphones and tablets; users do not need to own a Kindle or a Nook in order to use these apps, although the apps do come with some restrictions that the dedicated e-readers do not have. When connected to a network, mobile devices with e-reader apps are able to sync the user's dedicated e-reader or other device(s) with the e-reader app, allowing library practitioners to read a single document continuously while on the go. Other apps that e-reading library practitioners may want to consider include OverDrive, Google Books, and iBooks. Goodreads, the popular social networking site for readers and book recommendations, is a great tool for building lists of

Table 19.1

Mobile resources for professional reading.

E-Reader Apps	RSS Reader Apps	Web Reading/ Bookmarking Apps
Kindle	GoReader	Instapaper
Nook	gReader Pro	Pearltrees
Google Books	Feeddler	Gimme Bar
iBooks	Reeder	Kippt
OverDrive		Delicious

professional and popular reading material, and the Goodreads network of readers can help individuals discover new books that may be relevant to that individual's professional or personal interests.

Library practitioners can manage journal articles and blog posts through apps that deliver information directly from these sources to a central source. The simplest way to retrieve relevant information from favorite blogs, journals, and websites is through RSS feeds. Google Reader has apps for both iOS and Android operating systems, GoReader and gReader Pro, respectively. Other popular RSS readers for mobile devices include Reeder and Feeddler. Several existing RSS readers have also developed mobile interfaces for easy viewing on smartphones, tablets, and other small screens; these readers include Yahoo! Mobile and Bloglines Mobile. Other RSS readers offer mobile options, so be sure to check the RSS reader that you currently use and see how you can take it with you on your mobile device.

Tools for managing information from regular web pages also exist. In addition to social bookmarking apps like Pearltrees, Gimme Bar, Kippt, and Delicious, Instapaper allows users to clip web pages to a central online account. The web pages clipped to the user's account can be accessed by e-readers and an app for smartphones and tablets.

Interpersonal Networking

This chapter has already discussed the types of informal learning networks that organically grow from library practitioners' pervasive use of social networks. Interestingly, library professionals that use these types of mobile social networking tools to communicate with others in the field of librarianship do so for a variety of reasons and on a variety of levels. In her recent article on how librarians conceive relationships between themselves and social media tools, Hazel Hall indicates that many librarians incorporate "highly developed strategies for integrating social media tools into their personal professional lives" in order to complete collaborative project work, participate in new forms of networking, and raise their personal profiles, among other reasons (Hall 2011, 422). This means that librarians are using social networking tools to both maintain established relationships with colleagues and connect with new colleagues.

There are several mobile tools that can help librarians and library staff members develop these connections and communities. Facebook, Twitter, LinkedIn, Skype, foursquare, Flickr, and MySpace all have apps available for iOS and Android operating systems. To keep track of all of these different social media outlets, try using a social

Table 19.2
Mobile resources for interpersonal networking.

Social Media Apps	Social Media Dashboard Apps
Facebook	HootSuite
LinkedIn	TweetDeck
Twitter	Threadsy
MySpace	
Skype	
foursquare	

media dashboard, a tool that can aggregate social media accounts. Social media dashboard platforms like HootSuite, TweetDeck, and Threadsy all offer apps through the Apple App Store and the Android Marketplace.

Research and Scholarship

Library practitioners that engage in research and scholarship related to library and information science can take advantage of apps and mobile interfaces developed to assist the researcher in a mobile environment. Many databases of disciplinary literature now have either an app or a mobile interface, or both. Databases with efficient mobile interfaces include IEEE Xplore, BioOne, JSTOR, Medline, WorldCat, and EBSCOhost. True apps for scholarly databases include Gale Access My Library app and PubMed On Tap. As with library catalogs, scholarly databases more commonly offer mobile interfaces rather than true apps. Most of the time, the mobile interface will accomplish what the researcher needs. Researchers will also appreciate apps like iAnnotate or RepliGo Reader that allow readers to annotate and save PDFs on mobile devices.

For researchers who frequently collaborate with others, apps like Evernote and Dropbox ensure that collaborators are able to share documents and other information and to coedit papers with ease. Other popular file-sharing and syncing apps include Box.net, SugarSync, and SpiderOak.

Additionally, some citation- and reference-management programs have apps for tablets and smartphones. Mendeley and Zotero both have apps that sync with desktop reference libraries, and many of the apps developed for databases include functions for exporting records in the correct file format to a researcher's email so that the researcher is able to import the records into an existing library. The Pubget app, which facilitates life sciences research on mobile devices, is an example of an app that exports records to a user's email.

Virtual Workshops and Structured Courses

Online workshops, webinars, and structured courses have become increasingly popular for library practitioners as they are often inexpensive or free and can be worked into very busy schedules. Many platforms for webinars and live meetings have mobile versions; WebEx, Saba Centra, and Adobe Connect all offer mobile access. While

Table 19.3

Mobile resources for research and scholarship.

Database Tools	Collaboration Tools	PDF Tools	Citation-Management Apps
IEEE Xplore	Dropbox	iAnnotate	Zotero
BioOne	Evernote	RepliGo Reader	Mendeley
Medline	SugarSync		
JSTOR	SpiderOak		
EBSCOhost			
WorldCat			
Gale Access My Library			
Pubget			

participants may not want to view a webinar or participate in an online course from a smartphone or tablet, the option is available.

During online workshops, seminars, and courses, note-taking apps can help participants keep track of the information being disseminated. For the iOS operating system, Notes, iNotes, and Infinote are apps that library practitioners can use to take notes during meetings and webinars. For the Android operating system, Notetaker HD captures handwriting and can help users organize information into folders and export items as PDFs.

In order to organize and manage the information and tasks that these workshops and courses require of their participants, task-management tools may also be helpful. Popular task-management apps include Remember the Milk, Toodledo, and TeuxDeux. Each of these apps syncs with the desktop version and information on other devices, which means that tasks and to-do lists can be managed from anywhere.

Conferences

Finally, mobile technologies have much to offer both in-person and virtual conference attendees. Many conferences work with vendors, like Boopsie, to develop their own conference apps for smartphones and tablets. Conference apps often include easy ways for attendees to create a schedule, plan exhibit visits, meet with authors, connect with social networks, and manage hotel and restaurant information. Usually, the conference

Table 19.4

Mobile resources for virtual workshops and structured courses.

Mobile Platforms	Note-Taking Apps	Task-Management Apps
Webex	Notes	Remember the Milk
Saba Centra	iNotes	Toodledo
Adobe Connect	Infinote	TeuxDeux
	Notetaker HD	

Table 19.5

Mobile resources for conferences.

Conference App Examples	QR Code Generators	QR Code Reader Apps	Communication Apps
ALA Annual 2011	Kaywa	Red Laser	Twitter
Virginia Library Association 2011	GoQR.me	Scan	
	QRmobilize	Kaywa	
	QR Stuff	QR Reader	
		ScanLife	

will advertise the app, but most apps also appear in the Apple App Store and the Android Market. Recently, many conferences also have made use of QR codes and QR code readers to enhance participants' experience in exhibit halls and in programs. By quickly linking the physical world to the digital world, presenters and vendors can help facilitate conference attendees' management of related information and ideas.

Twitter also encourages conference engagement on an entirely new level. With hashtags—tags embedded in Twitter posts to organize message content—specific to conferences and programs, Twitter invites participants to discuss ideas in an informal, real-time forum. Smartphones and tablets have ensured that Twitter users have the ability to follow and participate in "backchannels," or online conversations that run parallel to spoken or even written discussions occurring during conferences or workshops. Furthermore, mobile technologies allow library practitioners to participate in both in-person and online conference environments while remaining in easy, continuous contact with colleagues, library users, and family members.

CURRENT AWARENESS AND MOBILE TECHNOLOGIES

This chapter would be remiss in not exploring some of the ways that readers of this book can continue to maintain a level of current awareness about mobile technologies and the changes that they are bringing to libraries and other institutions of learning. Many blogs, journals, conferences, websites, workshops, and wikis revolve around mobile technologies in libraries, and these are excellent resources for staying up to date on new trends and ideas.

Furthermore, for many librarians and library staff, the physical use of a mobile device also serves as a very important way to maintain current awareness about new and emerging mobile technologies. As technological change continues to drive library transformation, library practitioners need to feel comfortable with exploring new technology tools through experimentation and play. When libraries make new tools, such as tablets and e-readers, available for staff members to use, they are ensuring that staff members have the opportunity to investigate the ways that new technologies can be used to enhance or reinvent library services in order to sustain the vitality and relevance of the library. Most libraries either circulate various mobile devices or support users who own at least one type of mobile device, and such libraries are finding that staff

Table 19.6

Resources for keeping current with mobile technologies.

Conferences	Web Resources	Books	Blogs
Handheld Librarian	ALA TechSource workshops and publications	*No Shelf Required*	*No Shelf Required*
Computers in Libraries	Horizon Report	*Mobile Technology and Libraries*	*Mobile Libraries*
LITA National Forum	M-Libraries (Library Success Wiki)	*Libraries and the Mobile Web*	*Tablets in Libraries*
EDUCAUSE	EDUCAUSE publications	*Going Mobile: Developing Apps for your Library Using Basic HTML Programming*	*Handheld Librarian*
		Mobile Devices and the Library: Handheld Tech, Handheld Reference	
		Using Mobile Technology to Deliver Library Services: A Handbook	

members need to be well versed in the functionality of these tools. This type of knowledge is best gained through hands-on exploration, and library staff members should take advantage of every opportunity to get new technologies into their hands.

Similar to the other resource ideas discussed in this chapter, libraries can utilize free and inexpensive methods of ensuring that librarians and staff receive ample opportunity to explore new technologies, mobile or otherwise. Many libraries with staff that use various types of mobile devices hold user group meetings, where librarians and library staff discuss the technologies and how they can be used to enhance library services. Similarly, Steven Bell recommends regular, informal joint meetings among local libraries for the same purpose (Bell 2009, 2). By facilitating regular meetings among local or regional libraries, different library administrators and practitioners can embrace the opportunity to participate in discussions with other practitioners from their area. This idea remains particularly appropriate for maintaining current awareness relating to mobile technologies because the different libraries involved will undoubtedly have different technologies and expertise to share with their counterparts. This may be particularly true if different types of libraries (e.g., academic and public) are able to develop this sort of network or relationship in order to exchange ideas and facilitate time to play with new mobile technologies. Overall, librarians and library staff interested or invested in maintaining awareness about mobile technologies need to seek out and allow time for play and exploration with various devices. In addition to following blogs or reading journal articles on related topics, library and information professionals need to actually use the mobile devices they are reading about in order to truly maintain a fluency and current awareness surrounding these technologies.

Final Thoughts

A recent research study conducted among Australian librarians highlighted several characteristics of the successful twenty-first-century librarian: he or she has "an inquiring mind, enjoys playing and experimenting, and loves learning . . . [and] is also willing to share knowledge with colleagues and to mentor and coach others" (Partridge, Lee, and Munro 2010, 326). Along the same lines, the successful librarian of 1938 realized that "a certain mobility is our assurance in life" and chose to deal with this idea of constant change through inquiry and education (Waldron 1938, 442). Librarians have always had to cope with change on some level, working toward the ultimate goal of "sustaining the mission and vision of the library in its community and enabling library practitioners to strive for excellence in delivering its mission (Gutsche 2010)." Essentially, mobile technologies empower library practitioners to strive for excellence in new and exciting ways by changing the ways that practitioners communicate with each other, engage with the profession, and participate in professional inquiry.

REFERENCES

American Library Association. 2009. *ALA's Core Competences of Librarianship*. Accessed December 19, 2011. http://www.ala.org/educationcareers/sites/ala.org.educationcareers/files/content/careers/corecomp/corecompetences/finalcorecompstat09.pdf.

Bell, Steven. 2009. "Online or Out the Door: Continuous Learning for Academic Librarians in Economic Downturns." *Library Issues* 29(5): n.p.

Blakiston, Rebecca. 2011. "Building Knowledge, Skills, and Abilities: Continual Learning in the New Information Landscape." *Journal of Library Administration* 51(7–8): 723–743.

Collins, Jeannette. 2008. "Audience Response Systems: Technology to Engage Learners." *Journal of the American College of Radiology* 5(9): 993–1000.

Gutsche, Betha. 2010. "A Focus on Competencies Can Help Librarians Stick to Values while Absorbing Future Shock." *Library Journal*, March 1. Accessed December 21, 2011. http://www.libraryjournal.com/article/CA6719414.html.

Hall, Hazel. 2011. "Relationship and Role Transformations in Social Media Environments." *The Electronic Library* 29(4): 421–428.

Hanewald, Ria, and Wan Ng. 2011. "The Digital Revolution in Education: Digital Citizenship and Multi-Literacy of Mobile Technology." In *Mobile Technologies and Handheld Devices for Ubiquitous Learning: Research and Pedagogy*, edited by Wan Ng, 1–14. Hershey, PA: IGI Global.

Harrison, Rachel. 2010. "Unique Benefits of Conference Attendance as Method of Professional Development for LIS Professionals." *The Serials Librarian* 59(3–4): 263–270.

Johnson, L., R. Smith, H. Willis, A. Levin, and K. Haywood. 2011. *The 2011 Horizon Report*. Austin, TX: The New Media Consortium.

Kell, Susan E. 2009. "Technically Speaking: What Is in Your Professional Learning Network?" *Learning and Media* 37(3): 11–12.

Laster, Jill. 2010. "Report Measures Librarians' Time Reading Job-Related Materials." *The Chronicle of Higher Education. Wired Campus* [blog], March 5. http://chronicle.com/blogs/wiredcampus/report-measures-librarians-time-reading-job-related-materials/21641.

Liao, C. C. Y., Z-H. Chen, H. N. H. Cheng, and F-C. Chen. 2010. "My-Mini-Pet: A Handheld Pet-Nurturing Game to Engage Students in Arithmetic Practices." *Journal of Computer Assisted Learning* 27(1): 76–89.

Markgren, Susan. 2011. "Ten Simple Steps to Create and Manage Your Professional Online Identity: How to Use Portfolios and Profiles." *College & Research Libraries News* 72(1): 31–35.

Marshall, Joanne Gard, Susan Rathbun-Grubb, Deborah Barreau, and Jennifer Craft Morgan. 2010. "Introduction: Workforce Issues in Library and Information Science, Part 2." *Library Trends* 59(1–2): 1–5.

Ng, Wan, ed. 2011. *Mobile Technologies and Handheld Devices for Ubiquitous Learning: Research and Pedagogy.* Hershey, PA: IGI Global.

Pan, Junlin, and Karen Hovde. 2011. "Professional Development for Academic Librarians: Needs, Resources, and Administrative Support." *Chinese Librarianship: An International Electronic Journal* 29. Partridge, Helen, Julie Lee, and Carrie Munro. 2010. "Becoming 'Librarian 2.0': The Skills, Knowledge, and Attributes Required by Library and Information Science Professionals in a 2.0 World (and Beyond)." *Library Trends* 59(1–2): 315–335.

Pierce, Jennifer Burek. 2010. "The Pixelated Campus." *American Libraries* 41(4): 56.

Sands, Michael, and Soo Cho. 2011. "Mobile Technology Blurs Work and Nonwork Hours: Courts Have Yet to Rule on Overtime Issue, but Employers Should Address Potential Liability." *The National Law Journal* (January 10).

Siemens, George. 2004. *Connectivism: A Learning Theory for the Digital Age.* Accessed February 11, 2012. http://www.elearnspace.org/Articles/connectivism.htm.

Signorelli, Paul, and Lori Reed. 2011. "Professional Growth through Learning Communities." *American Libraries* 42(5/6): 56–59.

Smith, Aaron. 2011. "Why Americans Use Social Media," Pew Research Center. November 15. http://www.pewinternet.org/Reports/2011/Why-Americans-Use-Social-Media/Main-report.aspx.

Steyer, Robert. 2011. "Providers Going Big with Technology: From Phone Apps to Videos, Tools Being Used to Engage Participants." *Pensions & Investments* 39(22): 2.

Tomaszewski, Robert, and Karen I. McDonald. 2009. "Identifying Subject Specific Conferences as Professional Development Opportunities for the Academic Librarian." *The Journal of Academic Librarianship* 35(6): 583–590.

Waldron, Alice. 1938. "The Continuing Education of a Librarian." *Wilson Bulletin for Librarians* 12 (March): 442–443.

Index

About the Editors and Contributors

Lori Bell is in Information Technology Support at Graham Hospital School of Nursing Library, a part-time lecturer at the School of Library and Information Science at San Jose State University, and a part-time reference librarian at Illinois Central College. She has an MS in Library and Information Science from the University of Illinois and a certificate of advanced study in distance learning from Western Illinois University.

Thomas A. Peters is the dean of library services at Missouri State University. He studied English and philosophy at Grinnell College, and he has master's degrees from the University of Iowa (library science) and the University of Missouri—Kansas City (English). (tpeters@tapinformation.com)

* * *

April Karlene Anderson became the university archivist for Illinois State University in 2011. She received her MA in History—Public History from the University of Central Florida in 2007 and her MLIS from Florida State University in 2010.

Max Anderson is the technology coordinator for the National Network of Libraries of Medicine, Greater Midwest Region, located at the University of Illinois at Chicago Library of the Health Sciences. He advises health science libraries and health professionals in a 10-state region on emerging technologies and teaches classes on their use.

Robin Ashford is reference and distance services librarian at George Fox University, Portland Center. Robin earned her MSLIS from the University of Illinois at Urbana-Champaign. Her research interests include emerging technologies, mobile everything, social media, educational technology, gaming, augmented reality, near-field communications, Google, Apple, and chocolate.

Lisa Carlucci Thomas is the director and founder of Design Think Do. Lisa writes and presents on leadership, technology, and innovation in libraries, including e-books, mobile culture, social media, technology trends, training, and best practices. Lisa previously worked at the Yale University Library and Southern Connecticut State University. She is a 2010 Library Journal Mover and Shaker, a 2009 ALA Emerging Leader, and a MLIS graduate of Syracuse University. Follow Lisa on Twitter: @lisacarlucci.

Rene J. Erlandson is director of virtual services at the University of Nebraska Omaha Library, which encompasses all aspects of electronic resource management, digital collection development, digital asset management, web development, computer systems, and network infrastructure. Prior to joining the University of Nebraska faculty, she held positions at the University of Illinois at Urbana-Champaign and Iowa State University. Erlandson actively publishes in the area of library technology. Her work includes coauthoring a Library and Information Technology Association (LITA) Guide: *Technology for Small and One-Person Libraries*. (rene.erlandson@gmail.com)

Meredith Farkas is the head of instructional services at Portland State University and a lecturer at San Jose State University's School of Library and Information Science. She is the author of the book *Social Software in Libraries: Building Collaboration, Communication and Community Online* and the "Technology in Practice" column for *American Libraries*, and blogs regularly at *Information Wants to be Free* (meredith.wolfwater.com/wordpress).

Chad Haefele is the emerging technologies librarian at the University of North Carolina at Chapel Hill. His research interests include mobile web design, e-books, and gaming in education. (cHaefele@email.unc.edu)

Susan Kantor-Horning is the emerging technologies library specialist at the Contra Costa County Library in California. Her accomplishments within the library's Virtual Department include writing successful grant applications for projects such as Snap & Go and Discover & Go and participating in the My Info Quest collaborative text-a-librarian service. (skantor@ccclib.org)

Cate Kaufman is the library services director at Illinois Central College, where she has led the development and implementation of mobile library services for community college students and faculty. She has an MS in library and information science from the University of Illinois.

Deanna Lee is the vice president for communications and public engagement at the New York Public Library and is responsible for promoting—and engaging users in—the stories of the library. She worked for 20 years in broadcast journalism and is the recipient of eight News and Documentary Emmy awards.

Lili Luo is an assistant professor at the School of Library and Information Science at San Jose State University. Her primary area of research interest is digital reference, and she has been publishing actively in this area. Her other research interests include library education, information-seeking behavior, and human-information interaction.

Tammy A. Magid holds an MLIS from San Jose State University and a BS in kinesiology from Washington State University. Her area of research includes mobile-to-mobile messaging to deliver health information at the point of need. She has explored text-messaging programs related to family planning, reproductive health, and HIV/AIDS in both Kenya and the United States.

Chad Mairn is a librarian, teacher, author and technophile who frequently shares his enthusiasm for all things technology as a speaker at library and technology conferences. He is a librarian and adjunct professor at St. Petersburg College in Florida and is also the chief technology officer at Novare Library Services.

Rebecca K. Miller is the information literacy coordinator and college librarian for science, life sciences, and engineering at Virginia Tech. She holds an MLS from the University of North Carolina at Chapel Hill, a BA from the College of William and Mary in Virginia, and is currently working toward an MA in instructional design and technology from Virginia Tech. Visit her website (http://www.rebeccakatemiller.com) or email her (rebeccakate.miller@gmail.com).

Brittany Osika is the electronic resources librarian at Illinois Central College. She has her MLIS from University of Wisconsin—Milwaukee. Her interests include virtual library services and integrating emerging technologies into the library.

Dr. Harry E. Pence is a State University of New York distinguished teaching professor emeritus and presently serves as a faculty fellow for emerging technologies at the Teaching and Learning with Technology Center at the State University College at Oneonta, New York. He has written and presented frequently about emerging learning technologies and is a coeditor of the recently published book *Enhancing Learning with Online Resources, Social Networking, and Digital Libraries*.

Sue Polanka created the award-winning blog *No Shelf Required*, a blog about the issues surrounding e-books for librarians and publishers. Sue is the head of reference and instruction at the Wright State University Libraries in Dayton, Ohio, and the vice president/president elect of the Academic Library Association of Ohio. She was named a Library Journal 2011 Mover and Shaker for her work with e-books.

Andrew Revelle is a social sciences librarian at Miami University in Oxford, Ohio. His research interests include user attitudes about e-books and the ways data can be used to improve services in academic libraries.

Bonnie Roalsen is head of children's services at the Dover Town Library in Massachusetts and an independent consultant specializing in mobile technology, digital literacy, creative programming, and youth services. Bonnie was named a Library Journal Mover and Shaker in 2007 for her work incorporating digital media and tools into public library service. (wizardhere@gmail.com)

Alex Rolfe is technical services and systems librarian at George Fox University. Alex has an MA in medieval history and an MLIS from the University of Washington. His research interests revolve around board games, and he has recently started logging his plays on BoardGameGeek, his preferred social media site.